From Suburb to Shtetl

Egon Mayer

FROM SUBURB TO SHTETL

The Jews of Boro Park

Temple University Press

Philadelphia

Temple University Press, Philadelphia 19122
© 1979 by Temple University. All rights reserved
Published 1979
Printed in the United States of America

Library of Congress Cataloging in Publication Data

Mayer, Egon, 1944–
    From suburb to shtetl.

    Bibliography: p.
    Includes index.
    1. Jews in Brooklyn—Social conditions. 2. Orthodox Judaism—New
York (City) 3. Brooklyn—Social conditions. 4. Borough Park, New
York (City—Social conditions. 5. New York (City)—Social conditions.
    I. Title.
F129.B7M29   301.45′19′24074723   79-19111
ISBN 0-87722-161-8

For Daphne, our first born,
with a prayer that her world be as rich
as the one described in these pages

Contents

Acknowledgments

A first book, like a first child, evokes a special sense of gratitude to the ineffable power in the universe which has given one the inspiration and the strength to invest experience with meaning. I would be unworthy of this publication if I did not give expression to that sense of gratitude here.

This book was written not solely on the basis of inspiration and will. Its findings, its analyses, and its insights were acquired or created in the context of innumerable relationships with mentors, colleagues, friends, neighbors, and even strangers. I wish to acknowledge my intellectual debts and my gratitude (for these debts really cannot be repaid) at least to those whose influences and contributions I am aware of. It is in the nature of such debts that one remains unaware of the ones that are, perhaps, the most precious.

Reb Yitzchok Alster, formerly of the Kamenitzer Yeshiva, struggled mightily, and I would like to think not without some success, to teach me how to ask critical questions with a measure of humility. Professor Peter L. Berger, through courses at the New School for Social Research and at Rutgers University, through his written work, and, somewhat later, through friendship, gave me the conceptual skills with which to answer critical questions about the world of the faithful without demeaning its values or inhabitants. Professors Harry C. Bredemeier and Matilda White Riley were especially influential in helping me realize the sociologist's professional obligations to theoretical and methodological principles. Professor Arthur J. Vidich, of the New School for Social Research, first recognized, in a rather simple term paper I wrote, the rich possibilities of the Jewish community of Boro Park as a subject for a dissertation and a book.

My colleagues at the Department of Sociology of Brooklyn College, my academic home, have been a source of steadfast support and intellectual sustenance. Professors Marvin D. Koenigsberg and Mervin F. Verbit have been not only colleagues and friends but also my teachers. I have continued to learn from them in all these relationships. Professor

Laura W. Kitch has served as a mentor and critic, a confidante and a guide, and provided invaluable comments and suggestions throughout my work. Professor Sylvia Fava was a most helpful and generous resource on issues pertaining to urban sociology, and Professor Roberta Satow helped to clarify my thinking about theories of self and society. The various chairmen of our department, Professors Charles Lawrence, Deborah Offenbacher, Sidney Aronson, and Paul Montagna, along with Mrs. Sadie Altstein, have created an atmosphere which has fostered collegiality and creativity. Their tactful and generous managerial styles have surely enriched my career, and eased the burdens which inevitably attend the research and writing process.

Between 1972 and 1974 several generations of my students at Brooklyn College, especially those enrolled in my Sociology 19—Research Methods—course, voluntarily and generously gave their time and energy to collect information about the Boro Park community in general and its Jewish community in particular. Many conducted interviews of great depth with a sensitivity and professionalism that made me proud to be called their teacher. A few hardy souls also made their first attempts at computer-assisted data analysis. Some of the more outstanding volunteers were Laura Biderman, Joan Brandstein, Joseph Elnadav, Michelle Friedman, Heda Gelberman, Joseph Hochberg, Susan F. Hollander, Judy Horowitz, Renee Katz, Marvin Kirschner, Robert Koenigsberg, Marshall Korman, Rochelle Kurzman, Robin Lefkowitz, Norma Meyer, Naomi Nulman, Robert Solomon, Susan Weltz, and Harold Wilkes. Others whose names have faded from memory are no less deserving of my thanks.

The staff of the Brooklyn College Computer Center was helpful in all phases of data analysis. Professor James Wang, Mr. Julio Berger, Mr. Benjamin Klein, and Mr. David Pasternak consistently provided sound technical advice and good cheer.

Having lived in the Boro Park Jewish community during my formative years, I am bound to acknowledge many important relationships which contributed not only to the making of this book but to my evolution as a person. Friends at the Yeshiva Toras Emes, the Mesivta Kamenitz, and Young Israel have contributed in complex ways to shape my conception of Orthodox Jewish life. Many of their names have faded from memory, but their images remain with me vividly. To my parents and grandmother, the primary architects of the Orthodox Jewish family that I called home for twenty-two years, I owe an emotional and spiritual debt that I will never be able to fully repay. In many ways this work is an attempt to grapple with that debt, though I doubt that they will appreciate it in that light. My father-in-law, of blessed memory, served as my model of the unflappable Jew, one who has borne the marks of twentieth century Jewish history without losing his essential dignity as a man. Susan—initially a friend, now my wife and still my friend—a perpetually reluctant insider to the world of Jewish Orthodoxy and Boro Park, has continued to ask those critical questions that I should have thought of first, and has never refused to be impressed with convenient answers.

Lastly, I wish to express my gratitude to the Lucius N. Littauer Foundation and the Memorial Foundation for Jewish Culture for providing the financial assistance which helped to launch the publication of this study, and to my editors, Messrs. David Bartlett and Michael Fisher, for easing the transformation of this work from manuscript into book.

Egon Mayer
Lakeville, Conn.
Summer 1979

From Suburb to Shtetl

1 Jewish Orthodoxy in America
The Decline and Resurgence of Jewish Traditionalism

For one of the smallest minorities in America, Jews have enjoyed an extraordinary amount of popular attention in print. Not only have they written a great many books, but a great deal has been written about them. Why, then, another book about Jews? Because this book deals with a small segment of America's Jews about whom not much has been written, but whose ways of thinking and living provide insights into the dynamics of religious living and ethnic identity in modern America.

It is customary to divide American Jewry into three denominations or branches: the Reform, the Conservative, and the Orthodox. In the literature on American Jewry, however, the Orthodox have been less than equal partners. While an impressive body of social science literature has focused on the Reform and the Conservative branches, the Orthodox has remained a kind of "residual category"—neither Reform nor Conservative, but somehow more religious and traditional than either. The characteristics of Orthodox Jews, their ways of thinking and living, the organization of their communities, and their relationship to the larger society have remained conjectural. To be sure, one finds scholarly articles about them in journals here and there. But for the most part this segment of Jewry is unfamiliar, if not altogether unknown, to Americans—Jews and non-Jews alike.

The Orthodox is the smallest branch of American Jewry. Fewer than a million of America's nearly six million Jews include themselves under its rubric. Perhaps for this reason it is generally forgotten that Orthodoxy, as it is commonly understood, was the *only* form of Judaism until the early decades of the nineteenth century. During that period, Reform began as a religious movement in America; the Conservative movement began only at the turn of the twentieth century. As a matter of fact, while the Reform and the Conservative began as organized movements to change the prevailing patterns of traditional Jewish life, Orthodoxy was really not a movement at all. Rather, it was a state of mind and a way of life that prevailed unselfconsciously in the habits of most Jews until the turn of the century.

The waning and subsequent resurgence of Orthodoxy is a

3

"background" story that adds particular poignancy to the evolution and dynamics of life in the community explored in this book. But before we turn to that story, let us attend briefly to the question of what Orthodoxy is.

The religious life of Jews is based on the Torah, generally called the Old Testament or the Five Books of Moses. The patterns of "correct living" it prescribes, however, are not limited to strictly spiritual or religious matters. The Torah contains no fewer than six hundred and thirteen commandments, prescriptive and proscriptive, touching on every imaginable aspect of daily life: routine dietary habits are as meticulously regulated as sexual habits. Moreover, except in biblical times, Jews have never lived by the Torah alone. Rabbinic authorities have interpreted, refined, and augmented the original Mosaic rules for well over two thousand years. The accretion of local customs, codified as quasi-sacred norms by village elders during the long sojourn of the Jewish Diaspora, has also added to the corpus of commandments, the *mitzvas*, that Jews have lived by.

What are the first words that one should utter upon awakening in the morning? There is a rule. How many steps may one take from one's bed before washing at least the tips of one's fingers (known as *nagelwasser*)? There is a rule. At what age should a man marry? No later than eighteen, according to the rule. How is a woman to purify herself after her monthly menstrual cycle? In the *mikva*, of course, according to prescribed techniques of immersion. And how long after her period may her husband have sexual relations with her? Again, there is a rule. Rules, procedures, schedules, and prohibitions circumscribe traditional Jewish life. Orthodoxy, not as a particular religious movement but as a way of life, is nothing more or less than the fastidious observance of all of them.[1]

It is obvious to anyone acquainted with modern American Jews that very few of them live such a circumscribed life. The question is, did the majority ever live that way? It is difficult to establish with any precision or certainty how the "average Jew" lived and thought throughout history; the preoccupation of social scientists with Jews is a relatively recent development. We do know, however, that because of their pariah status, at least in the West, Jews nearly always have lived in segregated communities. They were a people apart both by choice and by necessity. In eastern Europe, where more than three quarters of America's Jews have their roots, the vast majority of Jews lived in *shtetlach* (the plural of *shtetl*—village or townlet), in which they constituted a relatively homogeneous population. Their cultural and everyday social life was carried on in isolation from their gentile neighbors. In these mini-municipalities local law, at least for Jews, was practically synonymous with religious regulation. Rabbis often were the equivalents of town officials, and they, along with other religious functionaries, had police-like powers. One may infer, then, both from the available literature and from the sheer social organization of traditional Jewish society in Europe, that, indeed, the great majority of Jews did live an Orthodox way of life.

The significance of the *shtetl* was that, perhaps because of its almost total cultural and social isolation, it was fundamentally religion- and tradition-centered. Human values were synonymous with Jewish values: pleasure was *nachas* and pain was *tzuris*. Basic human experience was mediated and apprehended through Jewish symbols. Space was defined by the location of the *shul* (synagogue), the *beis hamedresh* (house of study), the *mikva* (ritual bath), and the like. Similarly, time was punctuated by a prescribed schedule of daily prayers and by the calendar of Jewish holidays. Did Jews in the *shtetl* like that way of life? Would they like to have perpetuated it in the New World? We do not know. There were no social scientists around to survey their opinions. We do know that, almost from the moment Jews landed on these shores, Jewish life in America has been quite different from the established patterns of the *shtetl*.

Boro Park in the 1970s

Boro Park in the 1970s is neither a ghetto nor a *shtetl* in the strict sense of those terms; it is neither a Jewish suburb nor the kind of immigrant neighborhood that is so familiar on the New York landscape. It is none of these, yet it contains elements of each.

It has often been remarked that Jews in America are just like everyone else. But the visible majority of Jews in Boro Park are not at all like everyone else. And the community itself is far from typical for Brooklyn or for any other part of the country. The residents of the community look different. The men and boys wear various types of covering on their heads, from the fur-rimmed *shtreimel* to colorful knitted *yarmulkas*. Many also wear beards of various lengths as well as *peyes*, or sidelocks of hair. Many of the men clothe themselves in long black kaftans and, generally, dark-colored suits. Although women and girls are likely to wear more colorful clothing, their appearance too is bound to be a surprise. Adult women usually cover their heads with hat or kerchief or, more often, a wig. And women of all ages may be found wearing clothes that are far less revealing of their natural contours than is typical among modern Americans. Orthodox women of this community never wear pants.

The surprising appearance of the residents is echoed by signs in Hebrew and Yiddish in shop windows, offering such exotic services as *shatnes* testing for clothes and ritual purification for new dishes and cookingware. A stroll through the community reveals countless numbers of *shtieblach,* or little basement and store-front synagogues, *yeshivas,* or day schools for children of all ages, and several *mikvas,* or ritual baths. Eavesdrop on passersby, even on children playing in the streets, and you will easily catch unfamiliar phrases in Yiddish, Hebrew, or Hungarian. And if the conversation you happen to overhear is in English, you might be surprised to find young men or women discussing some subtle issue in the Talmud or some point of *halacha,* Jewish practical law. Of course, even local gossip might contain references to prescriptions and prohibitions, *mitzvas,* and *averas* that would strike the uninitiated as puzzling. In short, the unsuspecting visitor will have the uncanny feeling of having suddenly been transported into a wholly unfamiliar, if not foreign, environment.

Boro Park may feel like a foreign environment to a visitor, but an examination of some of the standard social indicators for this community, to be presented later on, reveals that this urban neighborhood is not too different from the American middle-class standard. Age, income, education, and occupational characteristics all point to the fact that this community is rather typically American—even though only one third of its population is third generation (native born of native parents).

Indeed, some might call Boro Park a "gilded ghetto":

> A second-generation community, located in the better neighborhoods of the city . . . whose social life was carried on exclusively with Jews of appropriate status. The institutions were all middle-class, but the participants were all Jewish.[2]

But Boro Park is not a "gilded ghetto." Kramer and Leventman state that residents of the "gilded ghetto" exhibit "a middle-class inclination to make distinctions between the sacred and the secular unknown in the ghetto where all of life came under the aegis of the sacred."[3] In the Jewish community of Boro Park, however, religious orthodoxy is, perhaps, the single most important criterion of membership. And, contrary to the observations of Kramer and Leventman, "money and what it can buy" is not the major source of status stratifying the community. Religious and secular education, observance of religious rituals, adherence to the tenets of the religious creed, and involvement in "Jewish affairs" seem to be equally important as vehicles for status achievement.

During the past decade the number of Orthodox and Hasidic *yeshivas* and synagogues has increased by nearly one hundred percent.[4] The only two non-Orthodox synagogues in the area were built before the Second World War.[5] No similar organizations have been established in Boro Park since then. And the vitality of the two existing organizations has been on a continuous decline. The overwhelming majority of Boro Park Jews seem to be fundamentalist in their adherence to the creed and practices of Judaism. The culture of the community can be characterized as Orthodox.

None of this is meant to suggest that the Orthodox Jews of Boro Park have recreated the Eastern European *shtetl.* This community is no simple transplant from another world that rigid traditionalists have managed to protect from the influences of modern America. Rather, I would like to offer the *shtetl* as an evocative metaphor of Jewish cultural and social autonomy, which the Orthodox Jews of Boro Park seem to have created along uniquely American lines during the past few decades. A cursory glance at the Boro Park Jewish community compels one to acknowledge that it is a community that is simultaneously growing more "American," more middle-class, and, religiously, more Orthodox. But to speak of such changes is to speak of a phenomenon that has, so far, not been explored in American social science.

From Shtetl to Suburb:
Reflections on the Sociology of American Jewry

The assumption that Orthodox Jews and Orthodoxy as a way of life would inevitably disappear with the Americanization of the immigrants' children and grandchildren has shaped the views both of social scientists who have studied the lives of Jewish immigrants and their children and, perhaps more importantly, of the immigrants and their children themselves. A compilation of the letters to the editor of the *Jewish Daily Forward*, published under the title *Bintel Brief,*[6] clearly indicates the prevalence of this sentiment. Old-timers decry the "waywardness" of their children: "They smoke on the holy Sabbath, can you imagine. They eat the *trefa* [non-*kosher*] food in the Irish pubs. Is this what we came to this golden land for? What are heartbroken parents to do? And we can't even speak English." Young adults, on the other hand, decry the backwardness of their parents: "My mother cries and curses because I date an Italian girl from the shop where I work. She can't understand that here in America everyone is the same. What do I care that her parents were Catholics in the Old Country? Neither her parents nor mine can speak English. They can't understand us, but we understand each other just fine. Please advise. How does one educate such ignorant parents?"

While these quotes are synthesized from a number of different letters, they convey the sentiments one finds in many individual ones. The elders see an ancient tradition, with all its rules, regulations, and complex structure of time and space, evaporating into thin air. Its elements are slipping through their fingers under pressures they cannot comprehend, much less control. To the young, the sooner it all passes, the better. Both agree that Orthodoxy as a way of life in America is bound to disappear in two or three generations.

To be sure, pessimism about the future of Orthodoxy, either as a religious system or as a way of life, was not universal. Religious stalwarts from the Old Country clung to the traditional habits of dress, lifestyle, and ritual and even built institutions, such as *shuls*, *mikvas*, *kosher* butcher shops, and *yeshivas*, to perpetuate them. But such stalwarts were exceptions, and their efforts were often perceived by others as well as themselves as "holding actions" against the inevitable tide.

Like the religious stalwarts, the literature dealing with efforts to perpetuate Orthodoxy in America departs from the main drift. This handful of publications is at the periphery of a much larger body of literature devoted to the culture and community patterns of non-Orthodox American Jews.[7] Sociological literature dealing with the Jewish experience in America, most of it written by Jews, relegates Orthodoxy to a residual category.

Marshall Sklare's is, perhaps, the best-known work in this area. Initially, Sklare attempted to show the impact of American society on traditional Jewish thought and communal life. He argued persuasively that Conservative Judaism, both as a system of religious thought and as a form of communal organization, has been the single most important consequence of the contact between Jews and America.[8] Moreover, he considered Conservative Judaism the wave of the future for American Jews:

It mediates between the demands of the Jewish tradition, the feeling of both alienation and nostalgia toward first and second settlement areas, and the norms of middle-class worship. It must in effect borrow something from each of these elements and synthesize them into a new pattern.[9]

Sklare provides no clear sociological explanation for the emergence and growth of the Conservative movement. He suggests several explanatory variables: (1) geographic mobility from an area of high concentration of Jewish population to areas of low concentration; (2) the status anxieties of middle-class Jews over what are considered lower-class religious practices; (3) the threat of anomie; (4) the need for group survival; and (5) the popularity of religious identification in America. But he fails to provide a clear line of theoretical explanation as to how these variables relate to one another, and how they collectively result in Conservative Judaism. In failing to offer a clear theoretical explanation for the Conservative movement, he also sidesteps the question of whether the type of adjustment to American life represented by Conservative Judaism might not be historically relative to the time and social circumstances in which it emerged. Certainly, Sklare's own reflections on his earliest work led him very close to that question. In one of his more recent works he acknowledged that "Conservatism is incorrect in its diagnosis of Orthodoxy and especially in its prognosis of Orthodoxy's future. . . . The full story of the renaissance of American Orthodoxy has yet to be written."[10] It is also interesting that in one of his latest works, on Jewish life in America, Sklare does not have a single reference to Conservative Judaism.[11]

The theme given so much prominence by Sklare was aptly summarized by Gans: "The main trends in the development of the American Jewish community can be traced most clearly in the changes that take place between the generations."[12] This theme has served as the central organizing principle in the works of several social scientists who have concerned themselves with Jewish life in America.[13] Goldstein and Goldscheider in their study of the Jewish community of Providence, Rhode Island, provide the most recent systematic expression of this theme.[14] They illuminate differences among three generations with regard to family ties, social class, education, and religiosity, differences that point to a general decline of Jewish distinctiveness and hence of Jewish Orthodoxy.

Community and Social Structure

All the works dealing with Jewish communities have tended to accept the scenario first outlined by Louis Wirth in 1929, and echoed in 1969 by Leventman—the movement "from shtetl to suburb"[15] (though, as the title of this book suggests, there is evidence, at least among America's Orthodox, of movement in the opposite direction as well). The suburbanization and concomitant Americanization of Jewry, it is argued, have resulted from a number of social structural changes, among them: changes in Jewish secular education, changing Jewish career patterns, changes in family patterns and the significance of the family, changes in communal organization, and the decline of traditional authority.

Put simply, various studies make it apparent that the American Jewish community has not been exempt from processes of bureaucratization and rationalization that have had an impact upon modern American life in general. These studies show that, if anything, the Jewish community has embraced such processes more readily than many other subgroups in American society. Still, the motivation for the apparent readiness of Jews to accept the processes of rationalization remains an open-ended question. Some observers point to a rationalistic tradition in Judaism. But it is likely that the explanation lies in the position of Jews in America at the time when these processes gained momentum on the American scene. As is clear from the contemporary debate over the "merit system" and university open-admissions programs, Jews had a lot to gain by accepting the processes of bureaucratization and rationalization. In any case, from our perspective, the important point is that, by and large, works dealing with the Jewish community implicitly have assumed the validity of a number of sociological generalizations that may be open to question.

Most significant among these generalizations is a thesis made popular by Vidich and Bensman in their study of the relationship between local community and mass society. They emphasize the intrusions of mass society into local communities, and view the community:

> as a limited and finite universe in which one can examine in detail some of the major issues of modern American society, . . . a stage upon which the major issues and problems typical of the larger society are played out.[16]

This thesis has been assumed willy-nilly in most studies of Jewish communities. No effort has been made to determine whether their religiosity and ethnic character have caused any modifications in how Jews adapted to those pervasive forces of modern life.

Another assumption that has casually insinuated itself into most studies of the Jewish community concerns residential patterns. Social scientists have assumed there is something natural, almost necessary, about the transition from what Fred Massarik has called the "Dense Jewish Urban Area" to "Jewish Suburbia."[17] This assumption has been buttressed by assumptions about the dominant features of the two types of community. Although Massarik allows that "the Dense Jewish Urban Area is the contemporary successor of the ghetto," it is their ghetto-like features that have been stressed in most studies of Jewish communities. Thus, the urban areas of Jewish settlement have been seen as populated by the elderly, the less mobile, the less Americanized, the lower in social class.[18]

In sharp contrast to this "ghetto" (Wirth), or "area of first settlement" (Sklare), or "Dense Jewish Urban Area" (Massarik), stands a type of Jewish community variously referred to as "the third area of settlement" (Sklare), "the gilded ghetto" (Kramer and Leventman), or simply "Jewish Suburbia" (Massarik). As Massarik points out, "The assumption is still widespread that Jewish Suburbia is a very homogeneous 'upwardly mobile, young couple, tract home' type of community."[19] Sklare's "Lakeville studies" not only support this assumption but see it as the future of the American Jewish community at large:

> just as differences in social characteristics between Jews and Gentiles are in the processes of diminishing, so do we expect that in the decades ahead the Jews of the nation at large will increasingly come to resemble today's Lakeville Jews.[20]

The acceptance of the "suburbanism as a way of life" thesis has not been explicit in any specific study of an American Jewish community. For this reason it has not been questioned. Yet the persistence of urban communities has received increasing attention in recent sociological research. Sociologists such as Ross, Mann, and Litwak have produced increasing evidence that specific forms of "local community" persisting in urban areas are meaningful for the residents who still live there.[21] Meanwhile, the study of American Jewish communities has continued to take as its premise the inevitable decline of urban communities and their relocation in suburbia. This assumption has been retained even in the face of near-violent struggles in the recent past over the issues of "community control" and "decentralization" in places such as New York City.

Thus, the sociology of Jewish communities in America can be seen as resting upon assumptions that, since the 1960s, have been a subject of contention, to say the least. The scope of this study does not allow a thorough investigation of the reasons why sociologists who study American Jews have been so willing to make these dubious assumptions. But it is clear that in making them they have neglected to study those patterns of community that have persisted or recently emerged among Jews living in urban centers.

Culture and Identity

Alongside the body of literature dealing with specific Jewish communities in America one finds a body of literature dealing with Jewish culture and, more prominently, with Jewish identity. The mid-1950s saw a sudden flurry of intellectual activity related to Jewish culture, culminating in several well-known publications. The dominant theme was spelled out by Gans, who, as we noted earlier, saw the shape of Jewish culture determined primarily by inter-generational changes among descendants of the immigrant generation. Thus, he saw the "second generation" as pivotal in the formation of the future of Jewish culture in America:

> The second-generation Jew, who has kept a custom here and a ceremony there from a once living complex, yet wants to experience them as "richly" and "fully" as if they were still the vital habits of old, has had to seek symbols, or tangible representations, outside himself in order to endow what he has preserved with concrete reality. These symbols have now become the appurtenances of what might be called an "objectified" Judaism.[22]

This generation has rejected its sense of "total Jewishness" and, as Herberg points out, has become like everyone else in the "triple melting pot" of America: Protestant, Catholic, or Jew.[23] According to Glazer, it has also fueled the "revival" of Judaism in America. As second- and third-generation Jews have moved out from communities with dense Jewish populations, "Jewishness" has declined. At the same time, "Conservatism and Reform have thus grown greatly, partly at the expense of Orthodoxy, for their new adherents have been defecting Orthodox Jews, and more significantly, the children of the Orthodox,"[24] giving rise to what Gans calls "symbolic Judaism": a collage of traditional practices and beliefs adapted to the tastes and needs of the American middle class. This transformation of integral Jewishness into Judaism is explained by Sklare and by Herberg as an accommodation of religious beliefs and practices to the demands of an open society, which—while it frowns on the particularism of ethnicity—accepts and even encourages the particularisms growing out of differences in religion. Thus, for Sklare, American Judaism developed into what he calls an "ethnic church," and, for Herberg, the Judaism of the second and third generation was just one way of being an American.[25]

Cultural change is seen, at least implicitly, as related to changes in identity. For most researchers, the "minority status" experienced by the second generation was the primary source of the identity crisis of American Jews that has had far-reaching consequences for contemporary Jewish culture. As Leventman has written, "Undoubtedly, a major dilemma for American Jews is how to participate as widely as possible in the general society and be as much like everyone else as possible while preserving a distinctive and separate in-group life."[26] The need to "be like everyone else" is seen as the driving force behind the transformation of "Jewishness" into "Judaism" (that is, the compartmentalization of religious identity). On the other hand, "Survivalism" (Sklare) or the "need to remember" (Rosenberg) is seen as the source of the cultural distinctiveness of Jewish Americans.[27] It should be pointed out that, though the connection between culture and identity is readily apparent, there has been no systematic formulation of this connection. Thus Sklare's exhaustive study of "Jewish identity" does not offer any conjectures as to how culture and identity might be related.[28]

Reflection on the various studies of Jewish culture and Jewish identity does reveal a number of assumptions from general sociology. On the cultural level these studies seem to assume that the "secularization thesis" is true. This thesis rests on the argument first proposed by Max Weber that the rationality inherent in the modern economy has a disenchanting effect on religion, leading to a displacement of religious, magical, or otherworldly symbols from everyday life. The general displacement of religious concerns and religious institutions from the center stage of everyday life is what students of religion in modern society have called the process of "secularization." The effects of this process on personal religiosity and on religious institutions have been the major theme of contemporary sociology of religion.[29] Though the sociological study of Judaism has assumed this process to be an important force in contemporary Jewish life, the specific relationship between secularization and Jewish culture has not been examined. Once again, a sociological generalization, tacitly assumed in the study of the Jewish experience in America, has prevented sociologists from exploring the relationship between certain general societal forces and a particular subculture. This lacuna in the sociology of Jewish life is particularly unfortunate in light of the literature on what Robert Alter labels the "fever of ethnicity" and the persistence of religion.[30]

An additional assumption underlying the putative secularization of Judaism is a sort of gravitational theory of identity. That is, it is assumed that there exist in the individual certain identity needs such that, if the individual belongs to a "minority group," he will seek to bring his identity into harmony with the norms of the majority. Sklare assumed this almost explicitly: "when the interaction is that between a dominant group and minority group, the similarities produced by the contact result from the modification of the minority culture."[31] Leventman's statement, cited earlier, about the need of Jews to be like everyone else also assumes an implicit theory of identity. A theory of identity, however, has not been made explicit in any study of Jewish culture or Jewish identity, with one notable exception—Verbit's use of reference group theory to explain the changes in the religious orientations of Jewish college students.[32]

The assumption apparent in all studies of Jewish identity is that the traditional Jew in modern America experiences what psychologists call "cognitive dissonance."[33] According to the theory of cognitive dissonance, as first proposed by Festinger, a stable identity requires cognitive consistency:

> The basic background of the theory consists of the notion that the human organism tries to establish harmony, consistency or congruity among his opinions, attitudes, knowledge and values. That is, there is a drive toward consonance among cognitions.[34]

The individual who experiences dissonance will seek to reduce it either by obtaining confirmation of his cognitions from his environment or by abandoning or modifying those elements of his cognitions that are dissonant with cognitive elements of his environment.

Studies of Jewish identity in America seem to take for granted the basic postulates of Festinger's theory. They suggest that in the confrontation between a minority identity and a majority culture the individual in the "cognitive minority" will experience some form of discomfort that will exert pressure on him to change his identity or, at least, to bring the more dissonant elements of his identity into consonance with the normative elements of the majority culture.[35]

Thus, Goldstein and Goldscheider refer to the third generation as the generation of security, clearly implying that for the first and second generation of Jews the experience of cognitive dissonance was too strong, preventing them from feeling comfortable in America.[36] On the other hand, the third generation have finally managed to bring themselves into line—cognitively speaking.

Recent analyses of what some have called the "post-industrial" era or the "post-modern" culture of America have pointed toward the tendency of "institutional isolation." Anton Zijderveld has explained this point as follows:

> This is the tendency of institutional sectors, such as the family, religion, government, education, the military system, etc., to grow autonomous. As autonomous sectors, they exert control over the individual only in so far as he falls within their "jurisdiction." . . . Living between various institutional sectors, each requiring from him a behavior that conforms to its autonomous norms and values, the individual will automatically develop a pluralistic identity.[37]

Although Zijderveld does not develop the theme of "pluralistic identity," the concept is of great significance for this study. It suggests that the social structural conditions of contemporary society produce individuals who, in fact, do not share a common, overarching definition of reality. The high degree of structural integration is not accompanied by a similar level of cultural integration.[38] Thus the cognitive orientations of individuals are controlled only within very limited bounds of jurisdiction.

Zijderveld calls advanced industrial societies "abstract."[39] The individual in such societies is:

> unable to experience an ultimate order in which each part obtains a stable position, in which truth and freedom are embedded in a taken for granted manner, and from which everyone and everything deductively acquires meaning and reality. . . . This loss . . . has deprived man of the solid ground on which his identity was founded.[40]

In such a society the individual recognizes only an abstract system of rules and regulations, designed to achieve goals with which he may be totally unfamiliar, and to which his value commitments are entirely unnecessary. Indeed, the individual must cultivate the ability to carry out his technical functions with a minimum of involvement: "The system needs detached and strictly functional experts—rational appa-ratchiks who are sufficiently dehumanized [in the public sphere] to be factors in the realization of calculable goals."[41] At the same time, as a way of coping with increasing dehumanization in the public sphere, "the private sphere emerges . . . as a refuge from the overwhelming and demanding powers of society."[42] Zijderveld seems to suggest, however, that the increasing privatization of personal life is independent of ultimate meanings or values. Hence, individual autonomy, which is one of the promises of the abstract society, is accompanied by the curse of alienation and anomie. Identity in contemporary society thus becomes compartmentalized, with a large compartment relegated to the private sphere.

Perhaps Zijderveld is overly pessimistic about the potentialities of post-industrial society. But his work does spell out the personal and cultural consequences of recent social change. While his insights are not altogether new, Zijderveld clarifies much about the impact of advanced industrialization on culture and identity—a subject that has been previously discussed in a far more abstruse manner by such critical thinkers as Mannheim, Marcuse, and Habermas; and in a far more sanguine manner by such American sociologists as Bell and Etzioni.[43] Each of these writers has recognized, albeit from different points along the theoretical and political spectrum, what Etzioni has stated most clearly:

> The modern period ended with the radical transformation of the technologies of communication, knowledge, and energy that fol-lowed World War II. A central characteristic of the modern period has been the continued increase in the efficacy of the technology of production which poses a growing challenge to the primacy of the values these means are supposed to serve.[44]

Thus, the post-modern period has been described by some leading contemporary theorists as one marked by the growing autonomy of major social institutions, placing them not only beyond moral con-straints that develop out of a shared value system, but also beyond direct manipulation by individuals.

Post-modern abstract society does, indeed, persist without the value commitments of its members. To that extent society at large has forsaken its role as the dominant source of social reality for individuals. But it must be recognized that for individuals living in abstract societies the concept of society itself is abstract. The new keepers of social reality are the various primary groups—religion, family, community, or otherwise (they all fulfill a religious function)—that are ready and able to offer individuals a symbolic universe of meaning.[45]

But what of "cognitive dissonance"? Would not that force individuals to abandon the worldviews of their separate primary groups, and, ultimately produce a "common culture"? As Berger and Luckmann put it, "The appearance of an alternative symbolic universe poses a threat because its very existence demonstrates empirically that one's own universe is less than inevitable."[46]

It could easily be argued, however, that empirical demonstration is not enough reason to abandon a value, particularly when an entire symbolic universe of meaning is at stake. Thus a diversity of symbolic universes in an abstract society need not lead to cognitive dissonance for members of the various cognitive minorities.

Indeed in the relative absence of cultural integration, the likelihood that an individual will experience cognitive dissonance if he is a member of a cognitive minority diminishes significantly. Instead we may find a situation in which all members of the larger society are alienated from the dominant structure, which they perceive as essentially abstract and meaningless, but which nonetheless offers enough physical benefits to warrant continued participation on a purely contractual basis. Once their contractual relationship with the abstract society is fulfilled, people promptly withdraw into finite universes of meaning which, by present-day standards, constitute paramount realities. Thus predictions regarding the fate of cognitive minorities in American society must be reevaluated. That is the larger theme of this work, and in the pages that follow we will explore its empirical ramifications as they apply to a particular minority—the Orthodox Jews of Boro Park. Specifically, we will provide support for the following statements about this community.

1. It constitutes a symbolic universe of meaning for its inhabitants, whose ultimate value commitments are to this community.

2. The fact that it is located in an urban center of an abstract society has little effect in eroding the community because the community and the society in which it is located are not in tension or conflict.

3. The individuals who inhabit this community and are committed to its values do not experience cognitive dissonance, nor do they show any

signs of redirecting their beliefs or rituals to bring them more into line with some putative dominant culture—because they do not perceive the broader culture of American society as dominant. They perceive it merely as desirable.

From Suburb to Shtetl: *The Renaissance of Jewish Orthodoxy*

Lest we put the conclusions too far before the study itself, let us take a few steps back and recall the highlights and purpose of this chapter. We have tried to sketch the basic ingredients of Jewish Orthodoxy as a way of life. So far as available evidence permits us to guess, Orthodoxy was the predominant way of life for the majority of Jews prior to their immigration to the New World. Social scientific study of Jewish life in the United States has presumed that Jewish Orthodoxy would not enjoy a long lease on life. Scholars and historians interested in the evolution of Jewish life in America have tended to ignore the Orthodox branch, convinced that it is a rapidly passing phenomenon in the New World.

The Jewish experience in Boro Park suggests, however, that modification of the general as well as some of the particular prognoses concerning the relationship between Jewish Orthodoxy and American society is in order. And in recent years there has been a noticeable shift in scholarly opinion on the Orthodox. Those who earlier wrote them off as a dying branch of Judaism have begun speaking of the "renaissance of American Orthodoxy." Indeed, such a renaissance can be documented in communities from Los Angeles to Boston, in scores of neighborhoods around the country.[47] But to this date there has been no effort to record, describe, or explain this so-called renaissance.

Lest we overstate, and thus distort the facts, let us be quite clear about this renaissance. It has not involved any mass movement among America's Jews. It has taken place *in pianissimo*, quietly, within the confines of relatively small communities. Boro Park is one of the communities where it has been most evident. But Boro Park is more than simply an example. It is a model. In fact, with a population of about fifty-five thousand Orthodox, it is the largest of the communities in which Orthodox Judaism has re-emerged as a vibrant model of Jewish living in a modern society.

Our choice of this minority community has, thus, been dictated by several considerations. First, Jewish Orthodoxy is a resurgent but anomalous phenomenon in contemporary urban America. Second, it is a phenomenon the reality of which is most evident at the level of specific local communities. Finally, we have chosen to study the Jewish community of Boro Park because it is, in the 1970s, the largest and most dynamic of all Orthodox Jewish communities in America. It is our contention that the renaissance of Orthodox Judaism can be best understood in microcosm, at the level where people actually live out such things, in the community. Therefore, it is the aim of this book to describe in rich, living detail the social history and the contemporary social profile of the Orthodox community in Boro Park.

2 From Shtetl to Suburb and Back
A Social History of the Jews of Boro Park

Since the landing of the Jewish pilgrims in New Amsterdam in 1654, the relative openness of America has made the yoke of the Torah increasingly more difficult to bear. Thus, as we have seen in the first chapter, Orthodoxy as a life style and as a movement has had a rather limping career in American Jewish life. As each new generation became more Americanized, it sprouted new communities and new forms of religious life consistent with modern, secular values. Boundaries between Jew and non-Jew became more permeable, and the Jewish communities of America shaped themselves in the image of the host society. This transition has involved both geographic mobility away from the so-called ghettos and social mobility up from the status of pre-modern, poor immigrants to modern, middle-class Americans. Leventman captured both the pathos and the cultural dynamics of this inter-generational process in his lively article called "From Shtetl to Suburb."[1] His title inspired the title of this chapter. We have, however, reversed the direction.

In this chapter we shall trace the evolution of the Boro Park Jewish community. Our objective here is to inform as well as to convince. We shall try to bring to life the process through which this unusual community has developed. At the same time we shall try to make plausible the direction of development suggested by our title.

Boro Park before Jewish Settlement

In his history of Brooklyn, Henry Stiles offers the following account of the origins of the territory known today as Boro Park (Map 1): "On the 10th of September, 1645, a tract of land on the bay of the North River between Coney Island and Gowanus, and forming the present town of New Utrecht, was purchased from its native inhabitants for the West India Company."[2] The local Indians—the Canarsee—gained from this transaction "a quantity of shirts, shoes, stockings, knives, scissors, and combs."[3] The town of New Utrecht itself was established by one Cornelius van Werckhoven, a member of the Dutch West India Company, on the basis of a petition granted by Governor Peter Stuyvesant in August of 1657. Available records indicate that the territory of New Utrecht was divided into twenty plots, fifty acres each, and apportioned among nineteen families of Dutch colonists. One of the plots, the twentieth, was reserved for the poor.[4] Although initially a sparsely settled agricultural territory, the area acquired more population and prestige in subsequent centuries. At the beginning of the twentieth century, residents reported that it was "one of the most beautiful residential communities in America." They also boasted of some historic notables.

> General Robert E. Lee planted a tree near St. John's Episcopal Church when he was vestryman of the church from 1842 to 1844. In this same church General Thomas J. (Stonewall) Jackson was baptized. Lee and Jackson were both stationed for a time at Fort Hamilton.[5]

The area appears to have included among its residents some of America's first and most respectable settlers. Jews came considerably later.

It is noteworthy that, as late as 1867,[6] Henry Stiles makes no mention of any Jewish organizations in his survey of "Hospitals, Dispensaries, Asylums, Benevolent and Religious Institutions and Associations." And there seems to have been no Jewish school or synagogue in Boro Park until 1881.[7] Farms were bought and sub-divided as early as 1891, and it was during this era that the neighborhood came to be known as Boro (or Borough) Park.[8] It was also during this period that Jewish residents make their appearance.

In many respects Boro Park is typical of the neighborhoods that came to be settled by upwardly mobile immigrants following the extending ganglia of the New York City subway system in the 1920s. Rows of modest single-family and multi-family homes face one another across tree-lined streets and avenues. Here and there a six-story apartment house breaks the suburban landscape, reminding the visitor that this, after all, is the city and not the suburbs. Or, perhaps more correctly, the landscape reminds us that communities like Boro Park were indeed the suburbs for eagerly Americanizing immigrants of the turn of the century. The name of the community itself appears to have been the invention of one of the many real estate speculators operating in the area at the time. The name has no legal status even today as there are no boundaries recognized by the State or City of New York that would define Boro Park per se. The allure of the name was obviously intended to attract Manhattanites to the "country-like" ambiance of the newly developing neighborhood.[9] An-

Map 1. Brooklyn, New York. Reprinted from Egon Mayer, "The "Objectivated Symbol System Technique," in *Urbanism, Urbanization, and Change: Comparative Perspectives,* ed. Paul Meadows and Ephraim Mizruchi (Reading, Mass.: Addison-Wesley, 1976), p. 161.

other contemporary observer reports that "Boro Park, newest of three communities in the New Utrecht area, is largely the product of the real estate boom of the 20's."[10] Another account in the *Brooklyn Eagle* fills in some of the details.

> About the turn of the century trolleys were running on New Utrecht Avenue from 39th Street to Bath Beach. McDougall's farm with the mansion and the windmill was on the hill west of the West Brooklyn Station on 44th Street and New Utrecht Avenue. A new station was added at 49th Street and New Utrecht Avenue, and the Blythbourne station was at 55th Street and New Utrecht Avenue. The space between the West Brooklyn and Blythbourne stations and between New Utrecht Avenue and 15th Avenue became known as Borough Park. The ex-State Senator, William H. Reynolds, a real estate man, developed Borough Park in collaboration with Edward Johnson, a builder.[11]

By coincidence, the name Boro Park surfaced in popular usage and newspaper articles at about the same time Jews began to settle there. Perhaps for this reason Boro Park has always been considered, at least by Jews, as a "Jewish neighborhood."

Jews and Suburbanization

The socialist-Jewish novelist Michael Gold recounts his visit to the area in the twenties:

> One Sunday we travelled to Borough Park to see the house and lot Zechariah was persuading my father to buy. . . . The suburb was a place of half-finished houses and piles of lumber and brick. Paved streets ran in rows between empty fields where only the weeds rattled. Real estate signs were stuck everywhere. In the midst of some rusty cans and muck would be a sign, "Why Pay Rent? Build Your House in God's Country." We came at last to Zechariah's. It was a large green house bulging with bay windows and pretentious cupolas. As we entered, there whined from within a petulant female voice, "Have they wiped their feet, Zechariah?" Mrs. Cohen, a fat, middle-aged woman, lay on a sofa. She glittered like an ice-cream parlor. . . . Her bleached yellow hair blazed with diamond combs and rested on a pillow of green velvet. She wore a purple silk waist, hung with yards of tapestry and lace. Diamonds shone from her ears; diamond rings sparkled from every finger. she looked like some vulgar, pretentious prostitute, but was only the typical wife of a Jewish nouveau riche.[12]

In a subsequent passage of *Jews Without Money* we find the fictional
Zechariah urging the author's father to stake his claim to a piece of Boro
Park real estate:

> Look, Herman, it's the best piece of property in Brooklyn! In five
> years it will be worth double the price! It is because you are my
> foreman, and I want to make a "mensch" out of you that I am giving
> you this chance. All the refined businessmen are moving here.[13]

Zechariah was, of course, correct. A great many of the successful
businessmen did move to Boro Park. By 1930 its Jewish population was
approximately 60,000, constituting a little over 50 percent of the
neighborhood. The other half was made up of Irish at one end and Italians
at the other. More important than the "Jewish density" of the area,
however, was its cultural ambiance. Both Jewish and other ethnic
residents of the area were on the beginning rungs of the American ladder
of success. Consequently, their homes, their lawns, their synagogues, and
their other public institutions tended to symbolize their material
achievements. Yiddish was falling into disuse, the synagogues took on the
architecture and decorous atmosphere associated with places of
Christian worship, and Jewish education was relegated to an "after
school affair" for most of the Jewish children in the area. The majority of
the homes were single or, at most, two-family dwellings, surrounded by
generous gardens. The public buildings that dotted the community
landscape, such as Temples Emanu-El and Beth-El, the Sephardic
congregation, and the YMHA, were imposing and expensive structures.
One of the first boys' *yeshivas* (all-day Hebrew schools), Etz Chaim,
founded in 1917 and closed in 1979, was a converted country club in the
heart of the community, on Thirteenth Avenue. While all these institutions proclaimed the traditional Jewish loyalties of the Boro Parkers,
they proclaimed with equal vigor the pride the residents felt in their
"Americanness," their financial success, and their general modernness.

Boro Park was never an area of first settlement, or a typical immigrant
enclave. The Jews who moved in and made their homes here were not
"just off the boat" or greeners. Boro Park was, and largely continues to
be, an area of second and third settlement. A move to Boro Park was, from
the start, a move up. The first Jewish residents in the area were the
successful, upwardly mobile immigrants, and, more frequently, the
children of such immigrants, who had settled some years earlier in either
the Lower East Side of Manhattan or in other Jewish ghettos, such as
Brownsville (in Brooklyn) or Newark (in New Jersey). A number of older

residents who participated in a family survey we conducted—which, along with the other methodology employed in this study, is described in detail in the Appendix—offered useful insights into the quality of mind that brought these early settlers to Boro Park. For example, Mr. P.W.'s father had immigrated into the United States as a lad of fourteen from Bialystock (northeastern Poland): "He bought property on the East Side. At that time the East Side was growing and he grew with the proper- ties."[14] Subsequently, the father moved his family to Prospect Park West, a park-like area in Brooklyn that was relatively accessible to lower Manhattan at that time. After some experiences with anti-Semitism, the family moved once again—this time to Boro Park. P.W. had lived in the Boro Park community since about 1920. His wife came to the community some years later from Brownsville, motivated by similar aspirations: to get out of the crowded ghetto into an aesthetically more pleasant area, yet one that had other Jewish residents and was easily accessible to the business districts of Brooklyn and Manhattan. They, and many others like them, saw in the Boro Park community the first signs of the fulfillment of America's promise: a home one could proudly call his own, a neigh- borhood in which one could take pride and feel secure, and neighbors with whom one shared some common fate and interests.

The settlement of Jewish residents in the area was facilitated by another, far less personal, circumstance: the extension of the subway system into the outlying reaches of Brooklyn. "The growth and extension of the rapid transit facilities connected what were once remote districts with the central downtown business district. . . . Boro Park with 'trop- ical gardens' and parks became increasingly accessible [in the early 1920s]."[15] By 1930 the size of the Jewish population in the area had just about tripled from what it had been at the turn of the century. By one reliable account it had increased to over 60,000 people.[16]

Mrs. L. moved into the community during the 1930s. Her parents had originally immigrated from Poland and settled in Trenton, New Jersey. She recalls how:

> We lived in Trenton and it was really a tough, tough thing to be a Jew. I'd walk the street and some of the kids would call me "sheeny, sheeny Christ killer." We lived in a section where we had to go three and a half miles to *shul* [synagogue]. We had to go three and a half miles to do our shopping at the *kosher* butcher. But in Boro Park if you want to be a Jew, and not eat anything *unkosher* you can do it.[17]

Her family, as well as her husband's family, had moved to the Boro Park community as a step toward improving their general life circumstances and their circumstances as observant Jews.

For the families of Mr. and Mrs. L. the move to Boro Park had not involved a move out of the immigrant ghetto, as it had for P.W.'s family. But for all three sets of families the move to Boro Park most assuredly constituted a step up on the ladder of social mobility.

In most cases the early Jewish settlers of the community clearly represent the second-generation phenomenon. One of the many studies on the subject summarized this phenomenon as follows:

> The alienation and marginality of the second generation and the different social situations they faced led them to develop parallel social structures to harmonize with their newly found success and status. Rejecting the Orthodoxy of their parents, they searched for new modes of religious expression more in congruence with their Americanized way of life.[18]

For the early Jewish residents of Boro Park the motivation to leave behind the immigrant ghettos was, undoubtedly, commingled with an aversion for the incoherent, exotic traditions and rituals that they associated with those ghettos. While they insisted on remaining Jews, and living in a Jewish neighborhood, their conception of religious identity was clearly an accommodating one. It had to suit their increasingly middle-class lifestyle. Such an attitude is corroborated by the early history of Jewish organizations in the community. The first temples, for example, were Temple Emanu-El (1904) and Temple Beth-El (1906). Both catered to the religious sentiments of the community in a manner that would be consistent with the principles of Conservative Judaism: an emphasis on decorum and style as opposed to traditionalism and emotionality. The first religious schools were also founded during this period: the congregational school of Temple Emanu-El and Machzike Talmud Torah (1908). The latter was a communal school which, by 1918, had an enrollment of over six hundred students and a staff of ten teachers.[19] It should be pointed out that, as early as 1918, the Boro Park Jewish community could boast that compared to all other Jewish communities in the New York area, it had the largest proportion of its youth receiving some form of religious education.[20] Another significant community organization established by the early Jewish residents was the Borough Park Young Men's Hebrew Association—the Jewish equivalent of the YMCA—founded in 1912 and built in 1914. The building cost one hundred thousand dollars. It contained, as it does today, a swimming pool, gymnasium, auditorium, game rooms, and classrooms in which classes were conducted in business and commercial subjects and citizenship training. Israel Zion Hospital was established in 1919. It had the distinction of being one of the few, if not the only, hospital in the New York area that served only *kosher* food from its kitchen.[21]

In all, the *Jewish Communal Register* listed twenty-seven permanent synagogues in the Boro Park area as of 1918.[22] Of these, fifteen were listed as Orthodox, seven as Conservative, and five as Reform. The language of prayer was restricted to Hebrew in seventeen of the synagogues, while in ten prayer was in both Hebrew and English. The language of sermons and announcements, on the other hand, was in English in seventeen of the synagogues and in Yiddish in ten. Thus, at least one third of the Orthodox synagogues were sufficiently Americanized to use English as the *lingua franca* outside of prayer. It should also be noted that twenty of the permanent synagogues erected their own buildings expressly for the purposes of the organization. Only seven occupied make-shift (storefront type) quarters that are normally associated with lower-class ethnic congregations.[23]

The construction activities of the early residents were quite amazing. Expensive, large edifices dotted the area, thus lending it a very specific definition. There were no structures built by competing religions or secular organizations to detract from the impressive shadow cast over the community by these early Jewish organizations. Most of these organizations are still extant. The sheer physical appearance of these structures testified to the success of the residents who built them. At the same time, both the structures and the activities pursued within them testified to the values these early residents had brought along from their ancestral homes.

Synagogues, which are the primary reflection of the commitments of the early residents to the traditions of their ancestors, clearly reflected the newly achieved status of Boro Park Jews. Decorum and dignity played a significant part in the services of even the Orthodox synagogues. Unlike the haphazard interiors of the ghetto *shtieblach*,[24] the synagogues all contained a separate prayer sanctuary with fixed pews and ornaments. The members, especially the officers and the clergy, were required to wear formal dress on Saturdays and holidays.[25] Yiddish, as was pointed out earlier, had been replaced by English in many if not most of the synagogues as the *lingua franca* apart from prayer. Membership itself was subtly restricted to those who would be a source of pride to the community.[26] And certainly those who would serve as officers in the synagogue had to embody the symbols of achieved status in both the religious and the secular world.[27]

The schools that were established to impart religious education to the young of the community operated only supplementarily to the public educational system that all children of the area attended.[28] In these schools children were taught the basics of Jewish religion and tradition (e.g. reading Hebrew, the Five Books of Moses, laws and customs pertaining to daily behavior, *kosher* food, and the observance of the Sabbath and other holidays). However, no attempt was made to inculcate a system of values that would radically differentiate the young growing up in the Boro Park community from youth in society at large. What was imparted was primarily a system of special practices rather than a worldview. It was an accepted fact that these children did go to public schools, would continue to pursue an advanced secular education, and would ultimately make their achievements in the professions or business. Nothing was taught in the religious schools that would conflict with that ultimate goal. The children educated in these schools (themselves being second- or third-generation Americans) looked upon their education as something "extra" added on to their "normal" education in the public schools. They did not see themselves as different from the other, non-Jewish children who went for religious instruction after school or on Sundays.

In a pre-Depression America that emphasized success through individual effort, the Jewish community of Boro Park exemplified success. Specifically, it exemplified the success of a group of people whose parents, or who themselves, just a few years earlier had come to America as Emma Lazarus had portrayed them: "the tired and poor; the wretched refuse."[29] The organizations that were established—health facilities, educational and recreational facilities, and facilities for business and social assistance—were signs of success and also ensured that Jews would not be a burden to the larger society. The organizations were, indeed, parallel to those of American society at large. As such, they mirrored the acculturating mentality of the first Jews of Boro Park. That mentality, typically, sought to make the meaning of "being a good Jew" consistent with "being a good American."

The fact that parallel structures were developed indicates that a dominant and imitable style was perceived. Moreover, the way in which the minority culture was taught and practiced within these structures indicates a distinct sense of defensiveness—as if the culture that was being perpetuated in these structures could be made tolerable to the dominant (American) cultural style only if it were properly packaged. An example of this attitude is clearly evidenced by the report of one resident, age 56 years, who was born and raised in the Boro Park community:

> In my days, even though we were religious, we weren't so concerned with wearing a hat. It didn't seem to be that important. In fact, I remember when we would go to Young Israel during the week for social occasions, we would walk to Young Israel and then put on the *yarmulka* [skullcap]. The neighborhood was not so fanatically religious. There weren't less Jews. But we weren't so conscious of it [the need to look Jewish] as today. . . . The Jews who came in [to Boro Park] in the '40s and the '50s brought in the custom of, shall I say, the need of identifying ourselves as Jews. . . . I went to New Utrecht High School. We would walk to school without a hat, sit in school without a hat or *yarmulka*. But when we came home, naturally, we put it on. My own boys think nothing of wearing a *yarmulka* on the subway or in college. But a hat they wouldn't put on.[30]

This respondent had received considerably more Jewish education than his peers and was raised in an Orthodox home. He has always considered himself personally to be an Orthodox Jew. His attitude is, therefore, all the more telling. It speaks of no desire to abandon traditional values and practices. But it does speak most clearly of a desire to contain those values and practices within the finite boundaries of privacy. Was he ashamed of those values and practices? Shame would be perhaps too strong a description of the phenomenon. A sense of inconsistency or cognitive dissonance is more likely. That is the signal feature of the second-generation phenomenon.

Excursus: The Spur of Cognitive Dissonance

What, exactly, did the second generation experience as inconsistent? It has been argued that much of the inconsistency may be attributed to their rapid changes in status. The religious expressions of their parents were associated with low status while this generation was moving into higher-status positions in American society. The fact that subsequent generations are readier to voice traditional religious expressions is attributable to their greater sense of security.[31] This explanation assumes that the second generation was, in fact, insecure, and that it takes about a generation to become secure in an achieved status position. The explanation is plausible, despite these assumptions. The Boro Park findings, however, seem to suggest an alternative explanation for the cognitive dissonance of the second generation.

The quality of religious education appears to be a crucial factor in both the commitments of this generation and its inconsistency. Specifically, most of this generation received religious education informally, in the home. Even those who received religious instruction at some congregational school or *yeshiva* were likely to receive it from individuals whose claim to knowledge was based largely on their traditional role. The instruction was likely to involve rote learning of the basics of religion, in the realistic belief that the home would provide the rest. The home itself did not ask more from these schools. On the other hand, the children attending these schools or receiving religious training at home were sent to public schools in which the training was far more rationally organized (in the formal sense of that word). One passed from grade to grade, earned awards (or, God forbid, failed), and generally moved through the system in a step by step process of achievement. Success was based on a series of rationally understandable steps. Thus, achievement in the secular world stood out in sharp contrast to lack of achievement in the religious world. As achieved status was highly valued by society at large, it was quite difficult for the upwardly mobile second generation to sustain a high level of interest in their development as Jews.

The inconsistency experienced by the second generation, then, was not so much that between high and low status, though, to be sure, that was part of it. Rather, it was due to the discrepancy between achievements in two different status systems. While these may not seem like greatly different explanations, the latter explanation is logically more consistent with the fact that the second generation experienced such great ambivalence toward its Jewishness. It also helps to explain the fact that in recent years Jewish religious education has become rationally organized, and the religiosity of Jews has become achievement oriented. These points will be elaborated below.

Phase II

The early period in the history of Boro Park Jewry corresponds quite closely to the period Kranzler has called "Phase I" in his study of Williamsburg Jewry.[32] This is not the only similarity between the two communities. A number of other subsequent developments in the two communities also reveal parallel patterns, which suggests that Kranzler's chronological divisions be adopted here.

At the turn of the century the community was still quite rural in character. By the 1930s the area had become a suburb within the city, and a Jewish community had been firmly implanted. As such, it could boast of all the organizations necessary for the maintenance of Jewish culture in an ambiance which no longer betrayed any evidence of the struggle and shame that had preceded the achievements of this generation. Moreover, it had become a community in which success was considered the fulfillment and continuation of the American dream. Practically, this meant that the children of the community were expected to surpass the achievements of their parents and grandparents. The so-called third generation was expected to move even further up the ladder of success. Many of them did. The community itself changed little from 1930 until the end of the Second World War. With Depression followed by war, it is understandable that few if any new organizations were established during this period. And those that already existed did not embark on any bold new programs.

The young people who came of age during this period, and began to establish homes of their own after the war, to a large extent moved out of the community into what has been referred to as the third area of settlement: the more spacious communities in Queens, Long Island, and Westchester. Their places were gradually taken by newly arriving refugees from war-torn Europe.Table 1 reflects this transition in the community.

TABLE 1
The Jewish Population of Boro Park, 1930–1957

| | 1930 | | 1940 | | 1950 | | 1957 | |
Age	No.	%	No.	%	No.	%	No.	%
5 and under	5,029	8.2	3,691	6.0	5,615	8.4	4,881	7.7
5–14	10,993	18.0	8,988	14.6	9,090	13.5	9,579	15.0
15–24	13,326	21.0	11,147	18.0	9,156	14.0	7,432	11.7
25–34	11,423	18.5	12,502	20.3	10,294	15.4	8,573	13.4
35–44	8,565	14.0	9,976	16.0	11,832	18.0	9,705	15.2
45–64	9,946	16.0	12,255	19.0	15,909	23.5	17,143	26.4
65 and over	1,901	3.1	2,953	5.0	4,880	7.2	6,191	9.6
TOTAL	61,335*		61,512		66,776		63,504	

Source: Morris Horowitz and Lawrence Kaplan, *Estimated Jewish Population of the New York Area, 1900–1975* (New York: Federation of Jewish Philanthropies, 1959).

The simplest way to summarize Table 1 is to note the overall change in population of the age group under thirty-five. This group holds the future of the community in its hands. In 1930 this group constituted approximately 65 percent of the total population. Boro Park was very much a young community. By 1940 the size of this group had declined to about 59 percent of the total Jewish population. While some of this decline may have been due to a lower birth rate in the 1930s, outmigration surely contributed to it. By 1950 the size of this group had dropped further to about 51 percent and by 1957 it had dropped below 48 percent. But a noticeable increase occurred among the older age groups. By the mid-1950s the community had aged considerably. This aging was especially striking because it occurred during the era of the post-war baby boom.

Apart from the change in the general age profile of the community, the pattern of moving away, referred to earlier, is evident from cohort analysis. Thus, the 15–24 age group constituted 21 percent of the community's population in 1930. But ten years later, in 1940, the 25–34 age group constituted 20.3 percent: some members of this group had moved out during this decade. The relative size of the 25–34 cohort also declined during the decade 1930–1940—from 18.5 to 16.0 percent. On the other hand, the relative size of the older age cohorts increased during this time. After 1940, however, the war intervened to slow down the transition.

The war years—in fact, the entire decade of the 1940s and the early fifties—have been described by one resident and observer of the community as a "dormant period." It may be assumed that during this period approximately 65 percent of the community was native born but of foreign parentage.[33] The largest proportion of the foreign born were from Russia and Poland. In much smaller proportions there were also Austrians, Hungarians, Germans, and Rumanians.[34] For the foreign born, naturally an older group, residence in Boro Park marked the culmination of their success in the new world. For the native born, who grew up in or had moved into the community at an early age, residence constituted a sort of stop-over on the ladder of upward social mobility. Following the war, this latter group began to enhance its achieved status, as is apparent from statistics for the community in 1949. In that year the median family income in the Borough of Brooklyn was $3,447.00, but in Boro Park the median family income was $3,955.00. And in Boro Park the median years of education completed by people over 25 years old was 10.5, which was one and a half years more than for the borough as a whole.[35] Presumably, those who grew up in the community and completed their education during this period were ready to embark on careers and lifestyles which would eventuate in their moving out of the community. But the war years and the period immediately after were not the time for major moves. These years were a time of waiting.

During this period of waiting, the history of the Orthodox community was developing not so much in Boro Park itself as in the Jewish communities of Williamsburg and Crown Heights. Newly arriving Orthodox refugees streamed primarily into Williamsburg. In reaction to the influx of those refugees, the more established and higher-status residents of the area began moving away into "the next rungs in the hierarchy of Jewish communities, particularly Crown Heights."[36] Many of the religious organizations that relocated in Boro Park at the end of the 1950s and throughout the 1960s were established in Williamsburg and Crown Heights.

In the 1960s blacks and Puerto Ricans began moving into Brooklyn in large numbers:

> There was a gain of 285,000 blacks for a new total of 656,000; and an estimated gain of 220,000 Puerto Ricans for a total of 399,600. The non-Puerto Rican white loss during the decade was 740,000 as black and Puerto Rican concentrations built up all through north and central Brooklyn.
>
> [On the other hand] vast stretches of south Brooklyn areas—Bay Ridge, Borough Park [Boro Park], Bensonhurst, Flatbush, Flatlands, Canarsie, and new developments along the South Shore—remained more than 90 percent white.[37]

At the same time, residents of these communities, who had been immigrants themselves just a few years earlier, were making a rapid and successful adjustment to the economic structure of New York City. They established themselves in the jewelry and garment trades, they set up retail shops catering to the special needs of the Orthodox community, and the better educated entered the rapidly expanding civil service job market. Widespread publicity about the suffering experienced by most of these former immigrants during World War II had fostered a climate of tolerance that permitted them to integrate into the economy of the city. There was little pressure on them to give up such religious practices as the wearing of the *yarmulka* (skullcap), *peyes* (side curls of the hair), and traditional dark clothing, or the observance of *kashrus* (dietary laws),

Shabbos (the Sabbath), and *yomtovim* (holidays).[38] The combination of economic success and a social milieu which had become quite tolerant of their cultural idiosyncrasies made the Orthodox Jewish community of Williamsburg much more resistant to acculturation than earlier immigrant communities.

Now the pressure of new neighbors, blacks and Hispanics, settling in their midst forced them to look for neighborhoods in which they might continue the lifestyle and organizations they had established for themselves in Williamsburg. The out-flow of Jews from Boro Park between 1950 and 1957, as shown in Table 1, served as a quasi invitation to the Orthodox and Hasidic Jews of Williamsburg. For a successful first generation of Williamsburgers, the tree-lined and high-status streets of Boro Park were the most popular choice as a second area of settlement.

Thus, the end of the 1950s marks a major turning point in the history of the Boro Park community. Upon revisiting Williamsburg in 1960, Kranzler wondered "whether there will be adequate serious, concentrated efforts on the parts of interested pressure groups to save Jewish Williamsburg as one of the, if not the, most important Orthodox Jewish community in the country."[39] With the benefit of hindsight on our side, it can be stated with certainty—but not without some sadness—that the concentrated efforts of interested pressure groups never materialized, and Jewish Williamsburg is no longer the most important Orthodox Jewish community in the country. Jewish Boro Park is.

Consolidated Orthodoxy

In 1960 Kranzler could still observe that although some of the Hasidic groups, such as the Skvirer, had moved out of Williamsburg and the city, "there are still numerous other Chassidic [sic] groups left that have their own leaders, such as the Vishnitzer, the Szigeder, the Papper, the Krasner and other [smaller] Rebbes."[40] In addition, Kranzler hastened to point out, the community could still point with pride to the "basic educational institutions which have helped make Williamsburg . . . such as the Yeshiva and Mesifta Torah VoDath, the Bais Yaakov Elementary and High School and the Teacher's Seminary."[41]

By 1970 all of the pillars of the Williamsburg community had relocated either in Boro Park or at the immediate borders of the Boro Park community. All of the "rebbes" (Hasidic leaders) mentioned by Kranzler had established costly, and apparently permanent, structures in Boro Park. Torah VoDath, one of the oldest of the all-day *yeshivas* in the

United States, had relocated into a multi-million-dollar complex of buildings in Flatbush, at the very edge of Boro Park. The Bais Yaakov school system had erected several large structures in the heart of the Boro Park community. The general growth of the Jewish educational system will be discussed separately later. The main point to be noted here is that throughout the 1960s groups that were the cultural and organizational backbone of the Williamsburg community either abandoned the latter entirely in favor of the Boro Park ambiance, or established major centers in Boro Park, leaving only token organizations in Williamsburg. The one exception to this trend had been the Szatmarer group, a fundamentalist group of Hungarian Hasidim.[42] But by the 1970s even members of this group had relocated in Boro Park in large numbers, establishing a school and several *shtieblach*.

In addition to the influx from Williamsburg, the fate of the Crown Heights community also had a significant impact on the history of the Boro Park Jewish community. Very shortly after the settling of the Williamsburg area by blacks and Puerto Ricans, a similar ecological pressure began to be felt by the Jews of Crown Heights. Many Crown Heights Jews, who only recently had left Williamsburg behind in their search for a socially more desirable neighborhood, were once again faced with the prospect of either accepting residence in an ethnically integrated area or moving. Though no precise figures are available, even a passing familiarity with the neighborhood indicates that most of the Jewish residents who could afford to chose the option of moving.[43]

It is important to recall here that the group of people of whom we are speaking is composed largely of post-war immigrants, and those earlier immigrants and their descendants who, for a variety of reasons, had chosen to remain in the ambiance of the Orthodox communities of Williamsburg and Crown Heights. In the late fifties and during the sixties, under the pressure of ethnic invasion, this group chose Boro Park as their next area of settlement. Their choice was dictated by a number of factors. Apart from the obvious desire to continue to live in an exclusively Jewish neighborhood, most selected Boro Park for practical reasons. The younger ones, trained in such free professions as law, medicine, engineering, accounting, and university teaching did, in fact, move to the suburbs. But those younger residents whose careers were tied to the civil service, or to the New York City Board of Education, in which increasing numbers of Orthodox Jews were employed during the 1960s,[44] and older residents whose occupations or business enterprises tied them to the city, saw Boro Park as a viable option. These several factors jointly contributed to making Boro Park the choice of Williamsburgers and Crown Heightsers, and thus a center of Jewish Orthodoxy in the 1960s.

According to the generalizations discussed in Chapter 1 concerning the process of Jewish acculturation and assimilation in America, one might have expected that, as these Orthodox elements moved into Boro Park, a fairly well-Americanized, modern second-generation community, they would swell the ranks of already existing organizations and modify their lifestyles and worldviews to suit their new community. In the 1960s, however, this was not to be the case.

A Decade of Movements: *The '60s*

The decade began, memorably, with the young, newly elected President John F. Kennedy calling on all citizens to ask themselves, "Not what your country can do for you; but what you can do for your country." As Richard Neuhaus has reflected, "Incredibly enough, it seemed credible then, and millions of Americans, young and old, spoke without embarrassment about service to American purposes in the world."[45] It certainly seemed credible enough to the residents of the Boro Park Jewish community, as well as to the newly arriving Jews from Williamsburg and Crown Heights. Kennedy took about 70 percent of the community's votes. This despite the fact that he was Catholic. Of course, the heavily Italian population helped. But Jewish Orthodoxy too was behind him all the way. The bewilderment caused by the assassination of that president and the nation's gradual—then more rapid—involvement in a war that still remains meaningless to the ordinary citizen, had as great an effect on this community, and not a very different one, as it had on the rest of the nation.

But the events that had some of the greatest impact on the community did not always make headlines. For example, Glazer and Moynihan report that "between 1950 and 1965 the proportion of Negroes and Puerto Ricans in Brooklyn rose from 9 percent to 29 percent of the population."[46] While this statistical fact by itself made no great impression on Boro Park residents, its ramifications were keenly felt. The non-white ethnics suffered the various ills of urban decay in the very neighborhoods which had once been occupied by Jews: Bedford-Stuyvesant, Ocean Hill–Brownsville, Williamsburg, and Crown Heights. And it was in these neighborhoods that the patience of these minority groups finally gave way to riotous destruction during several summers in the mid-1960s. Apart from the inevitable tensions which had built up between non-white ethnics and Jews in these communities,[47] the riots—which did get headlines—demonstrated to the Jewish community that minority groups can make demands on the majority. The question was no longer What can I do for my country? Rather, the question was, What will the country do for me (or us)?

The demands of the militant minority hastened, and perhaps caused, the passage of a series of federal laws safeguarding and enhancing the rights and welfare of minorities, especially the non-white ethnics.[48] Simultaneously, during this period, the federal government as well as local governments, large corporations, and foundations in the private sector, organized a massive effort to upgrade the welfare and economic opportunities of minorities.[49] The Johnson administration's "War on Poverty" made huge sums of money available to bona fide, and at times not so bona fide, groups in the minority community, in an effort to "clean up the slums" and to calm the passions that had led to the riots of the mid-1960s. And, to put it bluntly, as governmental and private funds poured into the so-called minority community, the riots stopped. Often the leaders of militant groups were co-opted and given prestigious administrative positions in programs that were designed to meet their demands. Thus, as Wattenberg and Scammon argue convincingly, in many ways the militant minorities succeeded.[50]

The two Democratic Presidents, Kennedy and Johnson, whose image and promise dominated the 1960s, had pledged to get America moving again. They certainly succeeded, but in ways they had not anticipated. The domestic programs inspired by the Kennedy administration, and carried to fruition by the Johnson administration, triggered off what can, perhaps, be called a movement spirit. In this spirit all minorities—ethnic, religious, political, and most recently, sexual—became aware of the possibility that they might make claims on society without becoming an assimilated part of it. That is, they could insist on being treated as equals without becoming like everyone else. Their increased self-awareness and assertiveness led minorities to demand that the abstract entity, society, accommodate their special needs. After all, it was argued by militants and liberals alike, colored minorities had to receive special consideration because of the extraordinary disadvantages they had suffered during the past several hundred years. This argument, in fact, elicited special consideration from most of the significant sectors of American society.[51]

And with that, other minorities made the same or similar demands for special consideration with the reasonable expectation that their demands too would be satisfied. Movements under all sorts of banners sprang up—some militant, others just noisy, all assured of at least a moment's worth of historic significance under the floodlights of the mass media, and all assured of a modicum of tolerance from the rest of society.[52] It was, perhaps, in reaction to this movement spirit that Nixon was able to capture the imagination of the voting public with his priomise to "bring America together again" in 1968. Whatever Nixon's election meant for the long-term future of minorities, the decade of the 1960s stands out as a moment in history when minorities in America achieved a heightened sense of awareness and assertiveness in the context of a—momentarily, at least—tolerant host society.

It is in this context that the development of the Orthodox community in Boro Park must be understood. The population that streamed into the community during the sixties saw itself as being "pushed out" from their previous communities. Moreover, they saw those who were doing the "pushing" as being rewarded by the Establishment. The reaction almost could have been predicted: Jews in increasing numbers, particularly in New York City, took on a cultural and political posture that was to become the explicit credo of the, by now notorious, Jewish Defense League (JDL).[53]

This is certainly not meant to suggest that the JDL was formed in response to some sort of broadly based grass-roots movement, nor that it received such support from New York's Jewry once it was founded. There is no evidence to support such contentions. The establishment of the Commission on Law and Public Affairs (COLPA), just a few years earlier, is probably a better reflection of the sentiments of the community during this period.[54] The point being emphasized here is, simply, that during the latter half of the sixties Orthodox Jewry became increasingly self-conscious and assertive of its interests. That self-consciousness and assertiveness took form in both militancy and legal defense. More generally, they took form in a conscious pursuit of a distinctive cultural style. A detailed description of this cultural style will be provided in subsequent chapters. But some additional comments are necessary here to complete our account of the societal context in which the Boro Park Jewish community underwent its consolidation as a center of Orthodoxy in America.

As important as national events were in the formation of the community, local city-wide events had an equal, if not greater, impact. The election of John Lindsay as mayor of New York City must be considered a turning point. For a variety of reasons, which need not concern us here, the impact of Lindsay's policies on the city was—and, more importantly, was perceived by the Jewish community as—strongly liberal. One memorable picture of the mayor shows him, during his first term in office, walking through a black ghetto in the midst of a riot, calming people and winning their confidence. While he, undoubtedly, did win the confidence of many in that ghetto, he just as surely lost the confidence of many in the white ethnic communities. In writing of Lindsay's bid for a second term, Glazer and Moynihan noted:

> In the end Lindsay won, though with a minority of the popular vote. But it is clear that the big issue of the campaign remains as the main issue of city politics: Do city policies favor poorer Blacks as against working class and lower middle class whites. . . . Had Mayor Lindsay done too much for Negroes? . . . Had he favored Manhattan over Brooklyn and the Bronx, what had he done about crime in the streets, what was his role in the teachers' strike [of 1968], . . . and even more directly, had his tenure in office increased racial and ethnic hostility?[55]

For the Jewish community in particular, and for the white ethnics around New York in general, the answers to these questions were unequivocal. Glazer and Moynihan themselves provide a clear sense of those answers: "Ethnicity and race dominate the city more than it ever seemed possible in 1963."[56] Among the facts that stood out most sharply in the minds of the thousands of Jewish residents who were fleeing the communities of Williamsburg and Crown Heights was that the very people who were "pushing" them out were receiving the full support and sympathies of the city administration. A particularly festering sore for many—who themselves only recently had experienced all the hardships of new immigrants—was the apparent ease with which the non-white poor received all sorts of financial assistance from all levels of government. Between 1965 and 1971 the number of Brooklyn residents receiving welfare more than doubled.[57] Table 2 shows the impact of this increase on ten Brooklyn neighborhoods, including Williamsburg and Crown Heights. In Williamsburg the percentage of the population on welfare nearly doubled, while in Crown Heights it nearly tripled. The New York City welfare system seemed to epitomize, for many, all that was wrong with the mayor, the city, and American society in general.

TABLE 2
Rise in Brooklyn Welfare Cases, 1965–1971

	Percent of Population on Welfare	
Neighborhood	1965	1971
Brownsville	22.8	38.4
Bedford-Stuyvesant	19.4	35.9
Bushwick	10.1	30.8
Coney Island	20.3	27.0
East New York	7.8	30.5
Fort Greene	18.9	30.5
Crown Heights	8.3	21.9
Sunset Park °	6.2	19.6
South Brooklyn	8.7	17.4
Williamsburg	15.8	28.8

° This community is contiguous with Boro Park on the west.
Source: Table adapted from *The New York Times,* April 10, 1972, p. 22.

The frustrations and tensions engendered by the Lindsay administration in the entire white ethnic community were brought to a head in
the Jewish community during the teachers' strike of 1968. In a school
system which had become largely black and Puerto Rican during the first
few years of the 1960s, a full-scale strike by a largely Jewish teachers'
union made for a clear-cut line of battle between Jews and blacks in the
city. The city government, being the employer against whom the
teachers walked out in an illegal strike, found itself in an inevitable
alliance with the black community against the Jewish community. The
fact that this local emergency came on the heels of the 1967 Arab-Israeli
war—an international emergency that had raised Jewish self-consciousness to a record peak—only served to make the community still
more militant and persistent in its self-defense.[58]

Thus, a decade that was ushered in with a plea for, and a more or less
public commitment to, shared national purposes increasingly saw that
commitment retracted from the public sphere, and rechannelled into the
private sphere, to more immediate, personal, communal purposes.

The Jewish community in Boro Park, which had been very much an
American-Jewish community and which had served in many ways as an
area in which Jews could become Americanized yet remain Jews too,
responded to the sixties by becoming more self-consciously Jewish, by
emphasizing the second part of the hyphenated identity over the first.

Jewish enrollments in local public schools declined to the point where the city was forced to lease portions of its school buildings to local *yeshivas*.[59] Enrollments in *yeshivas*, on the other hand, grew in significant numbers. The mobility aspirations of the residents, apparently, also underwent serious changes during this period. The question of moving out of the community was raised in all of the surveys which were conducted among the various sub-groups of the community. The most frequent response reveals the extent to which the perceptions of the residents changed concerning the opportunities or the desirability of further relocation. While earlier residents, especially the younger second-generation children of the Russian and Polish immigrants, saw Boro Park as but one step in their progress towards higher socio-economic strata and the suburbs, more recent residents, who settled in the community during the sixties, gave evidence of firm intentions to remain. Typically, the respondents averred, "Boro Park is a nice community. Where shall we go? Look what happened to Brownsville, Williamsburg, Crown Heights. We can't continue running. We have to stand up for what we have here." As to the question of the desirability of the suburbs, a similar disaffection was expressed:

> What's so good about the suburbs? People there are dropping out, getting divorced left and right. Their kids are becoming hippies and drug addicts. There is no *yidishkeit* there. Why should we want to move there when everything we want we already have here. The only thing missing in Boro Park is a park with some greenery so that the kids can play there.[60]

In our survey of the Young Israel Intercollegiates, a youth group in the community, most of the respondents were unenthusiastic about moving to the suburbs. Thirty-seven percent considered it unlikely that they would move to the suburbs when the time came to set up homes and families of their own. Another 36 percent were uncertain that they would ever make such a move. Fifty-two percent considered it unlikely and 36 percent expressed uncertainty when asked if they would ever move into an area that was less densely Jewish than Boro Park.[61]

Politically too, the community turned sharply inward. Communal and religious interests took precedence over broader national concerns. Richard Nixon swept the Jewish community in 1972 by as large a plurality as he lost it in 1960. He succeeded in 1972 largely because he promised continuing support for Israel and for the concept of financial aid for religious schools.[62] Young people in the community, who just four years earlier had rallied to the idealistic calls of Robert Kennedy and Eugene McCarthy, threw their support behind Nixon in 1972. In fact, the offices of the Democratic Party in Boro Park did not even carry the names of McGovern and Shriver in their windows during the '72 campaign.

In local politics too, the community became more self-conscious and communally oriented. A weekly column began to appear in the popular *Jewish Press* analyzing local issues in terms of their implications for strictly Jewish interests. Under the authorship of a professor of political science, himself a long-time resident of Boro Park, this column informed the Jewish public of its interests in city affairs, and of the steps they might take to protect those interests.[63] As an outgrowth of their increasing self-consciousness, Boro Park Jewry began to take a more active interest in such activities as police protection and community planning.[64] In response to organizing efforts of the Maimonides Mental Health Center, they began to take a greater interest in seeking assistance and services from outside agencies in order to meet local needs.[65] Perhaps one may best summarize the impact of the sixties on the Orthodox community by observing that pride in and pressure for communal interests replaced the patience that this community had traditionally exhibited in the past in the face of felt adversity.

Jewish Pride? Jewish Power?

In a decade of movements, during which all minorities pursued their own special interests with increasing self-consciousness and persistence, the reader may wonder why the fact that Jews did so too is so noteworthy. In fact, it may be argued that simply by following the dominant societal pattern, Jews did indeed become like everyone else. By organizing and asserting themselves more frequently and vociferously, Orthodox Jews were, indeed, showing signs of acculturation. Were these not steps in the direction of assimilation? The question is a compelling one!

It can be answered by first accepting a distinction between structure and culture, between form and content. If we focused solely on the forms of organization that the Orthodox community has adopted, we would certainly have to admit that the community has become quite Americanized. On the other hand, the ideology of the organizational process has been explicitly and unashamedly loyal to traditional values and precepts. Ironically, organizational changes in the community that led to a greater integration of Orthodoxy with the rest of American society also crystallized and strengthened the community's social boundaries. Instead of becoming culturally more similar to the host society, the community emerged from the decade of the sixties culturally more distinctive, more self-contained—very much more like an Eastern European *shtetl* than an American suburb.

A Community in Transition

In this chapter we tried to harness the winds of social change to portray a community in transition. But our focus was aimed essentially at the organizational structure of the community. We did not deal directly with people. Did people change during this decade of transition? How did they adjust to, and perhaps contribute to the changes in the community? How did they avoid the magnetic pull of cultural assimilation even as their community was becoming structurally more similar to the larger society?

These questions require more elaborate analyses of the internal organization and cultural dynamics of the Boro Park community, which shall be the subjects of subsequent chapters. But before we undertake such analyses, we should turn our attention to the people who make up the Boro Park Jewish community in the 1970s.

Because this is a study of a community, not of particular individuals or their families, it will lack the warmth of a photograph. It will, however, provide the precision of a portrait painted by number.

3 A Portrait Painted By Numbers
Demographic Characteristics of the Jews of Boro Park

        Perhaps because they have always been a minority, Jews have always been concerned about their number. Time and again in the Old Testament God promises the Patriarchs that their children shall be as numerous as "the stars in the heavens," or "the sands in the seas." Whatever the reason for this concern—be it metaphysical, political, or economic—it is clear that one can hardly give an adequate description of a community without including its numerical parameters. That is the purpose of this chapter.

The Problem of Finding Boro Park

One striking aspect of the Boro Park community is that there is no certainty about its real boundaries. Its general area falls under a variety of political and administrative jurisdictions that demarcate official boundaries to suit their own unique purposes. None of these boundaries, however, takes into consideration what is, perhaps, the most significant aspect of a locale, namely, its people. Our interviews with literally hundreds of Boro Park residents revealed that their way of demarcating the community's boundaries is distinctly different from that of official agencies that are in the business of drawing boundary lines. When asked "Why do you like living in Boro Park?" their unfailing answer was "We (or I) like living in an exclusively Jewish neighborhood," or "We (or I) like living among Jews." There is a problem, however, in trying to work with these social boundaries defined by the residents. The method by which these boundaries are drawn is often unclear. And often the specific geographic limits cannot be empirically determined.

To deal with the problem of discrepant definitions of a community by officials and residents, Ross has used a survey approach. He has successfully demonstrated that residents of an area can, in fact, recognize and name its official boundaries and can correctly identify the social status characteristics of its population.[1] But we are less concerned here with how accurately residents can identify the predefined boundaries of a locale than we are with how those boundaries come to be defined in the first place. Letting residents define the boundaries of an area—either explicitly or implicitly—is likely to reveal the meaning that the area has for them, and the extent to which the meaning is shared. And if shared meanings are one of the distinguishing features of a community, letting residents define a neighborhood's boundaries is likely to reveal whether that neighborhood can be considered a criterion of the concept of community.[2] Since we were trying to demarcate a religious community, we required definitions that were of a religious nature. At first, we discovered such definitions quite accidentally.

During the Christmas season Boro Park presents a curious image, even to the casual passerby. Its streets are dull and unlit in comparison with the streets that are at its official borders. Even within its official borders, those streets and avenues near the periphery are richly decorated with Christmas trees and electrical ornaments on doors and window frames of houses. It was from this observation that the first definition of the boundaries of the Jewish community emerged. It was found that the area grew more sparsely lit and decorated as one travelled from Eighteenth or Eighth Avenues, or from Thirty-fourth or Sixty-fifth Streets toward a hypothetical center—say, Thirteenth Avenue and Fiftieth Street. There were almost no Christmas decorations at all in the center itself. At the outset then, the density of Christmas decorations was used as an unobtrusive measure of the social boundaries of the Boro Park Jewish community.[3]

This unobtrusive measure was useful in two ways. It permitted the identification of the socially meaningful boundaries of the community and it also revealed the ethnic, religious character of the boundaries. It was within these boundaries that further sociological characteristics of the Jewish community were sought.

In order to obtain a more systematic measure of the number of Jewish residents and their pattern of settlement in the area, the neighborhood was subdivided into twelve sectors, using decoration density as the criterion. A count of the total population, the proportion of Jews, and their general distribution in the twelve sectors was obtained by means of the reversed street address directory, which lists telephone subscribers by address.[4] The use of this directory was especially important in obtaining a count of Jewish surnames.[5] On the assumption that most residents of the Boro Park area have telephones and listed numbers, a count was obtained of the total number of non-commercial subscribers, subscribers with Jewish surnames, and subscribers with the title of rabbi.

According to the U.S. Census Bureau the average household in Boro Park contains three persons, so totals were obtained by tripling the phone subscriber figures. As of March 1972, then, the total population of Boro Park was 76, 418; the total Jewish population was 38,259; and the total number of rabbis was 1,695. An independent study by the Hassidic Corporation for Urban Concerns, in 1973, found the Jewish population of Boro Park to be 47,437.[6] Our calculation was, therefore, a highly conservative, but once again a useful unobtrusive measure. A survey completed in 1979 by the Council of Jewish Organizations of Boro Park has established the average household size at 4.1.

With the overall area of Boro Park divided into twelve sectors whose boundaries were determined by the density of decorations at Christmas, and by the presence of major thoroughfares, distribution of the Jewish surnamed telephone subscribers in these sectors provided an index of Jewish population density. Table 3 describes the perimeters of the twelve sectors, and the proportion of phone subscribers with Jewish surnames in each. This table shows that the four sectors in the area from Eleventh to Sixteenth Avenues and Forty-third to Sixtieth Streets had the highest proportion of Jewish-surnamed phone subscribers.

An examination of the list of subscribers living just outside the perimeters described in Table 3 showed a decrease in the number of Jewish surnames as one moved outward. Thus, the density and distribution of the Jewish population in Boro Park could be accurately obtained from the phone directory. The method had the added elegance of being derived from the subjectively meaningful behavior of the residents themselves. Moreover, we also were able to graft this subjectively meaningful map of the community—the twelve sectors—onto the official census map, with its tract and block statistics.[7]

TABLE 3
Jewish Surnames Among Phone Subscribers in the Twelve Sectors of Boro Park

| | Percent of Phone Subscribers | | |
Sector	36th—42nd Sts.	43rd—50th Sts.	51st—60th Sts.
Eighth Ave.–Ft. Hamilton Pkwy.	18	50	30
Eleventh Ave.–Twelfth Ave.	16	61	70
Thirteenth Ave.–Sixteenth Ave.	40	81	55
Above Seventeenth Ave.	17	54	43

Source: New York Telephone Co., *The Brooklyn Street Address Directory* (New York, March 1972).

A Statistical Profile of Boro Park's Jews

Population statistics for the Jewish community are fraught with all sorts of difficulties. Apart from the philosophical question of "Who is a Jew?" there is the problem that American census records since 1957 do not enumerate people by religion. In New York City the official records of Jewish organizations are also notoriously unreliable. The problem of counting Orthodox Jews is even more complicated. Especially in Boro Park, most are not signed-up, dues-paying members of synagogues or other organizations. Charles Liebman, whose work was mentioned in the first chapter, has noted with appropriate frustration, "With respect to the numbers of Jews who consider themselves Orthodox, no reliable estimates can be made because we have no quantitative study of Orthodoxy in New York City."[8]

Enumerating Orthodox synagogues and estimating their average memberships, Liebman has arrived at a set of figures in which "the margin of error is surely quite high. The method employed to make the estimates would account for formal membership only; it does not include family members or others served by the synagogue. . . . If it did, the figure would be much higher."[9]

One way out of these complications, since we are studying an identified geographic unit, is to resort to an unconventional technique suitable for our purposes. Gutman has developed a useful list of non-conventional techniques for enumerating the Jewish population of the country as a whole.[10] Unfortunately, these techniques rely on a prior definition of community boundaries, or on the records of organizations, resources that were unavailable to us. But the idea of using a nonconventional technique was nonetheless a good one.

It was recognized that the most thorough statistical information on the community would be obtained from the records of the United States Census Bureau, provided that their data could be somehow narrowed down to the Jewish community that is the focus of our study. The narrowing or focusing was accomplished using the Jewish population density map described earlier in this chapter. That map was superimposed on the map of the area provided by the Census Bureau (see Map 2) to obtain a fairly reliable estimate of the size of the population and some of its demographic characteristics.

As we saw earlier, by using the telephone directory we estimated the total population of the Jewish community at 38,259, out of a total population of 76,418 people. Using Census Bureau maps, these figures

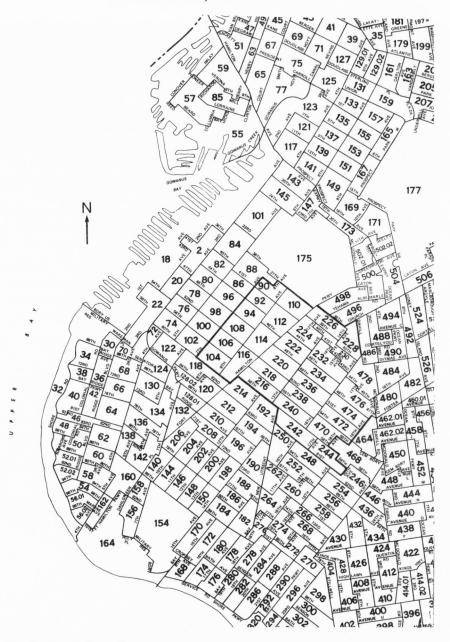

Map 2.   Boro Park area divided into census tracts (heavy lines indicate boundaries). Reprinted from U.S. Department of Commerce, Bureau of Census, *1970 Census of Population and Housing* (Washington, D.C.: Department of Commerce, 1970), Final Report PHC (1)-145, Inset 1A—Kings County.

were revised considerably upward. The total population was rees-
timated at 91,303, and the Jewish population at 46,103.[11] This final figure
is quite close to the independent estimate, mentioned earlier, of 47,437
by the Hassidic Corporation for Urban Concerns. Based on the findings
of the survey by the Council, mentioned above, the most recent estimate
of the Jewish population should be around 55,000. Jews thus constitute
just a little over 50 percent of the population within the perimeters of the
Boro Park area. This estimate of the proportion of Jews in the community
is slightly below the estimate made by Horowitz and Kaplan.[12] But it
must be remembered that their definition of the boundaries of the
community was somewhat different from the definitions used here.
Further, it should be borne in mind that the 50 percent figure is really far
less important than the fact that in some sectors of the Boro Park area
Jews constitute over 80 percent of the population, while in others they
may account for less than 20 percent.

These variations in population density in different sectors of the
community helped us estimate the extent to which other demographic
characteristics, reported in the census, are shared by Boro Park's Jews.
For example, in sector VIII, the sector that had the highest concentration
of Jews (81 percent), the mean family income in 1970 was $11,050. By
contrast, in sector IV, the sector that had the lowest concentration of
Jews (16 percent), the mean family income was only $8,741. Other
important differences between these two sectors included differences in
the proportion of foreign born, native born of foreign parentage, and
native born of native parentage, that is, first-, second-, and third-generation Americans. (See Table 4.)

TABLE 4
First-, Second-, and Third-Generation Americans in Sectors VIII and IV

Generation	Percent of Total Population in Sector VIII	Percent of Total Population in Sector IV
First	41	30
Second	38	31
Third	21	40

Source: "General Characteristics of the Population, 1970," in *1970 Census of Population and Housing* (Washington, D.C.: U.S. Department of Commerce, Bureau of Census, 1970).

The differences found between these sectors were found consistently throughout the area. Grouping the twelve sectors into those in which the Jewish population was less than 50 percent and those in which it was greater than 50 percent, similar differences were found with respect to income and generational status. The sectors that had 50 percent or more Jews had a mean family income of $10,843. The sectors with less than 50 percent Jewish population had a mean family income of $9,484. With respect to generational status, Table 5 is a summary of the distribution of generational groups in the two types of sectors.

TABLE 5

First, Second, and Third Generations in Areas with High and Low Concentrations of Jewish Population

Generation	Percent of Total Population in Areas of High Concentration	Percent of Total Population in Areas of Low Concentration
First	34.1	27.1
Second	37.8	32.5
Third	27.9	40.3

Source: "General Characteristics of the Population, 1970" in 1970 Census of Population and Housing (Washington, D.C.: U.S. Department of Commerce, Bureau of Census, 1970).

Turning to the age composition of the community, one again finds considerable differences between the more densely Jewish and less densely Jewish sectors of the area. Using census data, Tables 6 and 7 appear to confirm the description of the community presented by the Department of City Planning in 1969: "Boro Park is a stable, somewhat aging residential community."[13] Indeed, Boro Park is aging, especially its Jewish community. Table 8, which compares figures from 1957, in the work of Horowitz and Kaplan, with the 1970 figures presented in Table 6, reveals the extent to which the Jewish community aged during the 1960s.

The trend is obvious. Decreases have occurred in the relative size of every age group except for the two groups over 45 years of age. However, this trend seems to have reversed itself during the later half of the 1970s due to the high birth rate among the Hasidim. The out-migration of

TABLE 6

Age Composition of the Ten Most Densely Jewish Census Tracts in 1970

Age	N	Percent of Total Population
5 and under	2,672	7.6
5 to 24	8,125	23.3
25 to 44	7,338	21.0
45 to 64	10,722	30.0
65 and over	5,953	17.1

Source: "General Characteristics of the Population, 1970" in *1970 Census of Population and Housing* (Washington, D.C.: U.S. Department of Commerce, Bureau of Census, 1970), table P-1.

TABLE 7

Age Composition in the Four Least Densely Jewish Census Tracts in 1970

Age	N	Percent of Total Population
5 and under	940	7.9
5 to 24	3,731	31.9
25 to 44	2,548	21.4
45 to 64	3,036	25.5
65 and over	1,628	13.7

Source: "General Characteristics of the Population, 1970" in *1970 Census of Population and Housing* (Washington, D.C.: U.S. Department of Commerce, Bureau of Census, 1970), table P-1.

TABLE 8

Age Composition of Jewish Population in 1957 and 1970

Age	Percent of Population in 1957	Percent of Population in 1970
5 and under	7.7	7.6
5 to 24	26.7	23.3
25 to 44	28.6	21.0
45 to 64	26.4	30.0
65 and over	9.6	17.1

Sources: Morris Horowitz and Lawrence Kaplan, *Estimated Jewish Population of the New York Area, 1900–1975* (New York: Federation of Jewish Philanthropies, 1959); "General Characteristics of the Population, 1970," in *1970 Census of Population and Housing* (Washington, D.C.: U.S. Department of Commerce, Bureau of Census, 1970), table P-1.

young adults, referred to in the report of the Community Council of Greater New York, seems to have continued.[14]

The figures presented so far force one to conclude that, dating from its establishment in the 1920s, the Jewish community of Boro Park has been progressively losing that segment of its population on which, one would expect, the continuity of its culture depends. Moreover, the above figures suggest that if Orthodoxy has persisted in the community, its persistence has been due largely to the influx of first-generation immigrants. Thus, on the basis of the above figures it could hardly be argued—as we, in fact, argue in this study—that life in the Jewish community of Boro Park differs from the well-established pattern of growth and decline seen elsewhere. It seems to follow along paths which have been well described by other students of Jewish life in America. To support our novel thesis using demographic data requires evidence that points out the differences between Boro Park Jewry and other Jewish communities that have been densely populated by first-generation residents. Such evidence will be presented below.

The generalizations that have been used to characterize first-generation American Jews and their communities have emphasized their position in the lower class, their lower occupational status, and their tacit assumption that their children would be different from themselves. Perhaps related to these generalizations, it has also been generally assumed that their residential areas would tend to be shabby, standing witness to the gradual decline and ultimate passing of this group. These group traits, however, have not been found in the Boro Park community!

Perhaps the most striking feature of this community, both in the early stage of its development as well as at the present time, is that it is largely a successful community. According to informants who have lived in the community since the 1920s, early Boro Park Jewry included large numbers of doctors, lawyers, accountants, and successful businessmen.[15] Other residents were successful on a smaller scale, as local shopkeepers or craftsmen.[16] What is interesting for our purposes is that while the community has, indeed, aged and become more densely populated by first-generation Americans in recent years, it has not become less successful. The large numbers of first-generation ethnics who moved into the community during the late fifties and sixties have been quite successful by traditional American standards. In 1970 the previously mentioned mean family income for the densely Jewish sectors, $10,843, compared favorably with the median family income in the United States—$10,216;

in the State of New York—$10,617; and in the Borough of Brooklyn—$10,014.[17]

Data obtained from personal interviews with a randomly selected sample of Orthodox families in Boro Park indicated that the average yearly family income in the community may be as high as $14,573.[18] Such a high figure makes it rather difficult to sustain an image of Jewish Boro Park as lower-middle-class. To be sure, there are poor Jews in the community. But there are also some very rich ones, and the great majority seem to fall into the category of the comfortable middle class. The Jews of Boro Park may be slightly behind other American Jews as far as economic achievement is concerned, but, by generally accepted standards, they are clearly in the mainstream of the middle class.

The occupational pattern of the community also appears to contradict the ethnic-immigrant ghetto image. While it is probably true that pre-war immigrant Jews "came to the United States with little in the way of secular education . . . without capital or marketable skills,"[19] the Jews of Boro Park appear to have an appreciable amount of all three. The data in Table 9, obtained from U.S. census reports, support the more optimistic image of the Boro Park community.

Table 10 narrows the analysis of occupational patterns to the ten most densely Jewish census tracts. Census data are compared with the occupational data drawn from our interviews. Some of the larger differences between the census data and the survey data may be due to

TABLE 9
Occupations in Boro Park, 1950–1970

Occupation	Percent of Population		
	1950 (N = 53,861)	1960 (N = 46,471)	1970 (N = 41,361)
Professionals	7.3	9.0	12.5
Teachers			3.8
Managers	13.4	9.0	7.1
Self-employed	15.0	11.1	7.1
Sales	8.8	7.3	8.7
Clerical	17.7	22.0	26.8
Craftsmen	14.0	14.7	14.1
Operatives	20.4	21.0	14.7

Source: "General Characteristics of the Population, 1970" in *1970 Census of Population and Housing* (Washington, D.C.: U.S. Department of Commerce, Bureau of Census, 1970).

TABLE 10
Occupations in Densely Jewish Census Tracts and in the Family Survey Responses, 1970 and 1973

Occupation	Percent in Tracts, 1970 (N = 15,558)	Percent in Survey, 1973 (N = 115)
Professionals	16.1	28.8
Teachers	5.4	5.6
Managerial	8.0	1.8
Self-employed	9.0	26.4
Sales	10.8	7.5
Clerical	27.6	13.2
Craftsmen	13.6	5.6
Operatives	12.9	11.3

Source: Data for 1970 from "General Characteristics of the Population, 1970," in *1970 Census of Population and Housing* (Washington, D.C.: U.S. Department of Commerce, Bureau of Census, 1970); data for 1973 from author's survey of Boro Park families.

sampling error or to slightly different usage of terminology. Many women, for example, when asked to indicate their occupation, would simply write "housewife," failing to mention that they also held part-time jobs or even full-time jobs as secretaries. Thus our survey yielded an undercount in the clerical category. The overcount in the self-employed category may be explained by the fact that a large number of respondents simply indicated that they were "in business." We inferred that such a response meant "in business for myself." In fact, it is quite possible that some respondents did not mean that. Nevertheless, a clear occupational pattern did emerge. Both sets of data, albeit to different extents, point up the fact that the largest proportion of the present Jewish population is to be found in white collar and professional occupations. This pattern is hardly characteristic of an occupationally backward community.

Unsurprisingly, the level of secular education found in the community also differs sharply from the stereotype of an immigrant Orthodox community. Of the respondents in our family survey, forty-two (36.5 percent) indicated that they have completed or had some high school education; 11.3 percent had completed only elementary school. Only 5.2 percent indicated that they had not obtained any secular education.[20] On the basis of the 1970 census reports, the median years of education of residents in the most densely Jewish census tracts was 10.6 years, with some of the tracts reaching as high as 12.1 years. The median for the entire area was 10.0 years. Correspondingly, the percentage of high school graduates in the most densely Jewish tracts was 40.3 percent (compared with 35.9 percent for the area).

Apart from these conventional indicators of achievement, the community offers further, unconventional, indicators of its material successes. Newly built single-family and multi-family houses are to be found in great numbers on nearly every street and avenue. At a time when newspapers decry the crisis in the building trades, and the absence of new housing construction, new construction is springing up throughout the Jewish sectors of the community. Perhaps as many as 30 percent of all houses in these sectors have been newly built within the past decade. Newly built *yeshivas* and synagogues are also to be found in great number in the area. As was indicated in the previous chapter, these have nearly doubled in number since 1963. Unlike earlier immigrant communities, however, this organizational proliferation has not been accomplished by converting store-fronts and basements into *shuls* and *yeshivas*. Some such conversions may be found. But growth was accomplished primarily through construction for a specific purpose. Rents and land values have skyrocketed. Yet, people stay and build. The shops along Thirteenth Avenue, which cater primarily to the Jewish community, are stocked with expensive merchandise, from crystal chandeliers to quadraphonic stereo sound systems.

Perhaps the most significant way in which this community differs from previous immigrant Jewish communities is that the first-generation immigrants who settled in Boro Park entered the United States after World War II. Moreover, their roots are not to be found in the isolated *shtetlach* or ghettos of the Ukraine, Poland, and Russia. Large proportions of Boro Park's immigrant Jews came from the more modernized and urbanized areas of Hungary and Czechoslovakia. The first-generation Hungarian population of the community had risen from 882 in 1950 to over 4,000 by 1970. Similarly, Czechoslovakians had risen in numbers from 489 in 1950 to over 3,700 in 1970. While immigrants of Russian and Polish ancestry are still present in large number in the community, their proportions have declined consistently since the 1960s.

The changing mix of the first generation is of sociological significance for two reasons. First, the post-war immigrants had made their adjustments to modernity prior to their immigration. Thus, the impact of American life on their worldviews and lifestyles was not nearly as drastic as it had been for the pre-war Russian and Polish immigrants. The pre-war immigrants had to make most of their adjustments to modernity as immigrants. More significantly, the immigrants who came after World War II were conscious of being the remnants of a group that had been nearly exterminated in the Nazi Holocaust. The community they formed was intended not so much as a testimonial to their own achievements in the new world, but rather as a memorial for what they had lost. The community today is an amalgam: a testimonial and a memorial.[21]

Two important questions that have not been discussed thus far, and that the reader must undoubtedly be asking, are, How many of the Jews living in Boro Park are in fact Orthodox? and, What does it mean to be Orthodox there? The caveat offered concerning the enumeration of Jews in general applies even more so to the Orthodox. Liebman had defined Orthodox Jews:

> as all Jews who affiliate with nominally Orthodox synagogues. Alternate definitions would include Jews who view *halacha* or Jewish law as an obligatory standard for all Jews, or who behave as Orthodox Jews in ritual and *halachic* terms, or who define them- selves as Orthodox Jews without regard to their behavior.[22]

By any one of these definitions it would have to be concluded that nearly all of Boro Park is Orthodox. The fact is that, apart from one Conservative and one Progressive (like Reform) synagogue—both having small and decreasing clientele, all of the nearly 150 synagogues are nominally Orthodox and ritually adhere to *halacha*. The numbers of Jews who would consider *halacha* or traditional Jewish law as the obligatory standard for all Jews may be somewhat fewer, owing to the liberal sentiments of the younger generation, the American born, and those with more secular education. Approximately 85 percent of the respondents in the family survey indicated affiliation with an Orthodox synagogue. The respondents who did not indicate any affiliations allowed that while they did not consider themselves Orthodox they enjoyed the "atmosphere of the community." Only two out of the 115 respondents indicated affiliation with the Conservative or the Progressive synagogue. It would be safe to conclude that Orthodox Jews constitute the largest majority—perhaps 80 to 90 percent—of the community. More impor- tantly, it is the Orthodox who are the most visible segment of the community and who, therefore, define what it means to be Jewish in Boro Park. It is they who define the cultural style of the community's major institutions.

Before concluding this chapter a comment also must be made about the diversity in the community. In the preceding pages we have seen that there is considerable diversity in the community based on economic, educational, age, and immigrant status criteria. There are other sources of diversity as well, which are unique to the Orthodox community, and specifically so to the community in Boro Park. Familiar distinctions between *Litvaks* (Lithuanian Jews) and *Galitzianers* (Jews from Galicia) are replaced in this community by distinctions between Germans, Hungarians, and Russians, and, more recently, between new Russians and Israelis as well. Superimposed on the ethnic distinctions one cannot help but be struck by the distinctions between *Hasidishe yidn* (those who follow a particular *rebbe*), *frum yidn* (traditional European observant Jews who tend to affiliate with small *shtieble*-type synagogues), and modern Orthodox Jews who tend to be affiliated with such congregations as Temple Beth-El, or the Young Israel, or other major syngogues which are formally associated with the Orthodox movement in America. Among the *Hasidishe yidn*, of course, there are further distinctions to be made on the basis of dynastic allegiance. There are probably more than twenty Hasidic dynasties which make their home in the Boro Park community, some with followers numbering in the thousands, other with no more than an oversized *minyan*.

In addition to these highly visible facets, a communal portrait of Boro Park Jewry also includes some less visible, smaller components that should be mentioned for the sake of completeness, as well as for intrinsic interest. Since the late 1940s a handful of Yemenite families have made their homes in the community (from Yemen via Palestine and the Lower East Side to Boro Park). A chronicler of this exotic sub-community, Israel Grama, reports that since the end of World War II approximately 125 Yemenite families made their homes in Boro Park (about 90 percent of the entire Yemenite Jewish population in America).[23] Most Yemenites, according to Grama,

> have continued in the traditions of their forefathers and have pursued occupations as silversmiths, jewelers, masons, printers, and painters. The younger generation is veering away from such manual occupations and is pursuing professions. . . such as engineering, education, and music.
>
> The religious character of the Yemenite Jews has weakened throughout the years. This is painfully true among those Yemenite boys and girls who were born in this country. Most American-born Yemenites are but remotely aware of specific Yemenite practices and customs. . . . The greatest tragedy of all is that only a handful of Yemenite parents have realized the value of giving their children a yeshiva education.[24]

It is also interesting to note, though Grama does not, that it was Yemenite entrepreneurs who established the first *kosher* pizza shops in the late 1950s along Thirteenth Avenue. By the early 1960s these shops became important hangouts for the Orthodox teenagers of the community, where for the price of a slice of pizza (then only 15¢) made with strictly *kosher* "Cholov Yisroel" cheese, boys and girls from local *yeshivas* could mix and mingle outside of the purview of parents, rabbis, or teachers.

More recently, since the late 1960s, increasing numbers (figures not available) of Russian immigrants and Israeli *yordim* have blended into the social mix of Boro Park Jewry. A substantial number of Israelis have settled in the community, and several Israeli restaurants have opened along the main shopping street, Thirteenth Avenue. The new Russians are still a quiet minority, making their presence visible only on sunny holiday afternoons, when they congregate in noisy clusters along the main promenades of the area.

In view of the great variety of accents that make up the Jewish community in Boro Park, the reader may wonder how one can speak at all of a community here, as if it were a homogeneous entity. Yet, as Israel Grama reflected in the mid-1960s, "it would not be a misnomer to acclaim this locale as a 'Jewish melting pot,' " I share this appraisal, and shall try to demonstrate in the chapters which follow that, despite all sorts of ethnic cleavages, there is a core of values and beliefs, institutions and daily practices which transcend the sources of diversity and bind the many into one.

But what are these core elements, and how do they cement the community? These are the topics of subsequent chapters.

4 Ingredients of Holiness
The Social Construction of Religious Life in Secular Society

That the Jewish people are often called the Chosen People is more or less common knowledge. It is less commonly known that in the Old Testament they are frequently referred to as a Holy People or a Holy Community. As a matter of fact, one of the general commandments which accompanies the giving the Torah on Mt. Sinai, according to the Biblical tradition, is God's command to the Israelites, "You shall be Holy." In that context, of course, "being holy" meant conducting one's personal and social life according to the six hundred and thirteen prescriptive and proscriptive dicta layed down in the Five Books of Moses. Over the successive generations these six hundred and thirteen *mitzvas* have come to be known by Jews as the *ol Torah*, or the yoke of the Torah. It is probably fair to say that for well over two thousand years, since Biblical times, Jews have attempted—and managed more or less successfully—to conduct their lives according to those six hundred and thirteen *mitzvas*. Rabbinic exegeses and augmentations notwithstanding, every Jewish community throughout history has striven mightily to remain a holy community.

The threats to sustaining the way of the Torah have always loomed near. The history of Jewish communities is a well-known record of economic, political, and physical persecutions. Beginning with the Enlightenment in the late eighteenth century and the Emancipation during the nineteenth century, however, the threats to the way of the Torah took on a novel form. The threats no longer came from external constraint or compulsion. Rather, they now came from internal motivation. Jews increasingly were less coerced by a hostile social milieu, and increasingly were more seduced by an open one. The desire to live a holy way of life was gradually displaced by a desire for economic success and professional achievement. This transition is aptly captured in the concept of secularization, made famous by the German sociologist Max Weber. This transition is at its zenith in twentieth-century America as the children of immigrant Jews acculturate and assimilate into the most open and most secular of societies.

The pull of assimilation has led to the wholesale abandonment of traditional ritual practices, the six hundred and thirteen *mitzvas*, by the vast majority of America's Jews. It would be naive to think that the pull of assimilation has not exerted a seductive influence on Orthodox Jews as well. After all, most assimilationists once were themselves either Orthodox or the children and grandchildren of Orthodox or traditional immigrants. What is striking about the present Orthodox community, however, is that, by and large, its members still strive to live according to the way of the Torah. Yet how does one construct a style of life consistent with values and rituals meticulously laid down over a period of twenty-five hundred years? Moreover, how does one live in such a style of life and at the same time participate actively and successfully in the contemporary—highly secular—American way of life?

The last chapter traced some of the major steps in the development of Boro Park as a middle-class Orthodox Jewish community. Earlier we showed that, while the immigrant generation and their offspring who came into the community in increasing numbers after World War II became quite middle-class and Americanized, the community also became more singularly Orthodox in character. In this chapter we will give a detailed account of the inner world, so to speak, of middle-class Orthodoxy: its significant symbols and values, and its techniques of cognitive accomodation to the larger social milieu.

Shomer Shabbos—Bossor Kosher

A visitor walking along Thirteenth Avenue, the main commercial thoroughfare of the community, will frequently find two phrases boldly printed across shop windows and other commercial signs: Shomer Shabbos and *kosher*. If the shop sells meat products the signs will proclaim *bossor kosher*. What do these terms mean, and what is their social significance? The phrase Shomer Shabbos literally means "an observer of the Shabbos" (the Jewish day of rest). It refers to the fourth of the Ten Commandments, in which, according to the Bible, God commanded the people of Israel: "Observe the Sabbath day, to keep it holy, as the Lord thy God commanded thee. Six days shalt thou labor, and do all thy work; but the seventh day is a Sabbath unto the Lord thy God, in it thou shalt not do any manner of work."[1]

The term *kosher* literally means "prepared according to prescribed rules"—the complex dietary rules prescribed in the Old Testament—and generally refers to food.[2] These rules are particularly complex and restrictive in connection with meat—the phrase *bossor kosher* refers to *kosher* meats. Our present interest is not in the theological significance of these laws or rituals, but the role they play in the inner life of the community. The sociological question is of particular significance in view of the fact that, technically, Orthodoxy is hemmed in by six-hundred and thirteen Biblical commandments and hundreds of additional rabbinic ordinances derived from them. Thus it must be asked why two sets of rules receive such prominent attention in the Orthodox community?[3] Or, more correctly, what is the significance that the residents of the community attach to these two observances?

Among the questions asked of respondents in our family survey were the following: (*a*) "The most important thing that a person should consider in choosing a job or a career as a Jew is _____"; and (*b*) "Being religious today is easier or harder?" Apart from the general consideration of financial security and self-fulfillment, nearly all respondents thought it important that a person should choose a job or career that will permit him to "remain a Jew" or "remain religious." On the second item the overwhelming majority of respondents thought that it is easier to be religious today than it was years ago. In the course of the interviews respondents were asked to elaborate on what they meant by their responses. Without exception the elaboration of the responses to the above two items centered on (*a*) the desirability of jobs in which one can observe the Sabbath and keep *kosher*, and (*b*) the fact that such jobs are more available today than ever before. The pattern of these responses indicates that observance of the Sabbath and the laws of *kashrus* are regarded in the community as the principal ways in which one maintains his position as an Orthodox Jew. This attitude is readily understandable insofar as both observances function to maintain the separation between the community as an ingroup and the world outside. But the functional explanation misses the more intimate experiential importance of these two observances. For this, one must look to the actual ways in which these observances are carried out in daily practice.

To begin with, it should be understood that when one calls himself or another a Shomer Shabbos Jew much more is meant than that the person is observing the rules of the Sabbath. The phrase refers to a person who generally observes all the religious holidays according to the *halachic* precepts regulating them. More generally it refers to a person who participates in the activities and festivities of the community, deeming them more important than activities outside of the community. The experience itself is described eloquently and accurately by a "local patriot":

Yes, walk the streets of Boro Park on a Friday night, on a Yom Tov and even early on a Sabboth [sic] morning—and the sights you will see will remind you of Belz, of Meah Shearim, of Krakow and Warsaw as you have seen or imagined them. . . . On a Sabbath, you will find grocery stores, barbers, bakers, tailors sporting "Shomer Shabos" signs in droves along 13th and 16th avenues. . . . Early Shabat morning—as you rush to the First Minyan [early services]—you will see rebeyim and their Chassidim [sic] coming out of the mikvah [ritual bath] with the very spirit of the shechinah [God's inspiration] on their shining countenances. On Simchath Torah night you find that our cooperative police have closed off traffic on 47th Street from 13th to 14th avenues to allow B'nei Akiva, Pirchei Agudah, Young Israel Juniors—and adults too—to cavort to their hearts' desires. Before Shabat you will see Chassidim [sic] in long kaftans . . . running to greet the Shabat. On Shavuoth night you can make a 4:00 A.M. minyan [prayer services] in any one of a few places. During Selichoth week, you can take your choice of a 10:00 P.M., midnight, or early morning minyan. On Rosh Hashana, you need a traffic police to keep the mobs on their way to Prospect Park for Tashlich [a special prayer service recited near a body of water like a lake]. On Sukkoth you need more than a week to inspect all the kinds of sukkoth and their decorations which line our streets. And here, there, almost everywhere you can spot "eruv wires" strung across alleyways to allow for Shabat carrying.[4]

This account of the holiday atmosphere, an atmosphere which recurs in the community throughout all seasons of the year, was written twenty years ago. Yet, a more appropriate description could hardly be written today. The fact is that this atmosphere, which recurs at least once a week (Shabbos), is an enactment of community. The avenues and streets, though they are in the public domain, become the special territory of a special community. People dressed for the occasion of Shabbos or a Yom Tov can be found congregating at streetcorners and at the entrance ways of private and apartment houses for casual conversation, greetings, or visiting almost around the clock. It is a time when the residents of the community apparently have a need to see each other and to be seen by one another. Absence from one's accustomed clique either in the synagogue or at the usual streetcorner will be greeted with a mixture of concern and inquisitiveness by one's acquaintances.

The festive atmosphere also pervades the homes. Tables are freshly set, the best wares of the house are displayed, and the best foods are served to both family and visitors. It is a time to display, and through the display to identify and be identified. In a community where casual encounter between the sexes is very much curtailed, the festive atmosphere with its continuous promenades and visits also gives opportunities for the young of both sexes to be seen by and to see one another informally.

The atmosphere of festivity and the sense of at-oneness that recurs so frequently in the community are created within the framework of strict and complicated rules, prescriptions, and prohibitions.[5] Although these would seem terribly restrictive to the outsider, they are, in fact, rather casually managed by those who find their lives fulfilled within them. For example, the prohibitions against carrying any object from the private to the public domain and visa versa or the prohibitions against lighting a fire or turning electricity on or off are just some of the most obvious limitations imposed by Shabbos observance.[6] But, ingeniously, handkerchiefs become scarves carried around the necks or tied together to make a belt and thus carried permissibly and inconspicuously. A veritable industry has sprung up in the conversion of gold keys to pins or tie clips. Thus the prohibition is satisfied in a way that does not interfere with the accustomed practices of everyday life. Electric lights are turned on and off by means of electrical timer clocks, and modern gas stoves and ranges can be pre-set to maintain a desired level of heat without the necessity of rekindling the flame. Thus, what appear to be stringent prohibitions from the outside are actually routine behavior carried out without any noticeable inconvenience. What is important to note about the way the rules of the Shabbos are fulfilled is that it is a routine in which electric lights, house keys, gas stoves, and even handkerchiefs become artifacts in a special universe of meaning.

That universe may be understood by reference to rabbinic lore, which holds that observance of the Shabbos brings into the body of the Jew a *N'shama Y'thera*, or additional soul. In fact, when the Shabbos comes to a close, the celebration of that moment includes the inhalation of some sweet fragrance to compensate the individual, so to speak, for the soul he is going to lose for an entire week.

Like the other holidays, the Shabbos is a time during which one is truly being a Jew. Business and all extracommunal concerns are shut out, and all activities are focused on the celebration of God's commandments and one's identity. The celebration, thus, focuses and sanctifies time and very much defines space. It separates the week from the day of rest in a most radical manner, and it imparts to the community an atmosphere through which its actual space becomes like no other place in the rest of society.

Other significant holidays that structure time and space for the Orthodox Jew are listed below.

The Sabbath (Shabbos)	This holiday recurs weekly from Friday eve until Saturday night.
Rosh Chodesh	This is a monthly celebration of the new moon.
Rosh Hashono	This is the so-called Jewish New Year. It occurs sometime in September or October.
Yom Kipur	This is the Day of Repentance, a major fast day and a day of solemn prayer. It occurs a week after Rosh Hashono, usually in October.
Sukos and Simchas Torah	This is an eight-day autumn holiday celebrating the harvest, ending with a celebration of the Torah scrolls. It occurs about a week after Yom Kipur, in late October.
Chanuka	This holiday occurs sometime at the end of December, just around Christmas time. It is an eight-day holiday commemorating the victory of the Maccabees against the Hellenists who had desecrated the ancient Holy Temple in the second century B.C.
Purim	This is a carnival-like holiday in late February or early March.
Passover (Pesach)	This holiday occurs sometime in late March or early April. It is an eight-day holiday celebrating the return of the ancient Israelites from Egypt to the promised land.
Shavuos	This holiday celebrates the giving of the Ten Commandments and the Torah by God to the Jewish people on Mt. Sinai. It occurs seven weeks after Passover, in late May or early June.

Much the way that the observance of the Shabbos and other holidays consecrates communal time and space, the observance of the laws of *kashrus* (Dietary Laws) consecrates that activity which, perhaps more than any other, makes man what he is. Activities related to the preparation and eating of food in many ways define man and his relationship to his fellow man. It is for this reason that Max Weber recognized in the prohibitions of *kashrus* one of the major techniques for segregating the

Jewish community from non-Jewish society.[7] Dietary regulations serve to prevent commensality, and hence act as a buffer between Jew and non-Jew. But the functional analysis of this feature of Jewish life glosses over the myriad experiential details which shape the cognitive world of the *kashrus*-observing Jew.

Adherence to the rules of *kashrus* leads the individual to classify all items of personal consumption as either permissible or impermissible. This cognitive process is not without affective consequences. Items that are permissible become identified as Jewish food and their consumption becomes an event through which one reaffirms to himself and to others that he is, indeed, a Jew.[8] Thus, a simple trip to the local grocery or a restaurant becomes an occasion on which the Orthodox Jew's identity is hung on the scale, so to speak. The absence of permissible items from the shelves or from the menu may precipitate anything from mild irritation to existential dilemma. It is small wonder, then, that shops catering to the needs of this community broadcast their observance of *kashrus* in bold print and neon signs.

Outside of the community, where the availability of *kosher* food is limited, the observance of the *kashrus* rules will pretty much define the range of contact between the observant Jew and his fellow man. Admittedly, the range of strictness in the observance of the rules will vary from person to person. Some will simply not eat anything anywhere outside of their own homes, or the homes of Orthodox Jews like themselves.[9] Others will eat permissible foods even if these were not prepared in a *kosher* kitchen, especially if the foods and the utensils involved are cold.[10] But as long as one considers himself observant of *kashrus*, it is highly unlikely that he will sit down to a non-*kosher* steak dinner. The point is that while there is variation in what different Orthodox Jews will do in the name of *kashrus*, and all may not agree, all will agree on what is clearly a violation of it. It is this consensus that ultimately limits contact between the Orthodox Jew and the rest of mankind. More specifically, this consensus will limit the extent to which the Orthodox Jew will permit himself to identify with the rest of mankind. Perhaps there is something to the popular adage, "you are what you eat."

Because of the centrality of the rules of Shabbos and *kashrus*, and the amount of resources and activities devoted to their observance, they must be regarded as the key collective representations of the community. Through them time and space are organized and social intercourse with the rest of the world regulated. Further analysis of the way in which the rules are observed in the Boro Park community should reveal the prevalent organization of knowledge and cognitive style in this community.

In discussing differences in religiosity among three generations of Jews, Goldstein and Goldscheider have observed that adherence to both the rules of Shabbos and *kashrus* have changed greatly:

> always lighting candles on Friday night and adhering to *kashrus* (both purchasing kosher meat and keeping separate dishes) have minimal adherence and their practice has radically declined in three generations. . . . The proportions *never* lighting Sabbath candles has more than doubled in three generations.[11]

They emphasize, as others have, that those rituals that have served to distinguish Jew from non-Jew have declined in popularity while those observances that do not function to segregate Jew from non-Jew have enjoyed increasing popularity.[12]

From these observations of other researchers and from the ways in which these rituals are adhered to in the Boro Park community it would appear that one of the key values sustained through the practices of Shabbos and *kashrus* is the value of separateness. The prayer recited by all Orthodox Jews at the conclusion of Shabbos certainly reinforces such a conclusion. The prayer is called *Havdalah* [literally, separation]. Among its paragraphs it includes the following:

> Blessed art thou, O Lord our God, King of the Universe, who makest a distinction between holy and profane, between light and darkness, between Israel and the heathen nations, between the seventh day and the six working days. Blessed art thou, O Lord, who makest a distinction between holy and profane.[13]

The value of separatism in the Orthodox and Hasidic community has, of course, already been analyzed by a number of researchers.[14] However, it has generally been agreed that as these groups become more Americanized they will tend to shed precisely those rituals and beliefs—of Shabbos and *kashrus*—that serve to separate them from the rest of society. It is for this reason that the ways in which these rituals are observed in Boro Park strikes us as such a novelty.

We have already seen that while the rules of Shabbos are generally observed in the community, the ritual observance is assisted, if not made possible, by the incorporation of modern devices. The rules of *kashrus* have been less amenable to "modernization," but they certainly have not prevented Boro Park Jews from achieving a fully modern lifestyle. A United Airlines ad proclaims: you can keep the faith thirty thousand feet up in the air. Most recently the Holiday Inns chain of motels has instituted pre-packaged *kosher* meals around the country that are available upon request and are certified as *kosher* by recognized religious authority. Orthodox vacation resorts offer all the comforts expected by the American middle class. At the same time they offer such apparently un-American attractions as supervised *kosher* kitchens, elevators that operate automatically on Shabbos and religious holidays, separate swimming and sports facilities for men and women, entertainment by well-known cantors in climate-controlled synagogues that are built into the very premises of the hotels. The religious festivals, which further serve to heighten in-group solidarity, are frequently marked by musical concerts that are held at the conclusion of the festival. At these concerts the music and the instruments are thoroughly modern: everything from bongo drums to electrical guitars. The lyrics, on the other hand, are often from sacred prayers or Biblical literature. The popularity of this curious cultural amalgam is attested to by the thousands of stereophonic records featuring such music which have become available and popular in Boro Park in recent years. Also available in the community are a variety of sound systems on which these recordings may be played. By the accounts of the shop keepers in the area both the recordings as well as the stereophonic equipment have been selling well. It seems then, that the pursuit of middle-class lifestyles has not led to the wholesale abandonment of those rituals that are the life blood of Jewish Orthodoxy. Rather, those rituals and requirements have been incorporated among the many amenities made possible by the modern world. (See Figures 1–4.)

Respondents to our family survey provided explicit verification for this conjecture. In responding to the question of whether it is easier or harder to be a religious Jew today than it was years ago, the overwhelming majority believed that it had become easier, particularly because of the five-day work week, increased attention to civil rights (e.g. "If they [blacks] can wear their afros, why shouldn't we wear our *yarmulkas* [skullcaps]?"), and a general increase in Jewish pride. Correspondingly, among rabbis in the area who we surveyed, 65–70 percent indicated that they perceived an increase in the observance of the rituals of Shabbos and *kashrus* along with other ritual practices in the last decade. It would appear that, in fact, it has become easier to sustain the separation between the community and the larger social milieu, thus making ritual

Friendly, yes. But kosher?

If you're on a kosher diet, how do you keep the faith 30,000 feet up in an airplane?

Bring your own? Not eat? Not so. In the friendly skies, we've a simple, kosher answer.

Just ask.

Specifically, when you make your advance reservations. (At least four hours ahead of flight-time, please. We have to order out.) Our friends at Manischewitz® will supply us a kosher meal. We'll have it on board, waiting for you.

And that goes for all breakfast, lunch, dinner or snack flights on United. Anywhere. Anytime.

Now. Is that friendship?

The friendly skies of your land.
United Air Lines

Figure 1. Advertisement for *kosher* air travel. Courtesy of Leo Burnett U.S.A. A Division of Leo Burnett Company, Inc.

Figure 4. Advertisement for *kosher* vitamins. Reprinted from *Kol Boro Park* (Brooklyn), June 1979, p. 10.

observances easier to sustain. This calls into question Leventman's popular analysis:

> that with a much wider range of occupations now opened, Jews are increasingly choosing those which offer greater participation in the wider society. . . [and] Judaism seems to surivive . . . only as it makes fewer religious demands and adapts itself to the social needs of a highly secular and mobile population.[15]

The participation of all Jews in the wider society has, indeed, increased, but the Orthodox, at least in Boro Park, have been fairly successful in imposing a separation even as they participate. The contrasting perceptions of an old-time resident and of a young Orthodox accountant reveal the changing circumstances. The old-timer told us this story.

> I know of an instance. . . . It is a tragic story as such. We had a man *davening* in our *shul*, he knew who my father was, he came from a little town, and he prayed with a big *talis* and *gartl*—a real *hasidishe yid*. After *davening* as it is customary, my mother made a *kidush* every Shabbos—to make a Hasidishe atmosphere. This man never came up to *kidush*. And she asked him, "come up, come up." "No, no, I can't." Finally she found out he had a grocery in Maspeth, Long Island. He had to go after *davening*—I want you to know he *davened* with a *talis* with an *atara* and a *gartl*—and he had to go to the grocery even on Shabbos to open up. Operators, people, had to go after *shul* to their shops."[16]

Another old-time resident summed up the position of Orthodox Jews during the first few decades in America: "the motto was: if you don't show up for work Saturday don't bother coming in on Monday."

The lifestyle of J. L., one of our respondents in the family survey, stands out in sharp contrast to that of the embattled Orthodox Jew of yesteryear. J. L. is twenty-three years old. He sports a neatly trimmed beard and small *peyes* (side curls), as is customary among the very Orthodox and the Hasidic. In 1970 J. L. finished college, majoring in accounting. Presently he is employed by the Federal Internal Revenue Service as an examiner. His observance of the Shabbos and other religious holidays is respected by his employer as a matter of course. In fact, it is protected by law. When asked about his relationship to his colleagues on the job, he replied that he considered it friendly, though he has not been to the homes of any one of them and none of them have been to his. (Privatization is most likely typical of his non-Orthodox and non-Jewish co-workers as well.) He expressed satisfaction with the arrangement and found no ill feelings on either side. He takes his *kosher* lunch along to work. Many of his co-workers also take a brown-bag lunch to work for economic reasons. Thus, they may eat together and talk of politics or sports without having the rules of *kashrus* interfere with normal social intercourse on the job. No one seems to be much concerned with the fact that he wears a *yarmulka* or *peyes*. The experience of a secular education and profession appear to have taken no toll on J. L.'s religiosity any more than his religiosity might have hindered his successes in the wider society. His career pattern is not at all unique among the Orthodox youth of Boro Park.

The symbols of Shabbos and *kashrus* that are so pervasive in the community seem to indicate a tenacious consciousness of being different and separate. At the same time, the manner in which the ritual practices related to this consciousness are carried out indicate that the traditional practices and values have not interfered with the enjoyment of the amenities and opportunities of the contemporary American life, nor with the entirely profane pursuit of success in the modern professions. In fact, it may be argued that it is precisely the availability of the modern amenities and professions that has enabled this group to successfully pursue its religious beliefs and rituals in late twentieth-century America.

Adherence to the rules of Shabbos and *kashrus* is of central importance, but there are other symbols and observances that characterize Orthodox Judaism. In previous studies these other appurtenances of Orthodoxy have also been regarded as the artifacts of the pre-immigrant Jew. One set of rituals that touch very closely on the issue of holiness derive from religious regulations known as the laws of *taharas mishpocho*, or family purity. The most exotic, and controversial, aspect of these rules is the traditional belief that people can become *tomeh*, or impure, as a consequence of certain bodily functions. According to the Bible's metaphysical biology, women become impure, or *nidoh* (a special form of *tomeh*), after each menstrual period. For seven days after the menstrual flow has stopped men are enjoined from having sexual relations with their wives. After this period women are required to go to a *mikva*, or ritual bath, in which they must undergo a purifying immersion. Men, too, may become *tomeh* after any sexual intercourse or nocturnal emission.

Perhaps because the concept of purity and hygiene seem to be closely related, modern norms of personal hygiene have taken a great toll on the rituals associated with *taharas mishpocho*. Not surprisingly, according to Charles Liebman, until the 1930s there were hardly any *mikvas*, or ritual

baths, in any Jewish community in the United States. Today there are
over two hundred and fifty *mikvas* throughout the country, with only six
states lacking any. In the Boro Park community a major million-dollar
complex of *mikvas* was built during the mid-1960s. Many of the Hasidic
synagogues in the community have built their own *mikva* in the base-
are built to ensure the privacy of the user. They are attractively furnished, often resembling a modern health club rather than an ancient
ritularium.

What is, perhaps, most interesting about the continued observance of
taharas mishpocho in this modern Orthodox community is that both
hygiene and psychology are used to make the rituals more palatable.
Time and again one finds articles in *The Jewish Press* or the *Brooklyn
Jewish Journal* (both popular in the Boro Park community) reporting on
the allegedly beneficial effects of *mikva* purification. Some have claimed
that observance of these rituals lessens the incidence of cervical cancer.
Others have argued that the monthly periods of abstinence increase
sexual satisfaction between man and wife in the Orthodox family. As with
the laws of Shabbos and *kashrus*, so too with the laws of *taharas
mishpocho* we see the successful amalgamation of modern and traditional or sacred values in an institution that incorporates the symbols of
both.

Appearance, Status, and Authority

In a colorful essay on the dressing habits of what he called "extreme
Jews," I. B. Singer has described "the fur-edged rabbinical hat, long
gabardines, big beards, side locks, women in wigs and bonnets that
were already obsolete in my youth in Warsaw."[17] Using the analogy of a
"soldier surrounded" Singer has suggested, and others have confirmed,
that the special clothing style helps the pious Jew to

> enforce ever-stricter and more rigorous measures in order to retain
> his historical role and to raise a generation that will follow his ways.
> Thus, if the worldly Jew dresses in short [modern] garments, the
> pious Jew must stick to his long gabardine. Since the former shaves
> his beard and side locks the latter must let them grow as long as
> possible.[18]

These exotic styles are frequently found on the streets of Boro Park, but
they are by no means universal. Many, perhaps the majority, of the
Orthodox Jews of the community do not wear the traditional Hasidic

garb. But the fact that some do highlights the point that membership in the Orthodox community makes certain styles and appearances normative. Minimally, men are required to wear skullcaps or hats. Women, married or not, must be modestly dressed. And married women must wear their hair covered either by kerchief or hat, or by wig.

In their study of a largely second-generation Jewish community in the Midwest, Kramer and Leventman noted a general attitude towards "Yiddish speaking men adorned with beards and sidecurls and garbed in black frock coats and hats," which associated such characteristics "with the poverty and lack of enlightenment of the ghetto."[19] It was expected and assumed that the newcomers would shed these habits of appearance as they moved into the mainstream of American society. Some shedding has, indeed, occurred. But particular habits of speech and dress have remained one of the significant criteria of membership in the Orthodox community.

From the point of view of general societal attitudes towards the habits of the Orthodox and the Hasidic, it had already been observed in 1960 by Kranzler that:

> Economically most of the recent newcomers who are capable of holding a job have adjusted normally, despite the fears expressed by numerous people that they could never become absorbed into the American economy unless they would cut their beards and *peyes*.[20]

Jobs were found and careers secured despite the persistence of the beard and the *peyes*. It must be allowed that beards were trimmed and the *peyes* came to be tucked quietly behind the ears—left to flow freely only within the boundaries of the community. But the norms of personal appearance so prevalent in American society—the clean-shaven or clean-cut look for men, and the colorful and coquettish look for women—have been considerably modified in the Orthodox milieu. Women's clothing tends to cover a great deal more of their bodies than is generally the rule in contemporary American women's wear. The wearing of pants by women is a generally observed tabu. Yet if religious prescriptions regulate the modesty of women's clothing, middle-class values allow that no expense be spared to be as elegantly modest as possible. Thus, restrictions placed on clothing in the name of religious modesty appear to be counterbalance by wearing expensive clothing—a combination of Jewish modesty with the norms of American consumerism. Walking down Thirteenth Avenue on any ordinary week-day, one will find the religious women of Boro Park dressed as if they were on their way to some ceremonial occasion. The shabbiness normally associated with traditional religious dressing habits is simply not to be found in this Orthodox community. Here, as in the larger middle-class world, clothes are an important symbol of status. But the status they symbolize in this community is two-fold: religious and economic. Previous analyses of the traditional dressing habit have erred by focusing only on the religious symbolism.

The dual symbolism of clothes is found in the habits of the men as well. While the traditional Hasidic garb is on the decline, one is not likely to find casual clothes popular among the Orthodox. Suit and hat—expensive and modern—are the most popular, along with *yarmulkas* of every variety. Expensive and somewhat modernized versions of the traditional Hasidic *beketch* and/or *kapote* and fur-trimmed headgear have emerged among some segments of the community as the thing to wear on the Shabbos and the holidays. But the function of this type of dressing habit is primarily to signify the status of the wearer within the community and not to differentiate him from his fellow man in the secular world.

For a variety of reasons American attitudes toward dressing habits have undergone a radical change in recent years. As a by-product of this alteration in general attitudes, the peculiarities of Orthodox and Hasidic appearance have come to be accepted as just one of the many varieties to be found on the streets of the metropolis. At the same time, due to the rising socio-economic status of the residents, Orthodox dressing habits have been modified to reflect the rise in status. The letter of the law continues to be satisfied by the strict adherence to the traditional rules of modesty. Women have their elbows and knees covered and show no cleavage. Men have their heads covered and show a preference for somber colors. But the actual items that are used to satisfy the strictures of the law and custom give wide play to the tastes and status needs of a middle-class population. Traditional dress modes, then, not only have not suffered in the course of Orthodoxy's entrance into the middle class but also have been given a wider range of variability and expression precisely because this group can now *afford* to exercise its preferences. To put it quite simply, Boro Park Jewry discovered—and thereby has shown the rest of the world—that dressing in the traditional manner is not just the privilege of the poor, unenlightened ghetto Jew. The middle class can do it too. A small item in the widely read *Jewish Press* reflects this amalgam of attitudes towards clothing and religiosity:

Orthodox Fashions

Zipora Goren, wife of Israel's Ashkenazic Chief Rabbi Shlomo
Goren, presided last night over a fashion show that featured what
the well dressed religious woman wears: no mini-skirts and no deep
decollete. The show was held at Beersheba where it attracted a large
crowd from the local religious community. The mannequins were
girls from the Mizrachi Religious Institute.[21]

While this fashion show did not take place in Boro Park, it might as well
have because it very much reflects local attitudes toward dress and
appearance. Ritual modesty is displayed with the full force of middle-
class gaudiness. The proliferation of wig and hat shops, featuring ever
newer and more expensive styles, give further evidence of the importance of stylish appearance within the limits of ritual Orthodoxy.

The change in aesthetics and meanings attached to personal appearance in the Orthodox community must be understood as part of a
broader change in the very structure and symbols of status. The traditional status system has been described by Wirth, quite nostalgically, as
one in which:

> each individual who was just a mere Jew to the outside world had a
> place of dignity and was bound to the rest by profound sentiments.
> . . . Through the organization of the synagogue, the family unit was
> given a definite status, based not so much on wealth as on learning,
> piety, and the purity of the family, and services rendered to the
> community.[22]

Presumably, the status system of the minority community is rooted in
resentment against felt inferiority. This line of analysis has been recently
reinforced by Kramer:

> In effect the minority community mitigates against social inferi-
> ority by permitting its members to see themselves as persons. Es-
> chewing the categories of the dominant group . . . the shared
> minority status of the members of the community provides peers
> who appreciate individual worth and recognize social
> achievement. With each other they do not have to overstate the
> legitimacy of their claims to status nor prove their qualifications
> without social validation.[23]

Similarly, in their studies of Williamsburg, both Kranzler and Poll
emphasized indigenous religious values as the primary basis of social
status in the community.[24]

On the other hand, it has been suggested by Gordon, as well as by others, that with entrance into the class and status structure of official society the Jews, as all minorities, will readily abandon (and to a large extent have already abandoned) their indigenous ranking system.

> The traditional stress and high evaluation placed upon Talmudic learning was easily transferred under new conditions to a desire for secular education, if not for the parent generation, at least for the children. ... Thus the Jews arrived in America with the middle-class values of thrift, sobriety, ambition, desire for education, ability to postpone immediate gratification for long range goals, and aversion to violence already internalized.[25]

With the entrance of the subsequent generations of native-born Jews into the mainstream of America's stratification system, Gordon suggests:

> it is clear to any close observer of the American scene that in extrinsic culture traits, native-born Jews at various class levels are very similar to native-born non-Jews of the same social class. In dress, appearance, manner, and speech pattern, the Jewish graduate of an Ivy-league college, for instance, appears virtually indistinguishable from his Gentile counterpart.[26]

Once again, contemporary sociological analysis of Jews and the Jewish experience in America focuses upon the extremes of social isolation on the one hand and the relentless tendency toward assimilation on the other. The question of what the status system of a middle-class, American, Orthodox Jewish community might look like has simply been disregarded. Yet Boro Park is such a community, and its structure and symbols of status do not correspond to either of the two extreme characterizations.

While it is true, as Kranzler has observed, that "failing to abide by the basic standards of daily prayers, Sabbath observance, kosher food, proper marriage and other requirements of the Jewish law automatically precludes acceptance and advancement,"[27] simply meeting the above criteria will not ensure one's high status in the community. Formal education, both religious and secular, has come to play a major role in the certification of status in the modern Orthodox community. While in the traditional community one's reputation and familial ties are of major significance, in Boro Park, credentials count. The phrases of social distinction made popular by Poll in his study of the Williamsburg Hasidic community are rarely to be found in Boro Park.[28] Official titles and symbols of accomplishment are the norm.

In the telephone book survey of Boro Park Jewry a total of 1,695 persons were found with the official title of rabbi. Although most of the people bearing that title do not actually practice or officiate in that capacity, the popularity of the title indicates something of its desirability as a mark of distinction. Young men attending *yeshivas* typically express a desire to obtain the *s'micha* (ordination). Yet very few of them express any desire to practice as heads of congregations. At best, some would like to make a career of teaching in *yeshivas*. On the whole, however, their occupational interests have little to do with the *s'micha* itself. A survey of the rabbis in the Boro Park area (N = 56) indicated that 41 percent considered themselves Hasidic, and 51 percent considered themselves Orthodox. Within these two groups a mere 14 percent, or eight people, ever actually served as rabbis. Some 45 percent of the entire sample were employed in a variety of professions, including engineering, accounting, teaching, law, and medicine. Another 21 percent were in business, including self-employed butchers, real-estate men, salesmen, and so forth. While 32 percent of the sample did not provide usable information about their own occupations, all agreed to rank eight types of occupations as important in the community. Table 11 is a summary of their rankings.

The range of evaluations of the eight occupations seems to confirm the traditionally high esteem enjoyed by rabbis, especially in the eyes of other rabbis. It also confirms the status of businessmen, the traditional *balebos* [literally householder]. Interestingly, the respondents in the survey, who themselves were rabbis, were engaged in a variety of

TABLE 11
Rabbis' Ranking of Eight Occupations (N = 56)

Occupation	Percent of Choices Assigned, by Ranking							
	1	2	3	4	5	6	7	8
Rabbi	42.9	7.1						
Businessman	8.9	26.8	8.9	3.6	3.6		1.8	
Doctor	10.1	8.9	14.3	10.7	8.9	1.8	3.6	
Lawyer			12.5	7.1	14.3	5.4	12.5	5.4
Psychologist	5.4	3.6	3.6	12.5	1.8	12.5	5.4	12.5
Scientist	1.8	3.6			8.9	8.9	10.7	14.3
Craftsman	8.9	12.5	23.2	7.1	5.4	7.1		
Politician	1.8	10.7	5.4	12.5	3.6	10.7	1.8	10.7

Source: Author's survey of Boro Park rabbis.

professions. Correspondingly, some of the professions, such as medicine, psychology (surprisingly), and scientific research did appear as choices in the highest ranks. Even politics appears in the top two ranks with reasonable frequency. It would appear from this pattern of responses that the status system in the Boro Park community is marked by considerable ambivalence. Traditional roles are still highly valued, but success in secular and untraditional fields is coming to be accepted and even admired. What seems to be emerging is a dual status system that may be unique to the modern Orthodox community.

The concept of dual status in the context of minority communities has typically meant that a member of such a community might be considered of low status outside of his community, yet enjoy high status within the community. With respect to the middle-class Orthodox community the concept seems to have taken on a new meaning—the status achieved in the secular realm of education and/or career acts to supplement and enhance the individual's intra-communal status. Thus, the diligent *yeshiva bochur* (student) must not only obtain the *s'micha* (ordination) to rank high by community standards, but he must also obtain at least a bachelor's degree at Brooklyn College. Higher secular achievements in conjunction with religious learning are considered praiseworthy indeed. The attendance of *yeshiva* students, both male and female, in evening college programs and other programs of advanced secular education has become *de rigeur.* For example, according to the enrollment records of Brooklyn College, in the fall semester of 1971 there were 2,970 students attending the college from the four zip code areas comprising the Boro Park community. The U.S. census of 1970 showed a total of 6,089 students enrolled in college in the Boro Park area. It would seem that 48 percent of them are attending Brooklyn College. A further check of the college records revealed that the largest proportion of students coming from the general area of Boro Park reside in the most densely Jewish sectors of it. Not surprisingly, while the overall proportion of Brooklyn College students who attend evening session classes is less than 30 percent, among the students who reside in the Boro Park area the proportion attending evening sessions is 52 percent. Most of these students attend *yeshivas* during the daytime.

These statistical indications of the dual status system in the Orthodox community were further corroborated by the respondents in a survey of Young Israel Intercollegiates. Most of these respondents did not expect to obtain *s'micha;* however, they did indicate that their parents expected them to continue a *yeshiva* education through high school. All forty-four of them had attended, and most completed, *yeshiva* high school. Significantly, 84 percent of them indicated that they would provide the same type of religious education for their own children. The apparent enthusiasm for religious education, among both parents and children, is matched by a similar sentiment with respect to secular education their fathers had received; 21 percent indicated that their fathers had some college education. An additional 18 percent indicated that their fathers had completed college, and 9 percent of respondents' fathers had attained an advanced university degree. Nearly all of the respondents felt that their parents expected them to finish four years of college, and 32 percent expressed the feeling that their parents expect them to go beyond the four-year college education for some professional degree. Out of the forty-four respondents 77 percent expected to enter some professional career; only one respondent expected to become a practicing rabbi. It is important to recall that all of these respondents professed to be Orthodox in their religious beliefs and practices. Many of them had attended rather strict *yeshiva* schools.

The requirements of the dual status system seem quite clear from the two sets of survey data. Educational achievement is of cardinal importance. But achievement in either the religious or the secular sphere alone is simply not enough. Both are considered necessary. While successful businessmen, the *balebatim*, are still highly regarded, few of them actually expect their sons to follow in their footsteps without the appropriate amount of both types of formal education.

This alteration in the status system of the community has had a noticeable impact on the role of women as well. In neither Poll's nor Kranzler's study of the Williamsburg community is special attention devoted to the status of women. Rightly so, because in the traditional Orthodox or Hasidic community the woman's status is based directly on the status of either her father, if she is unmarried, or her husband. Because of the expanding range of opportunities for women in the job market, and the communal norms of educational achievement that apply more or less equally to both men and women, Orthodox women in the Boro Park community are increasingly emerging with personally achieved status. Particularly as young men are interested in pursuing and succeeding in two educational programs at once, the status of a prospective bride (not to speak of her market value) is much enhanced if she herself is capable of holding a job and earning an income that is adequate to support her and her husband while he is completing his professional and religious education. Also, as modern housekeeping has become less time-consuming, even in the Orthodox home and kitchen, the woman is also expected to be an intellectual companion to her husband.[29]

It would be naive to suggest that the only social forces that are helping to change the role and status of women in the Orthodox community are the technology of housekeeping and the status needs of their prospective mates. To be sure, these are important. Orthodox girls and women, however, have also been influenced in numerous and subtle ways by the women's movement of the 1970s. The popular jargon of women's lib and male chauvinism have crept into the common parlance of Boro Park Jewry as well. In this context it invariably means nothing more than that young husbands will change their own children's diapers—which their fathers would never have done. Or that young women will go off to evening courses at Brooklyn College while their husbands stay home to watch the children. Such apparently small changes in behavior, however, hint at much more profound changes in consciousness.

Since one dimension of the dual status system is universalistic, based on merit that applies to men and women equally, its influence reaches into the home, altering the way men and women perceive one another and altering their expectations of each other. Since much of the educational experience of young men and women, especially in secular subjects, is identical, it should hardly be surprising to find that their expectations for personal esteem, gratification, and even occupational achievement have grown more alike. The impact of these changes on marital relations is just now gradually coming to light.[30]

The status incongruence experienced by many of the earlier generations of Jewish immigrants in America seems to have been resolved in the Boro Park community in a way that was not anticipated in earlier research on the American Jewish community. Instead of isolating one system from the other, as studies of the Hasidic community have suggested, and instead of one system giving way to the other, as studies emphasizing assimilation have suggested, the dual status system that has evolved in the Boro Park community accepts the norms of both the religious and the secular status system (insofar as achievements are concerned) with little apparent concern for possible contradictions. The emergence of the dual status system cannot, however, be attributed solely to the economic advances made by the Orthodox community in Boro Park. In a large part it must also be seen as the replacement of the faltering *yichus* system.

The concept of *yichus* refers to the prestige and purity of one's lineage. In their study of life in the Eastern European *shtetl* (rural Jewish community) Zborowski and Herzog have suggested that *yichus* includes learning plus wealth, or wealth so used as to be translatable into learning through charity. The important point about *yichus* in the traditional community is that "within the community the yichus of every member is generally known down to the last detail, and to recite one's yichus to a new acquaintance is an integral part of an introduction."[31]

It is precisely this personal aspect of *yichus* that makes it a poor indicator of status in an urban community, and thus increasingly useless in the modern Orthodox community. In a community that consists of over ten thousand families it becomes quite impossible to familiarize one's self with the lineage of each one. Also, the often radical change of fortunes experienced by families during the war and in the course of immigration has rendered *yichus* a rather inaccurate indicator of one's present circumstances. Thus, the significance placed upon achieved status as opposed to ascribed status is the result of both internal as well as external conditions of the community.

One qualification that must be made with respect to *yichus* is that it does persist in a limited form in some of the small, ethnically based *shuls* (synagogues) that dot the Boro Park area. First-generation loyalists of such small town *rebbes* (rabbis who become cult figures) as the Belzer, the Bobover, the Debreciner, the Kereszturer, the Lubavitcher, the Munkacser, the Papper, the Stoliner, the Szatmarer, the Szanzer, the Szigheter, the Vizhnitzer, and a few others have succeeded in re-establishing *yichus*-based sub-communities within the larger Orthodox community in Boro Park. The way in which one of these sub-communities was re-established in Boro Park is quite typical of the phenomenon in general. According to one informant, who himself is a member of one of these Hasidic groups, the community was re-established as follows.

> How did it start? Well, there were a few people who even in Hungary were very interested in Reb ——. Years before there was even a rebbe [in the U.S.] these people got together and made a *beis hamedresh* [study and prayer hall] in Williamsburg. People who came from the same town of —— and were followers of the old rebbe decided to make the *beis hamedresh*. They decided they wanted to carry on.

In 1963, these followers of the old *rebbe* located his third grandson, a young man of twenty years of age then studying in an entirely non-Hasidic *yeshiva*. A few of the *balebatim* [financially established loyalists; plural of *balebos*] set this third grandson up in the *beis hamedresh* as the new *rebbe*. It is interesting to observe, here, that a number of other living descendants of the old *rebbe* were not selected. The above informant suggested that these other descendants lacked the appropriate achievements in scholarship. It is also interesting to note that the new *rebbe* was not discovered and installed in his position until ten or fifteen years after the old-time loyalists had been residing and established in the United States. They simply lacked the financial surplus to support the luxury of a *rebbe*. The re-establishment of this dynasty, then, depended very much on the former Hasidim achieving the secure financial status that enabled them to support the *rebbe*.

Throughout the above example *yichus* leans heavily on the crutches of measurable achievement. The *rebbe*, who occupies the highest status position in the hierarchy of this group, owes his position to his *yichus*—his grandfather—but could not have been selected by the old-time loyalists were he not also a highly accomplished talmudic scholar in a typically American *yeshiva*.

The way in which *yichus* does work in the small, sectarian Orthodox or Hasidic congregation (where it is possible to know the lineage of each member) is as a sort of credit rating. One's rating is presumed to be known until proven otherwise. But proof of one sort or another must be furnished in the form of recognizable credentials. While Kramer is correct in suggesting that within these communities the members do not have to "overstate the legitimacy of their claims to status,"[32] the claims must be legitimated by typically American standards of achievement.

One final point needs to be considered in connection with status and stratification in the modern Orthodox community, namely, social mobility. In the mainstream of the sociology of America's Jews, social mobility is one of the most, if not the most, important forces contributing to assimilation into American life. Typically, it has been suggested that as Jews—particularly the younger, native-born generations—rise on the American ladder of success, they will modify or entirely abandon their religious beliefs and practices to suit their newly achieved status. The assumption underlying this widely accepted proposition is that the traditional expressions of religiosity are necessarily associated with low status and poor secular education, and produce status anxiety in the upwardly mobile younger generation. It is this status anxiety that presumably leads the younger generations to abandon the ways of their fathers, as they abandon the communities in which those ways are still in practice.

A number of factors appear to converge in the Boro Park Jewish community that tend to suggest that a reconsideration of the prevalent assumption and analysis is in order. The extension of legal protection to those who wish to pursue any career in the public or private sector yet retain their religious practices has had both practical and psychological consequences for the community. Practically, such protection has ensured that Orthodox Jews can, in fact, pursue careers of their choice yet remain Orthodox. Psychologically, the availability of such a practical alternative has emboldened the coming generation of Orthodox Jews to, in fact, enter prestigious careers without fear that they may have to abandon the faith of their fathers in their attempts at secular success. The general liberalization of attitudes toward individual differences, at least in urban areas like New York City, has also contributed to the fact that those traditional Jews who did enter the job and career market during the sixties experienced less social pressure to conform than earlier immigrant generations.

The religious educational system has also matured considerably in the decades since World War II. Emphasis in the method and curriculum of these schools has shifted from the rote learning of precepts and practices to a greater appreciation of Jewish history, both ancient and modern, and a systematic understanding of the *halachic* principles (religious legalisms). Thus, students coming out of *yeshivas* are receiving a religious education that is every bit as rational and achievement oriented as their secular education. In this way the discrepancy between achieved and ascribed status has been reduced considerably, and aspirations toward occupational and social mobility need no longer be experienced as inconsistent with religious status.

As for the impact of social mobility on geographic mobility, the pattern here, too, has been a novel one. While some of the mobile young do prefer to settle outside of the Boro Park area, they move to nearby neighborhoods in which Orthodox communities similar to Boro Park have been established. The most preferred communities are in the vicinity of Boro Park itself: Flatbush, Belle Harbor, or since the early 1970s, Staten Island. More distant choices include Long Island communities, such as Lawrence and Great Neck. Another unusual direction of geographic mobility for Orthodox youth is a growing trend to settle in Israel. In the classified section of the *Jewish Press*—the most widely read

Jewish newspaper in the Orthodox community—housing opportunities in Israel and stories of families settling there are featured regularly.

Finally, the mobility aspirations prevalent in the community, particularly among the next generation, were reflected in the responses to our survey of the Young Israel Inter-collegiates. Their typical attitudes toward career and education have already been noted above. Also interesting to note is the fact that 70 percent were satisfied with the "density of the Jewish population" in the Boro Park area, suggesting that they would like to live in a similarly densely Jewish area. Quite consistent with this, 73 percent were satisfied with "those facilities in the community which make Torah-true *Yidishkeit* possible." Nearly a third of the respondents considered it highly probable that they would move to and settle in Israel. Another 14 percent considered such a move somewhat likely, and 36 percent wondered about the possibility of settling in Israel. About 23 percent of the respondents rejected such a possibility. Most of the respondents were ambivalent about moving to the suburbs, and indicated that they would not like to live in an area which was not as densely Jewish as Boro Park. In sum, the mobility aspirations of the young Orthodox in Boro Park combine the desire for secular success with an equal desire for a religious communal setting.

Habits of appearance tend to be the external expressions of status, but the inner dimension of status is found in the relations of authority and conceptions of legitimacy which are prevalent in the community. It is to this aspect of the modern Orthodox community that we now turn.

Two figures loom large as figures of authority in the traditional Jewish community: the rabbi, and the father.

> The rabbi, as the distinctive and unchallenged religious specialist of the Jewish community, emerged from the Soferic-Pharasaic tradition by the end of the first century [A.D.]. While the rabbi, like the priest and prophet before him, ultimately rested his authority on divine revelation, . . . he admonished the people through preaching and teaching. . . . In contradistinction to the priest and prophet, [he] based his authority on an intimate knowledge of the written and oral law, both of which, he claimed, were divinely ordained.[33]

Respect for parents was also divinely decreed according to the Biblical tradition; with special emphasis on "honor thy father." Accordingly, Poll has observed that in the Hasidic community:

> The husband [and father] has the authority in making family decisions. . . . Family norms are guided by religious convictions and

religious rules, and the husband [father] is the one who has received [the most] religious training. . . . [He] is the breadwinner and the overall supervisor of religious matters.[34]

The authority of rabbis and fathers could best be characterized by the Weberian category: traditional. And traditionally the status of these roles was rooted in a static social structure. With the erosion of that social structure, due to war, migration, and modernization, along with a general change in the very basis of status in the community, it was expected that the authority of these traditional roles would also be drastically reduced.

The confrontation of fathers and sons in the immigrant family is described poignantly by Handlin:

> The young wore their American nativity like a badge that marked their superiority over their elders. As they grew in knowledge and in craftiness, as their earnings rose above those of the head of the family, they ceased to bow to restraints and would no longer be ordered about.[35]

This account is corroborated by the colorful descriptions of Hapgood and Golden.[36] The second generation, the children of the immigrants of the turn of the century, did, indeed, deny much of the legitimacy of parental authority, especially the authority of the father. Phillip Roth's portrayal of the fictional Portnoy's impotent father is but the most extreme example of the denial of that authority.

The authority of the rabbi has, similarly, undergone a great deal of alteration. As Carlin and Mendlovitz have argued, "the American rabbi can best be understood as a religious specialist responding to a loss of authority."[37] Leventman's description of the modern synagogue amplifies the point:

> The synagogue has become a kind of middle–class settlement house. In the process, the status of the rabbi is often devalued to be replaced by the social director. It is somewhat ironic that a people with so great a religious heritage should have become so a-religious that the rabbi can hardly be spoken of as a spiritual leader. At best he is a pastoral psychologist, at worst, a sympathetic overseer.[38]

In both our family survey and our survey of rabbis in the Boro Park community, an effort was made to probe the relationship between the traditional figures of authority and their traditional subordinates. Parents, especially fathers, were asked to comment on the quality of their relationship with their children. In the survey of the Young Israel Intercollegiates the respondents were asked to comment on their relationship with their parents, rabbis, and teachers. While most of the rabbis were not practicing as such, they were asked to comment on how they thought residents of the community regarded clergymen. Other practicing rabbis were interviewed and asked to express their views on the same question. All the responses point to a change in the status of traditional figures of authority. But the pattern of that change is not simply one of erosion. Rather, the basis of legitimacy has come to reflect or parallel the dual nature of status in the community.

Of the two traditional figures of authority, it is the father who has suffered the greatest setback. The reasons for this may be readily understood if we compare the educational achievements, both religious and secular, of the community's youth with that of their elders. The figures in Tables 12 and 13 were obtained from our survey of fifty-six families in Boro Park.

Both tables indicate the increased importance of formal education, both religious and secular, which is being received in the greatest proportion by the American born generation of Orthodox Jews. Of those under thirty, 69 percent were born in the United States, while of the over-thirty group 60 percent were born abroad. Furthermore, those in the under thirty age bracket who indicated "high school" or "some college" as their level of education were nearly without exception students currently enrolled in educational programs. All had intentions of finishing college; some even to go on for some advanced academic or professional degree. In Table 13 it was generally the women who received "home training only." Among the under-30 group, those who were receiving elementary religious education were by and large continuing on to *yeshiva*.

Thus, even when it comes to matters of *halacha* (religious law) or ritual, parents can guide their children primarily on the basis of their own strongly ethnic *minhagim* (customs). Their children, on the other hand, can more frequently refer to a precise knowledge of *halachic* texts and historical precedents. When conflicts arise, as they often do, between parental guidance and youthful wisdom, the vocabulary of the conflict invariably reflects the battle between knowledge based on tradition and knowledge based on formal education. To the extent that the father is traditionally supposed to represent reverence for religious knowledge—which he often may not, in fact, possess—he is fighting a

TABLE 12
Extent of Secular Education among Respondents in Two Age Categories

Amount of Education	Percent of Respondents under 30	Percent of Respondents over 30
	N = 58	N = 57
None		5.2
Elementary	6.8	8.7
High school	37.9	36.8
Some college	5.1	7.0
College	29.3	8.7
Advanced degree	8.6	
Foreign and coder can't determine	12.0	33.3

Source: Author's survey of Boro Park families.

TABLE 13
Extent of Religious Education among Respondents in Two Age Categories

Amount of Education	Percent of Respondents under 30	Percent of Respondents over 30
	N = 58	N = 57
None	1.7	3.5
Home training only	5.1	15.7
Elementary or *cheder* only	17.2	26.3
Advanced or *yeshiva*	67.2	29.8
Coder can't determine	8.6	24.5

Source: Author's survey of Boro Park families.

losing battle with his children, whose religious education he has subsidized

A persistent theme in discussions with parents concerning their children is their dissatisfaction with their children's preferences for modern clothing and hair styles. Their children's retort most often takes the form of a legalistic rebuttal. "There is nothing in the *halacha* about what color my shirt [or dress] should be, or how I should cut my hair. As long as I live according to the *halacha* they [parents] can't complain."

It would appear that formal religious education enjoys greater esteem and legitimacy than parents, who represent essentially the same values but on the basis of traditional authority. Thus, if the authority of parents, and the father in particular, is eroding in the Orthodox community, it is being undermined not only by the increased secular education of the young, but also—and perhaps more so—by the increased religious education of the young.

What we witness in the modern Orthodox community, then, is not simply the displacement of one figure of authority by another. Rather, a shift seems to have taken place in the very nature of legitimacy, in Weberian terms, from the traditional to the legal-rational. The religious teacher, unlike the father, guides by means of teaching a body of knowledge that is open to questioning and understanding. His guidance is based on rational principles of pedagogy and the limits of a formal school bureaucracy. In this respect the religious educational process is quite similar to the secular one, and very dissimilar, indeed, to established tradition.[39]

In subtle, yet pervasive ways this alteration in the nature of legitimacy has eroded the traditional authority of the rabbi as well. Some of the change can be appreciated from the complaints of one informant. His brother is the rabbi of one of the oldest and largest Orthodox congregations in the community.

> When my brother stands up to give his *drasha* [sermon] on Shabbos all the *frume yeshivaleit* [devout *yeshiva* students] are busy talking to each other in the back of the *shul*. Do you think any one of them would ever stand up [out of respect] for him? No! But let any little *m'lamed* [teacher] walk in, he may have ten *bochurim* [students] and teach a *blat Gemora* [a page of Talmud] a week, and they'll stand up for him and call him *rebbe*. I ask you, where is the respect? That's what all the *yeshivas* fail to teach. The *yeshivaleit* have no respect. They don't know what it means—a *rov* [a true Rabbi].

The rabbi who dispenses homiletic wisdom, keyed to a lay audience, week after week on Shabbos mornings, commands little attention or respect from those who, through a *yeshiva* education, have acquired a taste for more rational learned discourse. Thus, the officiating rabbis of established congregations have lost a good deal of their prestige and following in recent years. Correspondingly, membership and attendance, especially of the young, has also declined in the large, well-established synagogues in the area. At the same time, the number and popularity of the more intimate *shtieblach* (store-front and basement synagogues) has increased. The success of the *rebbes* in these small congregations derives from two sources. Some, as mentioned in an earlier example, trace their *yichus* to home town *rebbes* in Eastern Europe and thus enjoy the loyalties of an immigrant congregation and American born Orthodox who are enchanted by such a heritage. The authority of such *rebbes* is a mixture of tradition and routinized charisma. A significant number, however, appeal to the native born, *yeshiva*-educated population because they present themselves as compassionate teachers. In fact, in most of these *shtieblach* the learning of Talmud and other sacred texts is conducted daily, after prayers. While Carlin and Mendlovitz, along with others, have accounted for the decline in the status and authority of the rabbi because of a generalized erosion of reverence for religious learning, it would appear on the basis of the Boro Park data that some rabbis have lost status and authority precisely because of an increased interest in and reverence for sacred wisdom. Synagogue rabbis have, indeed, lost authority. But teaching *rebbes*, and religious teachers whose authority is rooted in the formal structure of a *yeshiva*, have gained in status. It is interesting to note that even those Hasidic masters whose position is based on *yichus*, and are themselves leaders of substantial congregations, have, in recent years, established their own school systems. Thus, they too stand not merely as representatives of dynasties but, perhaps as importantly, as deans of *yeshivas*. Certainly, for native born youth who have little feeling for the histories of Eastern European communities, the role of master-teacher is of far greater significance than the role of hereditary communal leader.

In general, it can be said that both the traditional authority of the synagogue rabbi as well as the routinized charisma of dynastic *rebbes* has undergone considerable rationalization in the modern Orthodox community. In the course of this rationalization process their authority has also had to be curtailed in scope—so as to accommodate the participation of their followers in the secular world. The report of a Hasidic informant, who holds a Ph.D. from one of the major universities in New York City, presents an interesting case study of the process of rabbinic accommodation:

> My parents agreed to my getting married provided that I agreed to work—the *rebbe* had thought the marriage advisable. I got married, so I agreed to work. I went back to ——, went to some business school,

and took a course in bookkeeping. Then I came back here [Boro Park] and worked for five months as a bookkeeper. Then I got fired. I wasn't interested in anything. I had some money in the bank and ran around for awhile. I worked in a knitting mill for a couple of weeks, worked here, worked there. About a year went by and I was extremely frustrated and shut up. I worked in the *yeshiva* for awhile in a very minor position. I confided in him [the *rebbe*], but we rubbed each other the wrong way at that point. His attitude was a very wrong one at that time; he felt that I had to be goaded into doing something. I don't think he appreciated my [upper middle-class] background. My background was not one which allows me to walk into a knitting mill or do jewelry and be content. Most of my friends who got married at the same time didn't understand what was bothering me at the time: that I wanted more out of whatever I was doing than just a check on Friday afternoon. I had to have some interest in my work and it had to be prestigious enough for me to do it. If I wasn't going to be a *rosh yeshiva* [head of a *yeshiva*], I was going to be a college professor. At one point I decided that I can no longer see any reason why I shouldn't go to college. For awhile I was afraid to ask the *rebbe*, so I was going to do it without asking. Then I decided I always confided in him, there is no reason to stop now. I went in and told him I wanted to go. He argued about the fact that there would be women in my classes, and that what is taught there is heresy. He argued with me for awhile, but I think his argument was half-hearted because he realized that I was going.

In response to my question of what he would have done had the *rebbe* withheld consent, the informant claimed that he would have obeyed the *rebbe*. I doubt it. And, I suspect, the *rebbe* doubted it too.

The authority of this *rebbe*, and many others like him, rests on his ability to appreciate what is more or less a forgone conclusion in the minds of his followers. His guidance will often be in directions in which his flock is already pulling. Accommodations similar to that described above have taken place in nearly every Orthodox *yeshiva* high school in the last decade. While secular education in colleges was considered tabu, the religious leaders of the *yeshivas* recognized that such a course of action was desired by most of their students (and even more so by the parents of their students). So much so, that many of the students actually registered in colleges in the New York City area, thereby risking expulsion from the *yeshiva*. Sometime during the 1960s the deans of most *yeshivas* began making deals with their students, permitting them to attend college on a part-time basis, so long as they devoted equal or more time to *limudei kodesh* (sacred studies). A potential threat to authority was, thus, averted through artful compromise. Interestingly, the compromise rarely, if ever, involved self-conscious negotiation. Rather, it was expressed in most cases as the tacit acceptance of an inevitable course of action. Traditional authority made a rational appraisal of its own limitations, and chose to act rationally.

One final reflection on the nature of authority in the community comes from responses on our family survey and our survey of rabbis. Respondents in both of these surveys were asked to indicate the names and careers of persons they considered to be influential in the Boro Park Jewish community. Five or six rabbis occupied the most prominent place in the pattern of responses among both sub-samples of the population. Two other names which appeared with notable frequency were the names of people made popular through the *Jewish Press* and known for having connections with various levels of the government apparatus. The only person placed in the category of influentials, without rabbinic, academic, or political credentials, is a local real-estate broker who is also on the local City Planning Board and is one of the oldest members of the Sfardishe Shul—the oldest Orthodox synagogue in the area.

The rabbis who are considered influential owed their popularity to a number of sources. Two were reputed to have close ties with the city administration. One was the dean of an established and highly respected rabbinic seminary. Three Hasidic *rebbes* were thought to be influential primarily because of the reputed size of their flock. One in particular, the Bobover *rebbe*, had made a great impression on the Boro Park community because he has established a multi-million-dollar complex consisting of a *shul* and *yeshivas* since moving into the area. According to Police Department estimates, he brought along from Williamsburg nearly four thousand people.

The basic theme that seems to emerge from the pattern of responses on both surveys is that those who would make a claim to esteem and authority on the basis of traditional roles, such as a rabbi, must be able to legitimate their positions through non-traditional performance criteria. Rabbis must be capable educators and politicians who show sensitivity to the status aspirations of their followers; at the same time they must sustain the image of the ethical scholar and talmudic sage. Others, such as professionals in secular fields, who in traditional Jewish communities have not, as a rule, enjoyed esteem or authority, now do so only to the extent that they demonstrate a genuine *ahavas Yisroel*—the application of their skills to the Jewish interests of the community.

Stock of Knowledge and Worldview

The previous sections of this chapter dealt with the ways in which ultimate values and dominant symbols of the Orthodox culture articulate with the middle-class status of an increasingly Americanized Jewish community. Essentially, we have been talking about the consequences of the contact between two systems of knowledge: the sacred and the secular, or the communal and the societal. Since we have been dealing with the ways in which individuals have experienced and responded to this contact between the two systems of knowledge, a more formal phenomenological analysis appears to be in order. Specifically, we need to inquire, what are the elements of the two systems of knowledge that have made the outcome we have observed possible? And, what are the shared meanings which have emerged out of the contact?

The value of separateness and the closed or exclusive structure of the Orthodox and Hasidic community needs little further elaboration. Whether in the ghettos of Eastern Europe or in the low-status ethnic enclaves of New York City, the world of the Orthodox Jew has been woven out of a special language (Yiddish) and particular values, along with specialized religious paraphernalia (clothes and institutions) which perpetuate the values. It has been this world that is intimately known and readily at hand. It has defined the experience of "here-and-now." The secular world had been known largely as "out there," often through second-hand contact. What was known about the world "out there" most often rendered it tabu and threatening. It included knowledge which flew in the face of traditional wisdom, and opportunities which could be taken only at the risk of self-denial; against forces which were openly hostile to Jewish survival. The intimacy of the "inside" stood out sharply against the formality of the "outside". It is probably this relationship between the two worlds of minorities which led Shibutani and Kwan to observe that, in general, "One of the characteristics of minority peoples is their extreme preoccupation with the affairs of their own world; they have detailed knowledge of the transactions within their own groups but only vague notions of what goes on outside."[40]

The inability to participate—for whatever reasons—and the fear of participation build on one another to keep the world of the minority securely closed. Alteration in this relationship between the two worlds becomes possible only if the mutual exclusiveness of the minority and the majority is interrupted significantly. Certainly, the changed relationship between the Orthodox Jewish community and the society around it cannot be understood apart from a number of cataclysmic interruptions: the Nazi Holocaust, the establishment of the State of Israel, and a number of profound internal changes in American society. The first undermined Jewry's faith in faith. The second radically altered the self-image of the Jew. And the third made available to Jew and non-Jew alike unprecedented opportunities for occupational participation.

The fact that community after community was sytematically deported and annihilated, especially in Eastern Europe, during World War II, with almost no organized attempt at salvation not only undermined many people's faith in the goodness of God, but more importantly it created a crisis of confidence in the traditional communal leaders. As one Orthodox respondent recalled:

> The — — *rebbe* and I slept in the same barrack in Bergen Belsen. He was dressed like everyone else and his beard was hidden by a kerchief as if he had a tooth ache. Do you think he went around comforting or assuring people? His few Hasidim gave him the food out of their mouths, even though they too were starving. His main concern was to get out alive. Then he wasn't quite as anti-Zionistic as now because it was the Zionists who were getting him out of the camp.

What traditional religious leaders could have done to avert the tragedy is, of course, an open question. But from the point of view of the average Jew, the important fact was that these established pillars of communal authority were shown to be impotent. In addition, the experience of the Holocaust revealed the naivete of the belief that the inside world of the community could be insulated from the forces of the "outside" world.

The catastrophic disruption of the traditional Eastern European communities was followed, almost simultaneously, by an equally cataclysmic disruption of the taken-for-granted nature of things by the establishment of the State of Israel. This event, coming on the heels of the tragedy of the war, easily introduced a new vocabulary of attitudes and heroes into Jewish consciousness. *Der eidele yid* (the timid or docile Jew) who was content to earn his daily bread and dutifully attend to his ritual and Talmudic concerns, was quickly displaced by such new folk heroes as Hannah Szenesh, the young woman parachutist, trained in Palestine, who jumped into occupied territories in Eastern Europe to save the lives of her brethren—losing her own in the process. The traditional plea of traditional leaders for *bitochon* (trust in the wisdom and mercy of God) was rapidly coming to be replaced by exhortations for the pursuit of *Torah im derech eretz* (Torah along with participation in the ways of this world).

Perhaps, the long revered *rebbes* were themselves no longer willing to shoulder the responsibility of counseling simple faith in such an insecure world, and recognized the merits of a more active engagement in worldly affairs and pursuits. Whatever the case may be, these two events—the Holocaust, and the establishment of the State of Israel—forced a radical reorganization in the notions of reality or stock of knowledge prevalent in the traditional Jewish communities prior to these events.

It may be fair to say that the immigrants who revitalized the acculturating and assimilating Jewish communities in the United States after World War II were sadder, but a great deal wiser about both the ways of the world and the possibilities of sustaining an exclusive and isolated Jewish community in the host society.

With the end of the World War II the United States entered what sociologists like Daniel Bell and Amitai Etzioni have called the "post-industrial" or "post-modern" era. This period is characterized by the great growth of technology and the ascendancy of technical and bureaucratic rationality over a more generally comprehensible substantive rationality. In this new era success becomes possible to the extent that the individual is willing to master and carry out purely functional tasks. The social structure, as such, has become relatively devoid of collectively shared values beyond the practical norms of the workplace, market, and political conduct.

It may be argued that the survival mentality with which the Jew emerged from the catastrophe of the war was well-suited to the demands of a value-free (equal opportunity) market place. The Jew found that while the world "out there" became more available and familiar, it did not and would not become intimate. It was growing less and less intimate, more anomic, for Jew and non-Jew alike. Nor did it demand that the Jew become more intimate with it. It demanded only what it demands from everyone: that he do his job efficiently. How he was to consume the fruits of his labor remained a purely private matter. Thus, the world at large presented itself as simultaneously more promising and less inviting just as the traditional Jew, the erstwhile Orthodox immigrant, was making his way into it.

Just as close adherence to tradition had been seen as the vehicle by means of which sacred knowledge could be realized in everyday life and communal identity perpetuated, the example of Israel and the opportunities of post-industrial America suggested that the development of technical skills and political know-how are the present-day vehicles by means of which the same values can be sustained.[41] Hence, occupational skills and careers have come to be regarded in the same value-neutral terms as the rest of the world regards them. Since the world at large does not presume to ascribe any special value commitments to the engineer, as an engineer, the religious community has also come to regard that occupation along with most others as essentially value-free. Those who enter into such occupations, presumably, may be perfectly committed to Jewish values and Orthodox practices. The occupation is merely a vehicle for making a living. It remains divorced from the concerns and commitments of the communal life, the private sphere. At best, since these occupations are highly esteemed in the world at large, those who are engaged in them bring more credit to the Orthodox community. Moreover, since the political and military security of the State of Israel depends on many such skills, the pursuit of secular knowledge and skills is seen as an integral part of the overall security and survival needs of the Jewish people.

In retrospect it would appear that the core values of separateness and maintenance of communal identity have been expressed through a body of knowledge and practices which is an amalgam of *halacha* (sacred law of the Torah, Talmud, and rabbinic texts), and *minhagim* (locally accepted and transmitted customs). In the traditional, antebellum, community there was little distinction made between these two sources of knowledge and legitimate authority. Both were perceived as quite antithetical to the ways of the world.

The catastrophes of the twentieth century, coupled with the structure of opportunity in post-modern America have forced upon the consciousness of the Orthodox Jew a distinction between *din* (law) and *minhag* (custom). The abandonment of customs, especially with respect to figures of authority and occupational patterns, has come to be seen as a way of sustaining a communal order which is consistent with *halacha*. In due course, elements of secular knowledge and *derech eretz* (ways of the world) have come to be seen as accessories that, while not equal in value or importance to sacred knowledge, are necessary for the maintenance of those institutions which insure the viability of the Jewish way of life.

While secular knowledge has been integrated in the religious community in the form of an accessory, the secular world itself has come, increasingly, to regard its knowledge and techniques as value-free, and therefore, in principle, assimilable into any culture that wishes to buy it. Thus, in a very important sense, the cognitive minority and the cognitive majority agree on the definition of the situation: most of what is public or secular knowledge is value-free and contains no normative imperative or ultimate meaning. The cognitive minority merely adds a further stipulation: that such knowledge is a useful accessory to its special world. That special world, on the other hand, is sacred.

Secularization and Orthodox Culture

This chapter has sought to discover the dominant values of the modern Orthodox community, and to describe the key elements of the symbolic universe through which those values are expressed. Separateness and sanctity, as these are defined by ancient biblical rules appear to be the core values of Boro Park's Orthodox. The most pervasive norms through which these values are perpetuated, as we have seen, are the Shabbos, *kashrus*, and *taharas mishpocho*. To be sure, these normative patterns do not exhaust all six hundred and thirteen *mitzvas*. But they do constitute a core of observances around which a great many of the other *mitzvas* are organized. More importantly, the observance of the numerous *mitzvas* which constitute these essential norms tends to impel the Jews of Boro Park to observe the many other *mitzvas* of the Torah as well.

We have also seen that the observance of the *mitzvas* is further expressed through symbols and styles of personal appearance, status and authority. What all of these behavioral styles disclose is a system of core values which may be summarized as an impulse to lead a holy way of life. At the same time, we have seen that although holiness and purity continue to be of central concern in the community, its forms of expression have been molded to coincide with the middle-class and Americanized status of the Boro Park Jewry. In a very real sense the process of secularization, so pervasive throughout modern American society, has been successfully contained within the cultural forms of Orthodoxy.

In this chapter we have seen how, and to some extent why, the Orthodox of Boro Park have blended the values and major norms of a Torah way of life with the American, middle-class way of life. What remains to be seen in subsequent chapters is the source of structural or organizational support for these essentially cultural amalgamations. It is a sociological axiom that cultural forms, and values, can neither be created nor sustained without structural support from such essential social institutions as the political and economic systems of the community. Moreover, particularly in the present case, important support to the culture of the community comes from such essential institutional structures as the family, the synagogue, and the religious educational system. The next chapter will examine the ways in which these various structural supports help to sustain the cultural vitality of Boro Park as a holy community.

5

Ramparts of Holiness
Family, Yeshiva, Synagogue and Other Institutional Supports

The Orthodox community has forged a cultural amalgam out of traditional and modern values. But values and cultural forms are only a part of what constitutes the social reality of any community. An equally important part of that reality are the more complex institutional structures which help to sustain the culture of the community. Earlier chapters examined the supportive structures of the political and economic life of the community, and the ways in which these supportive structures both sustain as well as mold the cultural style of the community.

It has been suggested in earlier chapters that the cultural amalgamation found in the Orthodox community resulted from a cognitive process—a psychological process that has been called cognitive bargaining. The present chapter examines some of the organizational supports for these cognitive bargains or cultural compromises. The family, the synagogue, the *yeshiva*, youth organizations, and self-help and self-defense organizations are the infra-structure of the Orthodox community.

They provide more intimate, more personal, and more traditional support for the culture of the Orthodox community, and have contributed to both conserving and modifying its values, habits of thought, and styles of life. Self-defense organizations in particular, because they are new to the Orthodox community, are an especially telling indicator of the profound changes that have occurred there in recent years.

In the pages that follow, we will examine these major organizational units of the community, and the ways in which their patterns of integration with the larger social system tend to shore up and help to make real the cognitive patterns discussed above.

The Family as Audience

Considering the alleged importance of the family in traditional communities in general, and in Orthodox and Hasidic communities in particular, there is a surprising absence of actual research on the nature of the Jewish family. Poll, in his study of the Hasidic community of

98

Williamsburg devotes a mere six pages to the subject. Most others have done less. A nostalgic portrait of extended, closely knit, stable families, observing holidays and rituals together, persists. Sklare has recently suggested that:

> It is safe to say that the normative Jewish family is neither the cozily secure unit suggested by the popular stereotype nor the hot-bed of neurosis characterized by certain novelists. In fact, we might ask if there is anything really distinctive about the Jewish family. . . . It is possible to respond that given the particular socio-economic level that Jews occupy there is nothing exceptional in their behavior.[1]

Nevertheless, Sklare sees the American Jewish family as a "carrier" of continuity with the past. The family in the Boro Park Orthodox community falls somewhere between the stereotypic extended type "with several generations of a family living in the same house or, at least, in close proximity," and the typical middle-class conjugal nuclear unit.[2]

In our survey of a random sample of the Jewish households in Boro Park it was found that the residents of this community by and large do live in families. Out of fifty-six households only two respondents indicated that they had no relatives residing in the same household or in the immediate neighborhood. Twenty-eight, or 50 percent, of the respondents indicated that apart from the members of the household—usually parents and children—they also had other family members—in-laws, cousins, grandparents, and so forth—living in the immediate neighborhood. In fact, when respondents were asked to indicate who influenced their moving into the neighborhood, 87.9 percent made reference to parents, children, in-laws, or other relatives as sources of motivation. This pattern was most consistently exhibited by those residents who moved into the community in the last few years—the largely first-generation and Hasidic elements. This evidence appears to confirm Poll's characterization of the traditional family. But the ways in which everyday life is experienced in most of these families deviates considerably from the traditional pattern. This, of course, should not surprise anyone. After all, we are dealing here with an Americanized, middle-class group.

From Biblical times up until the catastrophic destruction of the Eastern European *shtetl*, the traditional family—with mother as venerated housekeeper and father as sometimes benevolent patriarch—was the cornerstone and wellspring of Jewish life and identity.[3] Of course, this does not mean that the Jewish family did not undergo change throughout the centuries. It did. But in all its diverse forms it was a fundamental institution of the Jewish community. The ideal-typical family was based on two major institutions: property and dynastic marriage. The concept of *yichus*, discussed earlier, was an integral part of the traditional social system; it was the symbolic representation and promissory note of what each member brought into the newly established conjugal unit. The *shiduch* (arranged marriage) was the social control mechanism by means of which *yichus* was protected, enhanced, and, at times, even acquired. The persistence of this family pattern was intimately related to what Daniel Bell has called family capitalism, and the general break-up of that economic form has had profound consequences on the traditional Jewish family as well.[4]

Perhaps the most fundamental fact of everyday life in the modern Orthodox household, as, indeed, in most other households in middle-class America, is that most, if not all, of the members of the family are out of the house for the major portion of the day. Fathers are at work. Children are at school. And in many—and increasing—cases mothers are also employed on at least a part-time basis outside of the home. In the ten most densely Jewish census tracts described in Chapter 4, about 36 percent of the women over sixteen years of age were in the labor force. This figure appears to be consistent with an observation of the U.S. Labor Department that, "it is the middle income level that reveals the largest proportion of working wives."[5]

In our survey of Jewish families in Boro Park we found that, indeed, women whose children have matured enough to be enrolled in kindergarten—and certainly women whose children are enrolled in the all-day *yeshivas*—are most frequently employed outside of the home, at least in part-time jobs. Interestingly, this pattern is quite consistent with Rubin's findings among the Szatmarer Hasidim of Williamsburg, where 52 percent of the women whose youngest children were six years old or older were employed outside of the home.[6] While newlyweds prefer to have children soon after marriage, the young wives we have encountered in Boro Park all expressed a serious interest in going back to work just as soon as the first child was old enough to be enrolled in kindergarten. This attitude reflected a clear awareness of family planning—generally a tabu subject among Orthodox Jews. It was clear from the comments of most of the young women that they did not intend to bear children in an uninterrupted series, nor to devote themselves exclusively to a lifetime of wifery and motherhood. While the subject of birth control is tabu and it is generally assumed that Orthodox and Hasidic Jews do not practice it by artificial means, we found almost no woman in our survey who considered herself fulfilled as a career housewife and who had no desire to be employed outside of caring for her family. With but one or two exceptions we also found no women who continued to bear children throughout their fertile years. While the more religious families tended to have more children (e.g. four to six) very few women were having children in their late thirties or forties. This suggests that after having what they regard as a desirable number of children, even the most religious practice some form of birth control. We might add that the form of birth control practiced is not likely to be abstinence, since that is frowned upon by Jewish law and custom.

The newlywed Orthodox women we have encountered all tended to look upon the world of work as something to go back to. This is hardly surprising in light of the level of education they have achieved. The fact is that nearly all had been employed prior to and right up to having their first child. Socio-economic status and the nature of work in contemporary America have had a significant impact on the very idea of family even among Orthodox Jews. Specifically, family cohesion and *yichus* have been disrupted by the prevailing conditions of economic survival and status aspirations.

To be sure, among the first generation, family connections still play an appreciable role in organizing business ventures and/or finding jobs for various relatives, should the need arise. This is particularly true for males in the community. But first-generation females are also frequently absorbed into the economy through family connections. Examples such as Mrs. F., who for many years was a bookkeeper in her cousin's small jewelry manufacturing company, or Mrs. M., who manages her son's import-export office, are not at all uncommon. For the second generation, however, such career patterns would be the exception, not the norm. Careers based on talent and education, the professions, seem to be the preferred avenues of entrance into the economy.[7] Even in the few instances we have found of sons going into their fathers' businesses, the sons entered only after obtaining formal educational credentials. In one instance a son became a partner in his father's business, but only after obtaining an M.B.A. degree. Thus, while the family continues to play an important role in the emotional life of the community—particularly on Shabbos and other religious holidays—its relationship to economic life and the conditions of social status has been severely circumscribed.

Correspondingly, the mechanics and the function of the *shiduch* (arranged marriage) has also undergone considerable change. Match-making is still a serious profession in the Orthodox community, but its objectives are quite different from the historic purpose of protecting and enhancing family *yichus*. In a community where casual encounters between the sexes are curtailed by all sorts of religious proscriptions, the *shadchan* (matchmaker) serves partly as a simple go-between, notifying eligible individuals of each other's availability. The *shadchan* is also useful for checking out that the parties are, in fact, suited to one another. In contemporary Boro Park parlance this means that the *shadchan*, professional or amateur, will inform both parties of each other's religiosity and modernity. For example, will the young man require that his wife wear a *sheitl* (wig for religious purposes)? Will the young woman expect that her fiance continue learning in a *kolel* (rabbinical seminary) after marriage? And, if so, what will be the source of their financial support? Will the young lady go to work? Will her parents provide a dowry, and how much? Does the young man plan to finish college? What are his career plans? Does he dress in modern clothes? (See Figure 5.)

Answers to such questions are especially important because in terms of outward appearances it is all too easy to confuse the *chnyak* (fanatically religious male or female, naive to all worldly concerns, emphasis on naivete) with the *erlach* (religiously committed, commit-ment not based on naivete in either religious or secular matters). And it is similarly quite easy to confuse the *batlan* (ostensibly a *yeshiva* student, but essentially a wastrel who spends his time in daydreams) with the *masmid* (serious Talmudic student). In the absence of the American-style dating encounter with its attendant sharing of intimacies, it is quite easy to be mistaken about a prospective mate.[8]

> "The shadchan is much much more than just someone who distributes phone numbers," Mrs. Heller [a *shadchan*] states. "I find myself frequently assuming the role of guidance counselor, psy-chologist and social worker. For example: I always ask both parties to call me after the first date so as to give me their impressions. Then I usually act as intermediary. If the young couple are too shy to say things to each other, they will tell me and I in turn will tell it to them. I sometimes have to say 'I like you' for them. Such a couple just got engaged."
>
> "I am definitely more than a phone number distributor," confirms Mrs. Rabinowitz [also a *shadchan*]. "I have to be the go-between during the first few times, do screening to prevent hurts, interpret

emotional situations, explain certain statements, and, in order for a match to succeed, push!"

All of the matchmakers, who cater to a huge range of clientele (non-Orthodox to Chassidic, blue-collar worker to professional, teenager to senior citizen), and often find themselves working together rather than competing, staunchly maintain that their services offer the fastest, easiest, and safest route to the chupah [canopy].

"Shadchanim aren't *dating* bureaus; they're *marriage* bureaus." proclaims Mrs. Heller, noting that the difference between the two is a vast and significant one.

"Going to a shadchan eliminates the problem of the 'rat race,' " says Mrs. Rabinowitz, "and problems that arise as a result of unscreened meetings between boys and girls are eliminated.

"Matchmaking is also valuable because there are people who under ordinary circumstances would not be able to meet or approach members of the opposite sex, such as the 'wall-flower type.' Going to a shadchan helps in this situation. If this type of person is alone on display, he has more of a chance than if he's in a group where his individuality is lost and he fades. . . .

"The shadchan is great for preliminary screening. If one party wants a family with a good reputation, respectable in every manner, the shadchan can find out about any skeletons in the closet and avoid painful situations."[9]

Despite the persistence of religious concerns in the relationships between the sexes, the decline in family capitalism and the importance of *yichus* has permitted cupid to raise his irreverent head. Love and personal satisfaction are coming to be expressed as a desirable, even necessary, precondition for marriage.[10] Therefore, after the *shadchan* has made the essential inquiries, a 'date' will be arranged between the young couple. The pattern which follows—except among the most rigidly Orthodox or Hasidic—will be quite similar to standard American dating system. The young couple will go out, perhaps to a movie with a "G" rating or a concert, or an appropriately *kosher* restaurant, and get to know each other. If the first date is successful—they think that the *shadchan* was right and they like each other—the pattern of dating will be repeated a few times. Some sexual experimentation may even follow the second or third date: the young man may be emboldened to hold the girl's hand and kiss her good-night. The assumption at this stage would be that the relationship is serious, and will eventuate in betrothal. While no systematic evidence could be obtained from respondents on sexual activity and the dating and mating process, frequent references were made by young men to those portions of the Bible and other exegetic and *halachic* literature that indicate that physical contact between unmarried males and females is permissible under certain conditions, or at least, is not a serious violation of the letter of the law. Here, again, the formal law seems to be invoked in an effort to legitimate violations of established customs concerning the relations between the sexes prior to marriage.

As important as matchmaking is in the community, the *shadchan* is rapidly coming to be replaced by the organizational affiliations of young men and women. For example, the fact that a large proportion of the marriageable youth of the community attend Brooklyn College enables eligible partners to meet informally outside of the community, and do their own checking out in the *kosher* cafeteria or in the foyer of the college library. In addition, the various political activities and rallies on behalf of Soviet Jewry, Israel, and other ethnically or religiously legitimated causes have, increasingly, brought the young Orthodox of both sexes into informal contacts. Consequently, while strong social, and familial, pressure is exerted on the young of both sexes to marry early, the choice of mate is coming to rest with the individuals involved. And their choices rarely, if ever, take *yichus* matters into consideration. Marriages among the second generation willynilly cut across lines of *yichus*, and the lines that historically separated Hasidim from *misnagdim* (non-Hasidic Orthodox), as well as across the ethnic origins of the parents.[11] The typical language of this criss-cross is, "I am not marrying his/her family. As long as he/she is as religious as I am they (the parents) have no reason to complain." The term "religious" in this context is clearly not limited to conformity or familiarity with familial *minhagim* (customs). The responses of the Young Israel Intercollegiates amplify this orientation to religion on the one hand and family on the other. While about 84 percent of the forty-four Intercollegiates indicated an intention to remain Orthodox Jews, more than 54 percent indicated that they either did not care about or were dissatisfied with their elders' opinions of decisions made by the students affecting their own lives.

The family, then, has receded from the economy as well as from the business of ensuring dynastic or ethnic continuity. Its role in the socialization of the young has also undergone considerable contraction. The *yeshiva*, which extends educational and day-care services to the young from pre-kindergarten through the collegiate years, has lifted the burden of socialization, especially religious socialization, from the family. What is passed on to the young, these days, as their sacred heritage, is more likely to come from the lips of the *rebbi* (religious instructor in the *yeshiva*) than from parents or other family elders. Perhaps recognition of this state of affairs and the efforts to cope with it have led to the establishment of the large number of small *yeshivas* in the community in recent years. Parents seem to desire a school for their children which most closely mirrors their own nuances of religious belief and practice. Thus groups like the Hasidim, who possess a rich body of *minhagim* (ethnic customs) have established their own *yeshivas* in order to perpetuate their particular religious style. But the very establishment of such *yeshivas* bespeaks the predicament of the modern Orthodox family. It has been relegated to the sidelines by virtue of its entrance into middle-class occupations and a middle-class life style. It can support financially, but otherwise merely passively observe, the religious education of its young. The family thus becomes a sort of paying audience at a show it has helped to produce, but whose script it cannot manipulate and, indeed, at times cannot fully understand.

This audience-like character of the family is a frequent source of complaint among the young:

> I can't walk down the street without an aunt calling to inquire about the person I was walking with, or to ask about where I bought the new clothes I was wearing. I often have the feeling that I am being watched, like somebody was looking over my shoulder. Everybody here knows everyone else's business. If I stay up late one night to study for an exam, a cousin or aunt, or maybe even the next door neighbor is going to ask me how I did. It really gets annoying sometimes. But at least its a fairly safe neighborhood. I guess it's nice to know that people do care about you. But they're so damn nosy.

The immediate, as well as the extended, family, while playing no active part in the daily lives of individuals, especially of the young, is ever present as an audience in front of whom one's activities are played out and evaluated. But the ability of the family to actually affect the lives of individuals has been greatly curtailed. The father is no longer the final authority on sacred matters, not to say on secular matters. He is simply a part of the general familial audience whose approval is sought and appreciated, but whose attempts to control are frequently dismissed as an irrelevant annoyance.

How, then, does the family as an organizational unit of the community contribute to the general viability of Jewish Orthodoxy? As strange as the answer may seem, the family contributes by its very passivity. We have argued in the previous chapter that the major cultural bargain that Orthodoxy seems to have made with the prevailing conditions of post-modern America is to play down the traditional elements of the religious life style in favor of its more legal-rational dimensions. To the extent that the family has been, historically, the primary carrier of custom and tradition, it has also been the major source of conflict between tradition and modernity. The playing out of that conflict has been the familiar theme in other Jewish communities. The large scale transfer of the socialization function from the family to the *yeshiva* in the modern Orthodox community in general, and in the Boro Park community in particular, may have served to neutralize this conflict in recent years. By becoming middle-class in character, the modern Orthodox family has facilitated the rationalization, in the Weberian sense of the word, of religious education; thereby contributing to the survival of Orthodoxy by meddling in it as little as possible apart from its financial support.

How the *yeshiva* has rationalized religious education and how it contributes to the viability of an American Orthodox community will be discussed later in this chapter.

The Shul: *Ties compartmentalized*

Although the modern Orthodox family seems to have lost many of its traditional functions, the sentiments on which those functions were once based, such as the need for religious fellowship and collective experience, are still very much alive in the Boro Park community. The synagogue, or the more familiar *shul*, and the *yeshiva* appear to be the organizational responses to these persistent needs. Of course, these organizations have existed in the Jewish community throughout the Diaspora. But their current forms seem particularly well suited to take up where the family appears to have left off.

Perhaps the most significant social fact that can be used to characterize the Boro Park community is the sheer proliferation of religious organizations. (See Table 14.)

The figures in Table 14 were verified by officers at the 66th Police Precinct. They estimated that in 1973 there were approximately fifty *yeshivas* and about 145 *shuls* or synagogues in the general area of Boro Park. In the course of one decade exemptions for clergy and religious

TABLE 14
Three Categories of Tax-exempt Property in Boro Park, 1961-1972

Category of Property	Number of Properties Listed		
	1961–62	1966–67	1971–72
Clergy°	57	94	165
Parsonage+	26	39	64
Religious‡	109	149	180
TOTAL	192	282	409

Source: New York City Tax Commission, *Detailed List of Tax-Exempt Properties of the City of New York* (New York: Department of Taxation and Finance, 1961, 1972). This list was used previously in Charles Liebman, "Orthodoxy in America Jewish Life," in *American Jewish Yearbook* (New York: American Jewish Congress, 1965), pp. 21–92.

° Tax exempt property of clergy.
+ Residential property attached to a *yeshiva* or synagogue.
‡ *Yeshiva* or synagogue or other religious institution.

organizations more than doubled. The Jewish population of the area also went up during this time, but at a much slower rate.[12] Clearly, the sheer quantity of religious organizations is an indication of their centrality in the value system of the residents. The amount of money spent on the building and furnishing of these structures can only be guessed at. Many have been newly built in recent, tight-money years. Nearly all have been renovated within the last five years. Sklare's observation that "the American synagogue is a vital institution: it is by far the strongest in the Jewish community,"[13] can be aptly applied in the case of Boro Park.

The question that remains to be answered is: what is the meaning that Boro Park Jewry attaches to the *shuls* they have built in such great numbers and at such great cost? Unfortunately, with respect to this question, Sklare's insights are not very helpful: "The prototype of the contemporary American synagogue is the synagogue center . . . [which] seeks encounter with the Jew on his own secular level."[14] But the Orthodox *shul* in Boro Park, and probably elsewhere too, has made few compromises with the secular culture. True, the buildings and interior decoration are new. But the rituals, prayers, and passions that transpire within them are very old. Bingo has not replaced the daily *mincha* and *ma'ariv* (afternoon and evening services); nor have breakfast clubs come to be substituted for the daily *shachris* (morning service). It would appear that, while the Conservative and Reform synagogues have managed to survive by extending themselves into secular activities, the Orthodox *shul*, at least in Boro Park, remains at the center of community life despite (or maybe because of) the fact that its activities are rather narrowly religious in character.[15] What, then, happens within the *shul* that makes it such an important structural unit in the life of Boro Park's Jews?

While learning sessions are conducted in most, if not all, of the *shuls* in Boro Park, much of its role as a house of study has been surrendered to the *yeshiva*. The quality of the learning that one is likely to find in *shuls* is ritualistic rather than scholarly or intellectual. With rare exceptions, *balebatim* (established members) sit down to read a few paragraphs from the Mishna or Talmud in order to fulfill the Biblical prescription for learning, not in quest of new insights or answers to burning ethical questions. A possibly important clue to the importance attached by Boro Park's Jews to the *shul* may be found in Alfred Schutz's reflections on music. He saw in the process of making and listening to music together a social mechanism of "mutual tuning-in."

> The flux of tones unrolling in inner time is an arrangement meaningful to both composer and beholder because and insofar as it evokes in the stream of consciousness participating in it an interplay of recollections, retentions, protentions, and anticipations. . . . this sharing of the other's flux of experiences in inner time, this living through a vivid present in common, constitutes what we called in our introductory paragraph the mutual tuning in relationship, the experience of the 'We' which is the foundation of all possible communication.[16]

The reason that people in the area give for attending one *shul* as opposed to another is that they like the *nusach* (tonal style, and sequence of the prayers) that is found in the *shul* of their choice, and the companionship of the clientele. Familiarity with the particular sequence and tone of prayers, then, is of great importance in the Orthodox Jew's appreciation of his *shul*. To be able to participate in the services, which often requires the aloud verbal contribution of each individual to common chanting, requires that the individuals present be all more or less equally familiar with the *nusach* of the particular *shul*. In terms of Schutz's analysis we may now say that the prayer service, like a musical experience, involves a "mutual tuning-in" whereby the participants relive the inner time of their ancestors as well as enter into the on-going experience of their fellow men.

With the decline of its legal and educative functions, the synagogue has become a center the maintenance of ethnic self-consciousness.[17] In a community where religious orthodoxy is an overriding value, ethnic origins—whether one is of Hungarian, German, Polish or Roumanian ancestry—are of secondary importance. Yet because of the *minhagim* (local customs) which had played such an important role in Orthodoxy, religion is experienced in peculiarly ethnic terms. The *shul* seems to have become the repository of the *minhagic* elements of Jewish Orthodoxy; fostering a good deal of sectarianism in an otherwise consistently modern and consistently Orthodox community. The *shul* has become the arena in which each ethnic sub-group of the community can continue to participate in its unique ancestral experience of Judaism. By localizing or compartmentalizing the sectarian *minhagim* and *nusach*, the community as a whole is left relatively free of conflicts based on ethnic differences, and individuals may comfort themselves in the thought that their special brand of the Jewish heritage is alive and well in *shul*.

The musical analogy also helps to explain the relative decline of the older, larger, more formal and more secularized synagogues in the area. Further, the musical analogy suggests a possible explanation for the anomalous popularity of the *Hasidishe shtieblach* (richly ethnic, Hasidic *shuls*) among the younger, second- and third-generation residents of the community. M. E.'s reflections on the popularity of the *shtiebl* among this group is quite revealing. Both of his parents had immigrated to the United States as children. M. E.'s mother had received her education in the public schools of New York. He himself is a native son of Boro Park. Age fifty-six, he owns his own home jointly with his in-laws, and is a successful and widely respected businessman. Talking of his father's ancestral village in Poland, he muses:

> The only thing I have to do with —— is that I *daven* [pray] in a *shtiebl* which originated there. Today, with all the *shuls* in Boro Park, I split my time between the bigger *shuls* and the *shtiebl*. How can I explain it . . . in the *shtiebl* we sit around a table . . . the *davening* is warmer, more *heimish* [homey]. The big *shul*, well . . . it's big and empty. Today most of the big *shuls* are empty. I imagine people are running to the *shtieblach*. Years ago when people weren't so involved with religion they went to the big *shuls* to listen to the rabbi on Shabbos morning [giving his customary sermon]. But today everyone knows as much as the rabbi.

This respondent's eldest son was studying in a rabbinical seminary and was already teaching in a *yeshiva*. For him, as for many others like him, the *shul* is a place where one goes not so much for moral guidance or prayer as for contact with the deepest sources of identity and a reaffirmation of those ties that have receded from the praxis of everyday life. The large, formal congregations with their ethnically mixed membership and bureaucratic organization offer no opportunity for such contacts. Hence, the popularity of such congregations has, indeed, declined. Unfortunately, no precise statistical evidence is available for this last assertion. But all who were questioned on the subject agreed with the observation.

It is in the *shul*, more than anywhere else, that the "we-feeling" is experienced and expressed through the participation in the commonly shared *nusach*. The demands of middle-class life style reinforce the compartmentalization of primordial ties. In some cases it is not even the first generation but their children and grandchildren who seek out the ancestral wellspring of the *shteibl*. The native born Orthodox have received their religious training largely as an intellectual experience in the *yeshivas*. Yet they hear from their parents and grandparents how it used to be, in the old country and are intrigued. One writer, describing a neighborhood *shtiebl*, reports that:

> there is an unusually large percentage of college graduates and/or students within [this] *olam* [congregation] that has probably the youngest average age of any Chassidic [sic] shule in New York City.
> Many of these collegiates are still cautiously feeling their way around Yiddishkeit. . . . Part of their feeling of acceptance comes from the presence of a large number of *seforim* [books on religious subjects] in English translation. . .
> Last June the shule made history when the rabbi, a linguist who speaks a brilliant Yiddish but a broken English, departed from tradition and spoke at a *shallosh seudah* [Sabbath afternoon communal meal] in the American vernacular, in deference to the high percentage of his listeners who know little or no Yiddish.[18]

We thus find a curious turn of events in Boro Park: strictly sectarian *Hasidishe shtieblach* which were established by dynastic descendants of Eastern European *rebbes* are frequented and supported by second- and third-generation, *yeshiva*-educated Orthodox. These *shtieblach*, by virtue of their hybrid clientele, enjoy a renewed lease on life as well as the status of being associated with the better educated native born youth. The second- and third-generation sectarians, on the other hand, enjoy participation in a quasi-ancestral community without being fully tied to its rules, *minhagim*, and structure of authority. This last point is essential: the primary experience and function of the sectarian *shtiebl* is atmosphere and identity, not authority. The larger, more formally established synagogue is likely to have many of the organizational features, the bureaucracy, in which people already feel trapped in their work-day world. Religious services in the synagogue are conducted by hired specialists: the rabbi, the cantor, the *shamos* (sexton), and elected lay officials. Such an atmosphere hardly makes for an expressive experience. In the *shtiebl*, on the other hand, individual members will take turns at conducting the rituals and chants associated with the service. Unlike in the synagogue, where congregants sit in fixed pews and follow a routinized service, in the *shtiebl* the participants sit around tables in loose arrangement, often moving chairs around to be closer to a friend or to the *rebbe* or the Holy Ark in which the Torah scrolls are kept. Amidst the collective recitation or singing, individuals will often express themselves in a spirit of exultation above the hum and murmur of the group. *Shokling,* swaying one's body to the rhythm of the prayers, is found much more frequently in the *shtiebl* than in the synagogue. In the latter, decorum is a far more important norm than expressiveness, not to say ecstasy.

From the discussion so far, it is apparent that these two units of communal organization: the family and the synagogue, which have traditionally bound the individual to the community, have undergone considerable specialization and constriction with modern Orthodoxy as we find it in Boro Park. The scope of these organizational units has come to encompass a more limited range of the individual's time, personality, and commitments. Even the most loyal members are, inevitably, involved in other organizational affiliations—minimally, a job—outside of, as well as within, the community. It is in this sense that we speak of these institutions as having become compartmentalized in the experience of their clientele. This phenomenon of compartmentalization is especially true of the most Americanized, second- and third-generation Orthodox. It would be somewhat less typical of the older, first generation, the poorly educated, and the lower class Orthodox.

The Yeshiva

In discussing the family and the synagogue our analysis has been focussed on the compartmentalized quality of both. We have shown that through the process of compartmentalization a greater share of the individual has been liberated so that he may participate to a greater extent in the world at large. The *yeshiva* (religious day school), more than any other organizational unit of the community, serves to ensure that the wider participation of the Jew in the secular world does not endanger or erode his commitments to religious and communal values and practices.

The statistical record of growth of the *yeshiva* movement in America speaks proudly of the significance of the institution. Approximately 91 percent (271) of the *yeshivas* in existence today were established since 1940, according to Schiff.[19] In fact, it could be argued that most of the second and third generations of Orthodoxy in Boro Park have been introduced to the secular world through the *yeshiva*. Two of the earliest all-day *yeshivas* in America were founded in Boro Park: Etz Chaim for boys in 1917, and the Shulamith School for girls in 1929. And, historically, attendance of Jewish youth in *yeshivas* has achieved the highest proportions in the Boro Park community. The *yeshiva* has thus played a pivotal role in defining for the residents the boundaries of the religious and secular spheres of everyday life, and the proper relations between. In due course the *yeshiva* has also had its impact on the religious conceptions of the first generation. In relinquishing its educative function to the *yeshiva*, the family and its traditional elders have implicitly ensured that religious values and practice become a matter of professional definition.

As Table 15 shows, *yeshivas* enjoy an impressive record of enrollment in the Boro Park community during the decade of the sixties. An attempt was made to survey all of the *yeshivas* in the area by means of a questionnaire which was sent to principals in the spring of 1973. Sixteen

TABLE 15
Enrollment in *Yeshivas* by Grade

Grade	N	Percent
Kindergarten	656	8.5
1-6	2,513	32.3
7-8	1,916	24.7
9-12	1,591	20.5
Rabbinical seminaries	1,086	14.0
TOTAL	7,762	100.0

Source: David Cole, "A Survey of Public and Parochial Schools Serving the Catchment Area of the Maimonides Community Mental Health Center," (Mimeo.; Brooklyn, N.Y.: Research Unit of the Maimonides Community Mental Health Center, 1971), p. 27.

out of thirty-two schools responded. Of the sixteen, 44 percent were founded since 1965. While longitudinal data on enrollments was not available, most of the principals indicated that their latest registration, September 1972, was the largest in the school's history. The size of enrollments in the sixteen *yeshivas*, as of September 1972, ranged from a low of thirteen students to a high of 1,129 students. The median was 212; the mean 301. Additional details were obtained from the information resources of the Maimonides Community Mental Health Center. According to the Center, enrollments in thirty-one *yeshivas* as of September 1970 came to a total of 7,762 students: 57 percent male and 43 percent female.[20] One may presume that the total figure for *yeshiva* enrollments would be greater in September 1978 than it was in 1972. Some claim that this figure has nearly doubled by 1978.[21]

While it is difficult to specify the exact proportion of Jewish school-age children in Boro Park who attend *yeshiva*, one statistic may be suggestive. Of the forty-two families, responding to our survey of families, who indicated that they have school age children in the house, all but three, or 93 percent, indicated that their children attend *yeshiva*. One may safely conclude that the *yeshiva* experience is common to the overwhelming majority of the Jewish youth in Boro Park. As Table 15 indicates, the *yeshiva* can encompass the entire early biography of the Boro Park Jew.

These figures, of course, do not permit us to distinguish between residents of Boro Park and students who merely come to attend school in the community. The figures also fail to account for those residents of the community who may attend a *yeshiva* outside of Boro Park. This problem is especially bedeviling as there are far fewer *yeshiva* high schools in Boro Park than are needed; consequently many young men and women attend *yeshiva* high schools and seminaries outside of the community. *Yeshivas* inside and outside of the community offer courses in subjects ranging from computer programming, electronic technology, accounting to dental hygiene and medical technology. (See Figures 6–8.)

Apart from the scope of its program over the biography of the individual, the *yeshiva* is remarkable for the intensity of its program. *Yeshivas* are so organized that all subjects, religious and secular, are taught within the system. It is quite possible, that an individual's entire education up until college will take place within the *yeshiva*—even in the same *yeshiva*. If the individual should so desire he or she can also continue post-high school training in a *yeshiva*. Because the standard

RABBINICAL CONFIDENTIAL
Screened Personal Introductions
THRU THE RABBI
Write of your desires to RABBI YEHUDA LEIB 98 Stonehurst Blvd, Freehold, N.J. call (201) 780-9339

FIELD'S (212) 391-2233
Friendship, Love & Marriage Free bklt "Find Happiness" Open 7 days, all ages est 1920 152 W 42 St Rm. 523 NYC 10036 Nationwide Service, all religions. We make arrangements for your sons & daughters without their knowledge

ALONE? WHY? 744-6300
MEET LADIES & GENTLEMEN
Free Brochure & Consultation
APPEARED ON RADIO TV
PHONE 9-12 AM, 7-9:30 P.M.
RAE LEIFER 400 E. 85 ST N.Y.C.

JEWISH INTRODUCTIONS
ORTH: NON-ORTH ALL AGES
Meet The Finest & The Best
Start Living Now!
(212) 645-0857 — Mr. Bruce
Screened & Confidential
Free Consultations By Appt Only
MR. PHILIP BRUCE
1601 Ocean Pkway. Bklyn NY 11223

SHAPIRO'S SELECTIVE INTRODUCTION SERVICE REALLY WORKS, 245-0026 ANYTIME

Meet Your Ideal Mate
Computer Introductions Est. 1966
Only $20. Free Questionnaire
Team 1270 Bwy NYC
563-3669-or 244-4270 eves

ISRAEL Matrimonial Happiness awaits you at fashionable marrg office. Globus, 245 Dizengoff St., Tel Aviv. Tel. 03-443749

SCIENTIFIC DATING SERVICE Guar dates. All ages. Visit hrs 11-8 P.M. 279-4358 147 W. 42 St, Suite 324

ATTR, yng charming, energetic warm hearted widow, w/children likes fam liv wishes Orth man till early 40's, obj matri. Send photo Box 1065 c/o JP

ISRAELI Girl Europe bkgrnd 23, coll grad, tall, good fam, seeks man w/similar bkgrnd 26-29 pls det & phone. Matri Box 1152 c/o JP

ATTRACT. Sincere lady mid 60's, 5'6" tall wishes to meet nice Balbat. Gent. pref up to 70 young & active for gd friend, later Marr. also drives a car Box 1167 c/o JP

ATTR Jewish woman late 40's enjoys tennis, ballroom dancing, seeks male companion for caring relation Box 1166 c/o JP

WIDOW European bkgrd charming 5'7" tall many interest indep. seeks a sincere fin. secure non-orth, gentl nice personality late 50 to early 60 only marriage minded Box 1163 c/o JP

Figure 5. Advertisements for matchmaking services. Reprinted from *The Jewish Press* (Brooklyn), March 23, 1979, p. 69. Courtesy of *The Jewish Press*, 338 3rd Avenue, Brooklyn, N.Y. 11215.

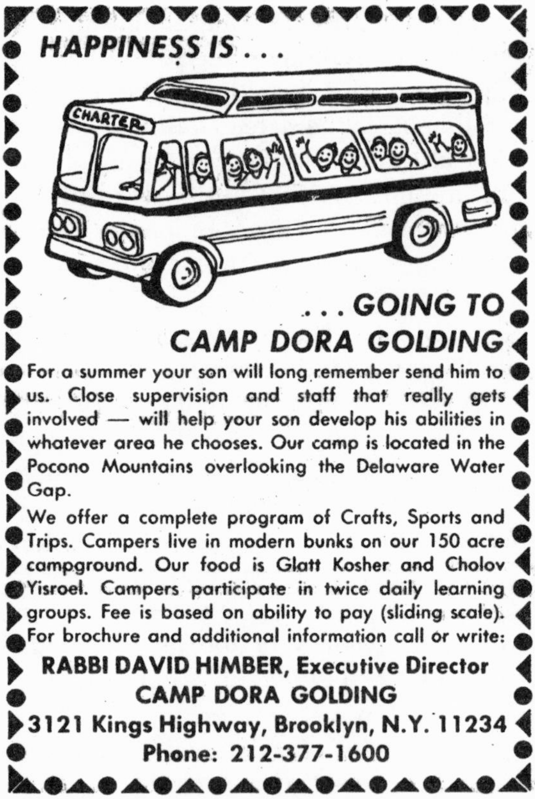

Figure 6. Advertisement for *kosher* summer camp. Reprinted from *The Jewish Press* (Brooklyn), April 13, 1979, p. 53.

DON'T JUST SETTLE FOR ANY JOB

As you know, well-trained secretaries can now command excellent salaries. Those with legal training can earn even more. There is no reason why you as a Bais Yaakov graduate, should not share in these opportunities. Our Vocational Institute trained girls with no background in typing and shorthand skills, and after one year they were placed in law offices at top salaries.

Bais Yaakov of Brooklyn can train you too, without leaving the warm Bais Yaakov atmosphere you have become accustomed to. Here are the facts'

- classes meet Monday through Thursday from 12:00 to 5:00 P.M. or in the evening Tuesday and Thursday from 6:00 to 10:00 P.M.;
- no previous training is required;
- full scholarships are available;
- you will be placed in a top paying job.

● REMEMBER Don't just settle for any job-get the best.

We'll be pleased to talk to you about the program.

Write to us at 1362-49th Street, or call
(212) 435- 7776 to arrange a convenient appointment.

Figure 7. Advertisement for a *yeshiva* offering vocational training. Reprinted from *The Jewish Press* (Brooklyn), April 13, 1979.

Figure 8. Advertisement for a *yeshiva* summer school.

A GREAT SUMMER EXPERIENCE
PERMEATED WITH TORAH TRUE INSPIRATION

OHOLEI TORAH
DAY CAMP
667 EASTERN PARKWAY
PR 8-3340-1   778-4773
778-3612   773-4960

MORE THAN "JUST ANOTHER DAY CAMP"

Special Programs Designed For:
Ages 3-5 Kindergarten Program
Ages 5-13 Day Camp Program
Ages 13-15 C.I.T. & J.C. Program
DOOR TO DOOR TRANSPORTATION
can be worked out for most places throughout N.Y.C.
SCHOLARSHIPS — FIRST COME FIRST SERVE BASIS
10% DISCOUNT — On All Registrations Completed Before May 18, 1979
For More Info Call Any Weekday or Eve.
Rabbi Yehoshua Yarmush   **773-4960**

curriculum includes both sacred as well as secular subject matter, a student will, typically, spend the entire day within the confines of the school. It is not for nothing that it is called a day-school.

The typical day in the life of the typical *yeshiva* student will begin sometime between 7:00 and 8:30 in the morning. In many schools attendance at *shachris* is obligatory. In such schools students will also take their breakfast meal at the *yeshiva*. Classes begin at 9:00 A.M. The most notable feature of the daily program is the separation between *limudei kodesh* (religious studies) and what is generally referred to as "English," meaning secular studies. In all Orthodox *yeshivas* the morning hours are given over to *limudei kodesh*. No mistake is to be made as to what must come first. English is taught only in the afternoon. It is frequently pointed out by principals and *rebbis* that the mind is more alert in the morning than at later hours, therefore they want the students to be exposed first to the *limudei kodesh*. Students are generally under the supervision of a *rebbi* (endearing diminuative of rabbi, teaches religious subjects) from the start of the school day until around 2:00 P.M. This will, of course, vary from age group to age group. Younger children will have shorter hours of instruction. The average morning session runs about five hours. Secular instruction for the lower grades begins around mid-day and ends around three or four o'clock in the afternoon. For the upper grades, that is seventh through twelfth, the afternoon English begins around two or three o'clock and ends around 5:00 or 6:00 P.M. The average afternoon sessions lasts approximately three hours. In addition, male students in the upper grades will be encouraged, and in some places obliged, to return to the *yeshiva* once or twice a week after they've had supper for *mishmar* (a special learning session). Clearly, the scheduling of the *yeshiva* program is organized not only to separate *limudei kodesh* from English, but also to ensure the primacy of the former. Apart from the actual content of the curriculum, the schedule and the intensity of the program conveys a lesson to the students that they carry with them long after they have left the confines of the *yeshiva*.

The method and style of the actual instruction also differs considerably from the morning to the afternoon sessions—with predictable consequences. In nearly all Orthodox yeshivas in Boro Park, as elsewhere, instruction in the *limudei kodesh* is organized by class and instructor instead of by department. One *rebbi* teaches one class for an entire morning session each day for one year. The curriculum will encompass such subjects as (1) *Chumash* (The Five Books of Moses and appropriate exegetical literature): (2) *T'nach* (The Prophets), (3) *Gemora* (Talmud and commentaries); (4) *Shulchan Oruch* (Practical Code of Jewish Law and Daily Practice); and (5) *Musar* (ethics) and anecdotes. The *rebbi* is allowed a great deal of latitude in how he will organize the scheduling and sequence of these subjects. Students themselves can often negotiate effectively, especially in the upper grades, to stay with a topic or to move along to others. Parenthetically, it should be noted that males are taught by male teachers. Females are most often taught by females, called *morah* or, if the instructor is married to a *rebbi* or rabbi, *rebbetzin*. In addition, the *rebbi* is also likely to supervise the students' participation in prayer services—at the afternoon *mincha*—and their proper ritual behavior at lunch—washing the hands and saying the proper benedictions and formulae before and after eating. In general, the *rebbi* will make a conscious effort to act as a role model for his students.

In sharp contrast to the *limudei kodesh*, "English " or secular study is organized, particularly for the upper grades, by department. On a typical afternoon an eighth grade *yeshiva* student may be exposed to as many as four teachers. English teachers are addressed as Mr. ——, or Miss ——, or Mrs. —— in contrast to the more venerated titles of *rebbi* or *morah*, or *rebbetzin*. Identification between students and teachers is not encouraged by the *yeshiva*. In fact, in many cases it is explicitly discouraged. As Poll has observed, these teachers are hired to teach their subject matter, not their students.[22]

The desired relationship between *limudei kodesh* and secular studies was forthrightly explained by Rabbi Joseph Elias to a seminar group of teachers of secular studies in 1961:

> It is one of the great leaders and spiritual guides of modern Judaism, Rabbi Samson Raphael Hirsch, who first formulated our stand concerning the relationship between Jewish survival, Torah study and practice on the one hand, and the modern world and its teachings on the other. He summed his approach up in the slogan *Torah Im Derech Eretz* which often is wrongly taken to mean a synthesis of Torah and general knowledge, but really stands for the *pursuit of general knowledge in the service of Torah.* . . . In effect, this means that some very definite control must be exercised over the General Studies Department.[23]

According to Elias, *yeshiva* education should make clear to the student that "secular aspirations are sterile and futile except through the specific contribution which the Jewish people was chosen to make to the redemption of mankind through its dedication to Torah."[24] Among his recommendations for the *yeshiva* curriculum are the following.

1. Allow only school-approved food in class.

2. There should be no prayers in general studies classes.

3. Avoid all discussions of religious matters and of non-Jewish holidays in general studies classes.

4. Point out that there are areas of knowledge in which the scientific method cannot lead to valid or meaningful conclusions.[25]

On this last recommendation, Rabbi Moses Tendler is even more specific about the viewpoint that the *yeshiva* should adopt.

> The facts of Science are not in conflict with the concepts of our Torah. It is the Mechanistic picture of a universe run by cause and effect without the mitigating influence of a personal G-d who sees and hears, knows and cares, rewards and punishes, that is in opposition to the truth of our Torah. But this is not the picture that Science paints. Science and the scientist realize their limitations. It is the atheist with or without a degree of Science that knows not or pretends not to know these limitations. . . .
>
> A lecture on evolution in the biology class, or atomic theory in the chemistry class or on meteorology in the General Science class without the mention of G-d's name, the wonder and majesty of His acts, is a denial of the goals of a Day School education. It is necessary for our students to receive a Torah outlook on life.
>
> No Day Schools dare tolerate a situation that was reported to exist in one of our oldest and largest Yeshivas in which the "Rebbe" warned his class against listening to the nonsense of the science teacher. The science teacher, on the other hand, constantly reminded his class "we are teaching science, no discussion of religion will be tolerated." When the theory of evolution was discussed the "good boys" walked out presumably leaving the majority of the class labeled as "bad boys" who are siding with science against religion."
>
> No! It is not even enough that Rebbe and science teacher leave each other alone—nor is it sufficient when a science textbook is chosen that is free of "objectionable" statements. The Day Schools earn their keep by professing a positive Torah point-of-view which must pervade the entire curriculum.[26]

The recommendations of Elias and Tendler are a fair summary of the philosophy one finds in the typical Boro Park *yeshiva*.

At this point it must be emphasized that while secular studies are made secondary in all respects in the typical *yeshiva* program they are by no means considered unimportant. Nor are students permitted to treat 'English' as unimportant. In order for the *yeshivas* to maintain their accreditation and to continue to receive various forms of governmental assistance, their students are required to take the Regents Exams and other standardized tests.[27] The successful performance of students on these examinations is considered by the *yeshiva* as well as by the parents and the community at large as a vindication of the religiously guided program. As one principal put it, "What do you care if our boys only get two hours of "English " a day, or if they read their math books in the bathroom. I'll match their Regents scores against any group of public school students." And, as a matter of official record, *yeshiva* students do, in fact, achieve superior scores on standardized exams.[28]

Yeshiva H. S. Seniors Are Regents Scholars

Fifty-six percent of the 330 seniors at the four Yeshiva University High Schools who were eligible to compete for New York State Regents College Scholarships have been named as winners or alternates Dr. Abraham N. Zuroff, supervisor, announced.

There were 136 winners and 49 alternates at the four schools. They are among nearly 19,000 winners throughout the State, representing 11 percent of the 166,000 who took part in the examination.

In addition, there were 13 winners at Yeshiva University High School for Girls of New York of State Regents Scholarships for Basic Professional Education in Nursing.[29]

While no separate statistics have been obtained for the achievements of *yeshiva* students in Boro Park, there is no reason to suspect that they would differ in any significant way from the overall pattern of *yeshiva* students.

From the perspective of this study, a crucial consequence of the dual *yeshiva* program is that students learn to define the parameters of the sacred and the secular. The secular world is defined in terms of highly specific and practical goals. Religion, too, is compartmentalized. Only, it occupies a larger compartment, so to speak. Rigorous training is encouraged in both, so long as the proper balance is maintained between the two. Perhaps that is the most significant statement one can make about the role of the *yeshiva* in the modern Orthodox community. In the absence of any other competent institution, it establishes proper proportions. This culturally dominant position of the *yeshiva* in the community may be due to the fact that it is the only formal organization among the other organizational units of the community which operates under formal state authority. It thus enjoys legal-rational as well as traditional legitimacy. This dual legitimacy enables the *yeshiva* to bestow intra-communal status along with universally recognizable credentials.

Apart from shaping the worldview of the second generation of Jewish Orthodoxy, the *yeshiva* has also succeeded in reshaping the definition and religious perspectives of the first generation. This generation, whose religious training was heavily traditional in character, confronted the modernity of America with trepidation. As tradition was all encompassing, so modernity appeared to be overwhelming; especially so, given the lack of familiarity with language and other social skills required for success in the new world. As Rabbi Jakobovits put it:

> The immigrants who came to America a generation or more ago had all been brought up in the homes of Isaacs and Rebeccas. They all stemmed from strictly religious stock. And yet, while some of them remained faithful to our tradition like Jacob, many turned their backs on their parents and became like Esau, renegades from Judaism.[30]

Those who did remain faithful probably bore the full brunt of the cognitive conflict between tradition and modernity. Compromises and resolutions of this conflict were worked out, if at all, in the privacy of the individuals' troubled souls. By providing a programmatic solution to the problem of religion versus modernity for the second and subsequent generations, the *yeshiva* has made the problem a matter of organizational policy instead of private conscience, and has generally allowed the first generation to be less concerned about the consequences of their personal struggles of conscience for the future of Jewry and Orthodoxy. The compartmentalization that is the distinguishing feature of the *yeshiva* program has become a model and a legitimation for the compartmentalized practice of Judaism for the first generation as well.

Youth Organizations

> Various types of youth organizations always tend to appear with the transition from traditional or feudal societies to modern societies.
> . . . The younger generation usually begin to seek a new self-

identification, and in one phase or another this search expresses itself in ideological conflict with the older.[31]

Eisenstadt arrives at this conclusion on the basis of a wide-ranging historical and anthropological survey of age stratification. One might wonder if it is not precisely this kind of problem that the prophet Malachi had in mind when he exhorted the ancient Israelites, "From the days of your Fathers Ye have turned aside from mine ordinances and have not kept them. Return unto Me and I will return unto you."[32] Universal or not, it is generally agreed that in contemporary societies youth forms a distinguishable social category; most frequently distinguished by its rebelliousness against adult or parental norms.

As Edward Bloustein of Rutgers put it in 1971, "The extraordinary fact which marks our days is that our children seem set upon rejecting our values."[33] This phenomenon has formed a part of the argument, discussed in earlier chapters, concerning the gradual disappearance of Jewish Orthodoxy in the United States.

Some elements of the youth phenomenon, or youth counter-culture, can be found in Boro Park as well. Although the *yeshiva*, with its extensive schedule, has managed to absorb most of the time, energy, and commitments of the young, its compartmentalized character has left some degree of unboundedness for the young. Indeed, youth in Boro Park, as elsewhere, is quite distinguishable as a social entity. It is the aim of this section of our study to examine the manner in which this social entity is organized, and the ways in which it functions as a source of social change and continuity in the community.

Three types of groups constitute the organizational universe of Jewish youth in Boro Park: synagogue-based groups, political-ideological groups, and religious-ideological groups. Apart from these, one service organization and the street-corner culture will be examined in some detail.

Perhaps the most successful of the synagogue-based youth groups is the Young Israel of Boro Park. It is a chapter of an international network of Young Israels which was, "formed in 1912 by a handful of Americanized Orthodox youth who felt themselves a part of American society, rejected many of the folkways and practices of their parents, but wished to remain Orthodox."[34] The Boro Park branch was, in fact, established by some of the original founders of the movement. Some still reside in Boro Park and are active participants in the local chapter. When we surveyed the Young Israel of Boro Park in 1973 it had approximately four hundred officially registered non-adult members in four divisions, including age groups from kindergarten through the collegiate level. The adult membership is not relevant to the present discussion, except insofar as a large number of the young members are the children of families who are members of the Young Israel synagogue. In this sense the organizational structure is quite similar to the Jewish centers found in the Conservative and Reform movement. In recent years, however, the Young Israel has also attracted a large number of young Jews whose parents, being first-generation and more traditional, would not be affiliated with the Young Israel synagogue.

> As late as World War II, Young Israel was looked upon as the least observant of the Orthodox group. . . . In developing an attractive social program, for example, Young Israel closed its eyes to such activities as mixed dancing, which few rabbinic authorities would sanction. Its lay leadership, which was [often] not *yeshiva* trained, refused to defer to an Orthodox rabbinate who, they felt, lacked secular training, sophistication, and community status comparable to theirs.[35]

This somewhat *risque* reputation of Young Israel attracted those children of the first generation who did, indeed, wish to break with the traditions of their parents but were not willing to go all the way. They chose to remain in the Orthodox fold. Interestingly, in recent years this membership itself has been a source of general movement to the religious right on the part of the organization. Thus, while some of the native born youth have successfully disengaged themselves from the organizational involvements of their parents by joining Young Israel, they have sought reforms (e.g. an end to mixed dancing on the premises) in the organization of their choice which would be consistent with parental values. In general, the members and fellow travellers of Young Israel do not seem bent on challenging or violating the core religious values of the community. Quite the contrary!

Some of the other large synagogues in the area also serve as a place of social gathering for their young members as well as young non-members. But they do not have anything resembling an official youth program. Young men and women use the occasion of Shabbos and holiday services to mix in informal groups at the entrance or rear corners of the *shul*. The organization of these groups is strictly cliqueish in character. Their function, however, is quite similar to Young Israel. They serve to bring young people into conversation groups in which they can realize a sense of shared identity and solidarity. Such synagogue-based youth groups have also sprung up in some of the larger, recently established Hasidic *shuls*. But these youth groups are very much beholden to the congregational hierarchy and serve primarily as learning groups or moral rearmament groups in which the young people of the *shul* are expected to participate during the time when they are free from the *yeshiva*. In general, the synagogue-based youth groups serve to contain the youth of the community, channelling their energies in the direction of fairly traditional activities, such as prayer, learning, and recreation which remain within the confines of religious norms—no hanky-panky between the sexes.

While the containment of youth may just be an unintended consequence or latent function of the synagogue-based youth groups, in the religious-ideological groups it is a matter of policy. The Agudath Israel is one such group, with roots in pre-war Europe. As a movement, it was founded in Poland in 1912:

> To stem the flood of both cultural and national assimilation, the rabbis and lay leaders of Orthodox Jewry ... founded Agudath Israel in 1912 in order to organize all those ready to maintain the inseparability of religion and nationality. . . to try to solve the problems concerning Judaism and Jews everywhere in the world in the spirit of Torah ... to substitute the modern form of voluntary organizational discipline for the cohesion and inner strength of the community life within the ghetto.[36]

Needless to say, the movement has undergone considerable change since its inception, both in the United States as well as elsewhere in the world. While in Israel it has become an active political force, in the United States it became a network of chapters which function as youth centers. Some observers, like Liebman, have seen this development as a weakness:

> Reb Aharon and other *rashe yeshivot* [deans of *yeshivas*] who were leaders in the Agudah trained the younger generation to value only one activity, *lernen* [religious learning]. The result was a devaluation of and contempt for political and societal activity in the Jewish community.... The organization never became an active communal force.[37]

In one of a series of meetings by the rabbinical leaders of the movement, in the spring of 1973, a new program, called *Rishum*, was instituted. This was designed to get the members of the organizations more actively involved in the Jewish concerns of the community. Since the early '70s the Agudah has become an active political force in the local Jewish community.

Whatever the weaknesses of the Agudah movement might be, its Boro Park branch remains one of the most popular religious youth groups in the area. Parenthetically, it may be noted that the national chairman of the organization, Rabbi Moshe Scherer, resides in the Boro Park community. While synagogue services are conducted in the Agudah, the synagogue itself is not the primary source of membership for the organization. It draws most heavily from the local *yeshivas* whose students are encouraged by the *rebbis* to join. The principal activities of the organization are learning, moral rearmament, and celebration of holidays. On the joyous festivals of Simchas Torah, Purim, and Chanuka, the Agudah is the locale for vigorous dancing, singing, skits, and games. Like Young Israel, the Agudah functions as a recreational organization which helps to structure the time during which the young are not in the *yeshiva*. The Agudah, however, is primarily for young men. It does not sponsor co-ed activities. Girls participate in a sister organization known as Bnos. Also, what passes for acceptable recreation is more narrowly defined by *halachic* terms in the Agudah than in Young Israel. Sports and mass entertainment (e.g. movies) tend to be excluded from the Agudah program, although sports has gained a measure of acceptance.

Official membership figures for the local chapter could not be ascertained, but, in any case, would have proven to be a poor reflection of the size of the active membership. On a Simchas Torah night there may be as many as two thousand young men crammed into the assembly hall, dancing and singing, shoulder to shoulder. On a typical Shabbos morning there may be only a couple of hundred at prayer services.

Learning groups of varying size and formality abound in the community; especially on Shabbos and holidays. Whether it be several *yeshiva* students getting together in a friend's living room to review a *blat gemorah* (a page of Talmud) or a group of young adults coming together in the basement of a house or a synagogue to hear a lecture on the relationship between science and religion, there seems to be an active interest in being associated with a youth group per se. But it has to be one which conforms to the ideals of Jewish Orthodoxy.

Whereas organizations like the Young Israel and the Agudah tend to contain youth, others, such as Mizrachi Ha Tzair, Bne Akiva, and most recently the Jewish Defense League and other politically motivated organizations attempt to educate and mobilize the young into particular political styles of thought and action. Although these organizations do not occupy permanent physical quarters in the area, [38] they appear to be quite successful in mobilizing large numbers of people through informal communication networks. Thus, schedule of meetings or rallies just seems to become known to the interested clientele. On the other hand, because of their more formal character, the local Agudah or Young Israel seem to attract a far larger membership than these organizations. Yet they undoubtedly enjoy the sympathies of most of Boro Park's Jewish youth. These organizations have served to politicize many of the young, and some of the older generation on behalf of Israel, Russian Jewry, and local Jewish concerns, such as street crime and welfare for the Jewish poor. Most importantly, these organizations have served to absorb the political-moral energies of the young. As commitment and political participation became the watchwords of American youth in general in the late 1960s, these organizations acted as a kind of substrate to which the political ardor of Orthodox youth could be attached. Not surprisingly, therefore, these organizations have been most successful in mobilizing the Orthodox and Jewish youth on the college campus.

The one threat to the Orthodox lifestyle and value system, which comes to the fore among the youth, and with which the various organizations mentioned thus far have not adequately coped, is what Wolfenstein called the "fun morality."[39] This ethic is found especially among the middle and upper-middle classes in advanced industrial societies. It legitimates the seeking of personal satisfaction, pleasure, and, especially, the seeking of fun in one's leisure. While the Orthodox value system could not possibly recognize leisure as a category of time, much less the activities associated with it, it is quite clear that Boro Park's youth find themselves with time on their hands during which they look to have fun.[40] The one formal organization which has served the fun needs of the community for the past half-century is the Young Men's and Women's Hebrew Association (YM & YWHA), affectionately called the "Y." The "Y" is also an excellent example of the cognitive and organizational compromises which are so typical of the hybrid culture of modern Orthodoxy.

The Boro Park "Y" was founded, at its present location adjacent to the

Temple Emanu-El, in 1912. According to its former Director, Abe Hershkovits, it was established by some well-to-do members of the Temple,

> who were motivated by the fact that they wanted to get their children out of the pool halls which then existed down further in the lower forties [streets] and into a healthy atmosphere for the young Jewish boy and girl. . . . The Temple itself gave the initial contribution.

The building was built to include a swimming pool, a large and well-equipped gymnasium, an auditorium which even today houses a local symphony orchestra, and a variety of game and recreation rooms on the upper floors. Its early clientele were mainly public school children whose parents saw in the "Y" an opportunity to provide them with all the varieties of fun within the context of a nominally Jewish organization. The only religious service which the "Y" provided was that its auditorium was converted into a synagogue during the High Holidays—Rosh Hashono and Yom Kipur. The parents of these children turned to the "Y" for their fun also. In due course the organization took on the character of a typical suburban Jewish center. It offered recreational opportunities from the cradle to the grave—it still has a golden agers club for retired clientele.

In the late 1940s and early 1950s the program of the "Y" was geared very heavily to teenagers, sponsoring a variety of clubs, teams, Scout troops, dances, and so forth. An estimated 650 teenagers were enrolled in the variety of programs. In addition, several hundred adults were enrolled in physical activities, hobby clubs, orchestra and glee club. The golden agers groups was established in 1947. At this point the organization still catered primarily to the early Jewish settlers of Boro Park and their children, a strongly acculturated and largely non-Orthodox group. The late 1950s and the decade of the sixties, as has been shown earlier, witnessed the transformation of Boro Park Jewry. The clientele of the "Y" changed accordingly.

As of 1972, the "Y" boasted of approximately 3,800 members. According to Abe Hershkovits, who was then its director, at least 75 percent of these members were Orthodox. The bulk of the membership is made up of the students who come from local *yeshivas* as part of a joint physical education program. Such a joint program was pioneered by the Beth Jacob girls' school in 1947, and was instrumental in making such a program acceptable to other local *yeshivas*. Of course, as Mr. Hershkovits pointed out, the "Y" itself has had to go a long way to accommodate its programs to the religious needs and restrictions of the new clientele.

> There are no co-ed activities at all. I haven't had dances here for maybe three, four, or five years. Game room, which used to be a big thing—well, now very few come around. The *yeshiva* kids are not interested in just socializing or hanging around the "Y.". . . . You see these cups? On Fridays the Beth Jacob girls come straight from school, the kids bring their lunches and we provide a place for them to sit and eat, separate for those who eat a meat lunch with a separate tablecloth. Well, they wanted cups with which to wash in order to say the *brochoh* [blessing before eating]. . . . Etz Chaim, Torah V'dath, Kamenitz, as well as most other local *yeshivas* come here and have their swimming and gym programs under our supervision. On a Sunday evening we have them with the *peyes* [earlocks], the real Hasidic kids. I work with all these schools—we literally walk on egg shells—we want to do nothing that might make them feel that we are unsympathetic to their needs.

Interestingly, while most of the local *yeshivas* make use of the facilities of the "Y," they will not acknowledge any formal affiliation with the organization which they still consider as somewhat *goyish* (un-Jewish). As Mr. Hershkovits mused:

> The "Y" is still considered as an 'institution.' Let me give you an example. Beth Jacob, with whom we've been dealing more than any other group here in all our years, they had a yearbook in which they wrote about their programs. They wrote: "our children use a local institution where they have gym and swimming." They would not even mention our name in their yearbook. I asked some of the administrators about this and they said, "Look, we have our problems too with some of our stricter parents. It is safer not to mention the "Y" by name."

Similarly, while many families join as members and make regular use of the facilities of the organization, their attitude towards the "Y" is strictly of a utilitarian nature. They do not look upon the "Y," as earlier generations of Boro Park's Jews have, as a community center in which friendships may be cultivated and with the values of which one might readily identify. The "Y" has come to serve the fun needs of the community, especially of the young, without that need and the organization which serves it having become a fully accepted part of the

community as a whole. The membership, along with other local organizations, continue to make demands on the "Y" to make its programs
more compatible with the Orthodox value system. The organization
survives—by walking on egg shells—to the extent that it successfully
makes those accommodations, even though Orthodoxy in Boro Park
appears to deny the legitimacy of the organization. It is this duality
which very frequently characterizes the Orthodox response to some of
the popular features of middle-class life and youth culture in particular:
participation at the level of practice, and denial at the level of ideology.

A similar duality can be found in the response to one of the most
authentic youth phenomenon in the community—the pizza shop scene.
During the mid-1960s several pizza shops were opened along the main
street of the community, Thirteenth Avenue. Two significant features of
these shops are that they are *kosher* and *shomer Shabbos* (closed on the
Shabbos and other religious holidays), and they have become hangouts
for Orthodox youth. Apart from selling pizza and refreshments, they
have sit-down accommodations and house juke-boxes which feature the
latest Hebrew records along with popular rock tunes. For a while many
of the local *yeshivas* made these shops 'off-limits' for their students.
Rebbis actually took it upon themselves to casually patrol the stores to
check on their students. At one point a rumor was spread that one of the
larger shops was owned by an individual who, personally, was not *shomer
Shabbos,* and that there were doubts about his *kashrus* observance as
well. That store was very rapidly abandoned by its youthful clientele and
it was soon under new management. Apparently the other shops
recognized the potential danger because at the present time they all
boldly post signs of their Shabbos and *kashrus* observance which are
confirmed by the signatures of well-known rabbinic authorities. They all
appear to be doing a booming business. On Saturday and Sunday nights
one might find hundreds of young men and women, mostly single and
some young couples, mingling around the shops. Music and conversation
mix freely with the sharp aroma of the pizza and *falafel, hoomis, and
tehina* (middle-eastern foods). While official opposition to these shops
and the social life surrounding them continues, the youth of the community seem to have voted with their feet, so to speak. So long as the
shops conform to *halachic* standards of Shabbos and *kashrus* observance,
the young of the community continue to patronize them in their pursuit
of fun. Whether the pizza shop scene constitutes a rebellion against
parental values remains a debatable question.

Self-help and Self-defense

The idea of self-help is not new to the Jewish community. It is rooted
in the fundamental religious precept of *tzedaka* (charity), the elements of
which make each Jew personally responsible for his Jewish brethren.
Essentially, it is this precept along with a sense of pride (of not wishing
to be dependent on strangers or government) which has given rise to the
multitude of charitable organizations found in every Jewish community
throughout the United States, indeed, throughout the world. "Whatever
one's orientation to Jewish identity there was a consensus about the need
to help the Jewish orphan, the Jewish elderly, the Jewish sick, the Jewish
unemployed, the Jewish family in trouble."[41] While in some of the gilded
ghettos of the acculturated third and subsequent generations of American Jews some of this consensus on *tzedaka* has been forgotten in recent
years, in the Boro Park community its spirit and practical expressions are
very much in evidence. *Tzedaka* is very much a vogue. Nearly all of the
large established synagogues as well as some of the larger *shtieblach*
sponsor interest-free loan funds for family and business emergencies. The
local *yeshivas* depend very heavily on the generosity of the residents of
the community. On the average, nearly 50 percent of the budget of the
yeshivas depends on voluntary contributions or governmental sources. It
is this last source that will concern us next.

While the traditional forms of self-help persist in the community, new
forms have also emerged which seem to imply an entirely new posture of
the Orthodox community *vis-a-vis* society at large. It was observed in
Chapter 5, that the decade of the sixties was a period of growing
self-awareness for America's minorities. Correspondingly, the American
Establishment during this period—under a Democratic administration
for nearly the entire decade—showed itself to be quite flexible to the
needs and demands of the various groups, especially blacks. Under the
Johnsonian banner of the War on Poverty a large variety of programs
were funded to help disadvantaged minorities or, as one recent Title I
brochure put it, "bypassed peoples." Because of the dangers of reverse
discrimination, or perhaps simply as a matter of pork-barrel politics,
many of these programs were sufficiently broad in design so that groups
other than blacks began to take advantage of them.

Since the sixties the idea of self-help has come to include all the
activities related to obtaining a fair share of governmental subsidies for
the Jewish community. This is a relatively new attitude toward public

assistance, and it is most readily noticeable among the post-war immigrants and their children. Where earlier generations of immigrants and their children proudly eschewed anything resembling the public dole, the post-war immigrants and their descendants see societal resources as equally available to all segments of the population: to Orthodox Jews as well as blacks. They have learned to fight for their fair share in a way that is quite novel in the American Jewish experience.[42]

Some of the more dramatic results of the new attitude may be observed in the extent to which governmental programs are utilized in the community. *Yeshivas* receive governmental aid through the following federal, state, and city programs.

Name of Program	*Source*
Breakfast Program (Title VII)	Federal government

Elementary and Secondary Educational Act, 1965
    Title I
    Title IV-B
    Title VII
	Federal government

Headstart	Federal government
Lunch Program (Title VII)	Federal governmmment

Neighborhood Youth Corps, CETA (Title VI)
    Summer Program
    In-school
    Out-of-school
	Federal government

Counterforce	New York State
Mandated Services	New York State
New York State Greenberg Law	New York State
New York State Textbook Law	New York State
Bus Transportation	New York City
Day Care Centers	New York City

Concrete examples of federal involvement in the Jewish community are provided in the following newspaper articles.

OEO Gives $198,542 to New York Jewish Poor

On the heels of a disclosure in the "Spotlight" column in the *Jewish Press* that New York City was harboring at least 300,000 Jewish poor, an announcement was made this week by Rabbi Sholem B. Gorodetsky, chairman of the Hassidic Corporation for Urban Concern (H.C.U.C.) that they will be able to distribute $198,542 to various groups to render services to the Jewish poor in Brooklyn and New York City.... Rabbi Gorodetsky said that a grant was received from the Office of Economic Opportunity this week through the N.Y.C. Council against Poverty.[43]

465 Teenagers in Summer Projects

465 unprivileged Jewish teenagers in the 14-22 age group including a number of handicapped, are currently involved in special summer project administered by Torah U'Mesorah—the National Society for Hebrew Day Schools. Funded by the Federal Government's Department of Labor through the Youth Services Agency of the City of New York, the program, known as Neighborhood Youth Corps, concentrates on teenagers from poverty families in Metropolitan New York who are either actual or potential high school dropouts.[44]

The Maimonides Community Mental Health Center, established in 1967 with Federal, States, and City funds, also stands as a monument in the community to the radically new role of public assistance in solving problems in the Jewish community. Although this organization does not cater exclusively to the needs of the Orthodox or even Jewish community in Boro Park, special programs for dealing with the emotional and welfare problems of the Orthodox have been set up and have been achieving a measure of success.

What is most significant about the governmental programs of assistance and the programs of other extracommunal agencies, such as the Federation of Jewish Philanthropies, is that the assistance they offer is not merely to the individual as a needy citizen. They are actually subsidizing structural entities of a recognized community, the Orthodox community. For example, when the Hassidic Corporation for Urban Concerns appeals for OEO funds on behalf of the Jewish Orthodox poor, it makes clear in its appeal that the families of such a group are large because of the prohibition against birth control. They make clear that the Shabbos observer faces job discrimination because of his religious practices, and that the price of *kosher* food is a good deal higher than the price of non-*kosher* food. As the above exhibits have shown, the OEO has responded favorably to just such appeals. Thus, Jews receive financial assistance not merely as needy citizens but as Orthodox Jews. They have also received public school buildings which the city has abandoned for one reason or another. From such evidence it would appear that the community has been relatively successful in sustaining its definitions of reality, and obtaining the assistance of agencies of the larger society in helping to perpetuate those definitions.

Similar instances of successful self-definition may be observed in the political arena as well. Here, self-defense has come to replace a more traditional attitude of huddling quietly under the sometimes tolerant protection of alien governments. Unlike self-help, self-defense has not been a common feature of traditional Jewish communities. Of course, in the United States the B'nai Brith Anti-Defamation League has been fighting discrimination and anti-semitism for nearly a century. But its approach has been strictly civil libertarian and individualistic in character. It has sought to protect the rights of Jews as Americans and not as Jews—and certainly not as Orthodox Jews. Until recent years the Orthodox themselves looked upon their practices and values as some sort of handicap, well-captured in the popular exclamation, *es is schwer tzu zein a yid* (it's tough to be a Jew).

As the late sixties witnessed a general politicization of American society, the Jewish Orthodox have also become politicized. Practically, this turn of attitude involved a number of events and actions both large and small. While we do not possess systematic information about the past political attitudes and activities of the Orthodox or the Boro Park Jewish community, we did obtain survey information on current political attitudes, expectations, and sense of competence. In an effort to discover the sense of powerlessness which is customarily associated with Jewish Orthodoxy, a modified version of the Neal and Seeman Powerlessness scale was administered to all respondents in our survey of families.[45] Out of the 116 individuals who were reached in our sample of families, 56 respondents filled out the seven-item scale. The instrument sought to distinguish respondents' feelings of political competence or sense of powerlessness in society at large as compared with the same attitudes within the community. Respondents were asked to select responses to a set of seven statements which would indicate mastery or powerlessness.

Two sets of scores were, then, computed for each respondent: a general mastery score and a communal mastery score. The highest possible score in each case was 21 and the lowest 7. The average general mastery score for the 56 respondents was 12.6, while the mean community mastery score was 14.9. The difference between these two averages does not appear to be significant, but it does seem to imply a greater optimism among the Jews of Boro Park regarding their ability to control their own immediate community than to master the fate of society at large. At this point the scores remain suggestive only, as no comparable scores exist for society in general or other comparable communities.

A far clearer indication of politicized Orthodoxy may be observed in the variety of activities and organizations which have been launched in the past five years aiming specifically to protect the interests of Jews as Jews (not simply as Americans with civil rights). The most vociferous and popular among these undertakings has been the Jewish Defense League, (JDL), founded in 1968. Although few people in the community are actually members of JDL, the slogan "NEVER AGAIN" has a very potent appeal among the post-war immigrants and their native born children. The challenge of that slogan has made the community quite active in pursuing its interests, whether they be the observance of Shabbos, sewage and sanitation problems, safety in the streets, or, as the following article shows, tenants' rights.

Boro Park Tenants Council Gets Underway

A new movement has been born in Boro Park. With the Maimonides Neighborhood Center acting as midwife, sixty tenants got together last Thursday and created the Boro Park Tenants Council.

They are fuming over the greed of those landlords who file for rent increases without removing violations. They wanted to know what their rights were. So the first priority of the meeting was a discussion of tenant rights. . . .

One thing that became clear at the meeting was that suits brought by individuals in court are often just so much water through a sieve. In the words of one staff member of the neighborhood center "The judges 9 out of 10 times are the biggest landlords in the community." So what recourse is left?

At that point Ron Lucas of the Center stood up and pronounced fighting words that probably have not been heard in this community since W.W. II.

"Let's have the beginning of a unified Boro Park." After a tense interval a small nucleus volunteered to continue the push for tenant rights. To keep it expanding at a time when the only thing that seems to be getting bigger is the rent bill. More volunteers were expected at a meeting later that day.[46]

In addition, the residents of Boro Park, along with Orthodox Jews elsewhere, have shown considerable tenacity in pursuing goals in the political arena—such as in school board elections, and in the mayoralty campaign; in monitoring the quality of local television programs, or the scheduling of classes in New York City colleges on Jewish holidays. This kind of self-defense has involved a confrontation by the Orthodox community with society at large as a quasi-independent entity insisting that its definitions of self be accepted. This confrontation in the political arena, especially in New York City, has proven quite successful.

Maintaining a Religious Community

A community, especially a religious community in the midst of a secular society, exists for its members not merely as a universe of values and symbols but also as an organized system of institutions which concretize and strengthen them.

In this chapter we have seen that the salient institutions of the Orthodox community in Boro Park have incorporated the process of cognitive bargaining, that subtle dance of social separateness and social integration which we described in the previous chapter, into their day-to-day lives. The family, the *yeshiva*, the synagogue, and the other institutions of organized Orthodox Jewish life have found ways to accommodate to the functional demands of the larger secular society. Yet, the accommodation has not been at the cost of religious values or practices that have ultimate importance for the community. Quite the contrary. The accommodation at the purely functional level has served to strengthen those habits of thought and lifestyle which are most distinctly in keeping with Orthodox Judaism. The question we must now consider is how durable these habits promise to be.

6

Glimpses at the Future
The Impact of Deviance and Change

The preceding chapters have a distinctly upbeat tone, with good reason. Institutions, such as *yeshivas*, synagogues, *mikvas*, *kosher* butcher shops, and the like, that are, for most American Jews, part of the fading memories of an ancestral world, have achieved a vitality in the Boro Park community that would have been unthinkable even for the first-generation immigrants of the turn of the century. The routine lives of the residents of this community are suffused with the living force of the Torah and its ancillary rituals and customs. As Irving Howe has written of the *shtetl* of pre-war Europe, Boro Park has emerged in the late twentieth century

> as a world in which God is a living force, a Presence, more than a name or a desire. He does not rule from on high. . . . The 613 *mitzvot*, or commandments, that a pious Jew must obey, which dictate the precise way in which a chicken is to be slaughtered; the singsong in which the Talmud is to be read; the kinds of food to serve during the Sabbath; the way in which shoes should be put on each morning; the shattering of a glass by the groom during a marriage ceremony—these are the outer signs of an inner discipline. . . . The community is a manifestation of God's convenant with Israel.[1]

What is perhaps most remarkable is that this community is not a cultural relic of the past, that staunch loyalists have been able to isolate and protect from the assimilationist ravages of modern society—quite the contrary. It is a community that evolved under precisely those conditions of modern life that enabled its members to enter successfully into the economic and political arena of the larger society. The upbeat tone of the previous chapters stems from this curious evolutionary twist.

But by focusing our descriptive and analytic lenses on the *shtetl*-like quality of the Orthodox community in Boro Park we have, perhaps, overemphasized the goodness of fit between the values and beliefs of people, the culture of the community, and the structure of organizations. While these three dimensions of social reality are profoundly inter-related they are never simple blueprints for one another. Amidst even the most homogeneous groups there are minorities who duck under the shadow of consensus or openly rebel. And communities also change—at times dramatically, at times imperceptibly—either because of internal

135

changes among their members or because of forces encroaching from outside.

We have traced the evolution of the Boro Park community from the turn of the century up to the 1970s as a case study in the reconstruction of a religiously based community, but our study would not be complete without some projections into the future. Such projections, however, cannot rest comfortably on the forces of communal solidarity alone. We must train our attention on the forces of discord and change as well. Throughout this chapter we shall be addressing the question of the future of Boro Park as an Orthodox Jewish community.

Deviance: *The Chronic Patterns*

The concept of deviance conjures up images of wild-eyed lunatics and hidden perversity. But that is not the technical meaning of the term. In sociology it is used to refer to all those forms of behavior which go contrary to accepted communal norms. To be sure, some deviations may be more extreme than others, and some people may violate a greater number of norms than others, but deviance need not involve bizarre or illegal behavior. Deviance is a persistent feature of all communities, and all communities exert some amount of effort to control it. Where deviance is not controlled successfully it becomes a potent source of social change. The very success of control, however, may change a community as well.

In Boro Park, as elsewhere, deviance occurs either as a result of inadequate conformity to communal norms, or as a result of overzealous conformity to them. What constitutes deviance in this community, however, is vastly different from what one would find in other communities throughout the United States. A *yarmulka*, or skullcap, that is too small or too colorful is interpreted as a sign of wavering religious loyalty. A hemline which is too short—immodest, or too long—modishly maxi, brings under suspicion the religious convictions of a young woman. On the other hand, a young man who devotes all his energies to prayer and Talmudic studies, to the exclusion of all other worldly interests, will readily earn the label of a *chnyak*. He will rarely be a desirable candidate for friendship or marriage. Similarly, a girl who is overly zealous in her prayers, or overly meticulous in the observance of all rituals, is perceived as a social misfit. Charity is a much admired virtue in the community. But one who devotes too much of his resources to it is suspect. He is either too eager for *koved*, that is, for the prestige which attends charity, or he is

irresponsible. Probably both. Devotion at prayer is also a highly respected trait. But one who prays too loudly, *shokls* too fervently, is
thought to be pretentious. The examples abound. But what do they
signify?

As we have seen in the previous chapters, the core value system of the
community is bifurcated, and its institutions are compartmentalized into
sacred and secular spheres. The one is basic, the other is accessory. But
both are important. The person is expected to perform an intricate ballet
of routine activities that acknowledge the proper significance of each of
these spheres. Daily prayer and the meticulous observance of all personal
rituals are admired. But not at the cost of professional or financial success.
Conversely, the admiration which is given to people who achieve success
in the professional or business worlds is readily withheld if success is not
accompanied by the regular observance of religious norms as well.

The educational and other institutions in the community are designed
to enable people to master the intricacies of this normative ballet, but the
cultural choreography is far from perfect. Not only does the bifurcated
value system leave many Orthodox Jews ambivalent but it also leaves
them without solid guidelines in the choice of careers, the use of leisure
time, and a whole host of alternatives pertaining to the individual's
relationship to the larger society. Therefore deviance is always im-
minent. Some people in the community are always too modern while
others are always too religious. But since there is no objective arbiter of
the middle ground, both the *frum* and the *moderne* stake their claim to
communal normalcy. Such competition over the definition of normality
not only leaves substantial segments of the community in a perpetual
state of deviance *vis-a-vis* one another but also is the source of a
simmering *kulturkampf* (cultural tension) in the community.

One of the practical consequences of this cultural tension is that such
institutions as *yeshivas* and *shuls* are multiplying, folding, and sub-
dividing in almost endless succession. What we have seen earlier as the
tremendous increase in the numbers of these institutions is, as least in
part, the result of people changing their minds and shifting affiliations.
As soon as a handful of people come up with a new configuration of the
proper balance between the sacred and secular spheres, they set about
establishing a new *shul* and, if their means allow, a new *yeshiva*. One
need not be a great logician to figure out that such an endless proliferation of new institutions tends to deplete the total resources of the
community in the long run.

The fact that some segment of the community is perpetually regarded as deviant by some other segment has adverse consequences in the short run as well. The ambivalence that such tension engenders, particularly in the young who are on the threshhold of adulthood and careers, motivates many to leave the community altogether. They hope that by changing locales, moving say to Flatbush or to Staten Island, or leaving the city entirely, they might escape the pressures of competing communal norms.

Finally, the lack of firm consensus on the contours of the straight and narrow path between the sacred and the secular leaves every Boro Park Jew feeling vaguely uncomfortable. At one time or another he is certain that his neighbors consider him, or at least his children, deviant. Thus, neighbors are feared as much as they are enjoyed. After all, what might they think?

This subtle tension, which insinuates itself into the consciousness of every person in the community, is one of the sources of a condition that might be called chronic deviance. This chronic deviance is evidence of the inner uncertainty that lies under the veneer of massive communal consensus. In the more technical language of sociology, one might say it reveals the anomie haunting the doorstep of even this cohesive system. The problem seems to be rooted in the nature of the bifurcated value structure of the community. And yet there is another form of deviance, also chronic, that grows not from the inner cultural strains of the community, but from the unavoidable contact between the world of the Orthodox Jew and the larger society. It is a kind of deviance observable mainly among the young people of the community.

The exposure of the young to secular education at all levels, and the pressure on them to pursue professional careers, brings them into frequent contact with lifestyles that are prevalent in the larger society. We have taken great pains throughout earlier chapters to describe the ways in which the Jews of Boro Park have avoided the magnetic pull of assimilation. We have seen, for example, how the styles of dress that are popular in the larger society are made *kosher* through conformity with *halachic* restrictions. Similarly, in such phenomena as *kosher* pizza shops, liturgical music set to jazz or rock tunes and instrumentation, night attendance at college while remaining in *yeshiva* during the day and *kosher* camping tours to the Southwest, we see varied attempts to thwart assimilation by incorporating elements of the tempting modern life style into the sacred system. To the extent that such cultural amalgamations work, they symbollize the ingenuity and success of the community.

But cultural forms carry within them, however imperceptibly, values as well. Two values that are, perhaps, fundamental and inherent to the modern life style are privatism and pleasure. The legitimacy of the pursuit of private pleasure, without concern for tradition, without concern for the opinions of elders finds support in virtually every facet of social life in modern America. As the journalist Tom Wolfe has observed, "we are now in the 'me' decade."[2] The fact that Orthodox Jews have been able to incorporate microwave ovenware, stereophonic music, and exotic vacation packages into the normative patterns of a religious community that is bound by ritual restrictions of a two thousand year old system is a tribute to their ingenuity. But their implicit belief that the incorporation of such elements does not in any way contaminate primordial values may be naive; 'me-ism' is a value woven into even the most minor accoutrement of modern social life.

Every new artifact of modernity that is successfully incorporated into the community's routine, diffuses a bit of its underlying value as well. Vacation packages and retirement communities, no matter how *kosher*, serve to remove the individual from continuous and intimate contact with his family and neighbors. Technological advances in the kitchen, no matter how *kosher*, tend to liberate the Jewish woman from her traditional chores, and willy-nilly lead to changing sex roles in the family. The availability of Talmudic lectures on tape-recorded cassettes or on the radio, on station WEVD, inevitably lessens the importance of those personal human ties through which such wisdom was communicated in the past. Thus, the successful merger between the artifacts of the modern lifestyle and the two thousand year old sacred normative system inevitably lead to the crystallization of values which are deviant by ancestral standards. The focus on self-realization and personal pleasure, which is inherent in the goals and lifestyles of young Orthodox Jews in particular, is a profound and chronic deviation from a religious system whose persistence over the millennia was based on organic continuity between the generations.

Although statistical evidence is not available at this point, there are numerous impressionistic indications of the consequences of 'me-ism' for the community. Despite the availability of *shadchonim*, or matchmakers, young Orthodox Jews increasingly prefer to make their own marital arrangements. Romance and personal compatibility are concerns that override more traditional considerations. When couples fail to achieve the kind of personal satisfaction that they have learned to expect in marriage, consultation with marriage counselors, therapists, and even the dissolution of the marital bonds are not uncommon. The attractions of leisure-time consumption are pulling families further apart, and the pull of upward social mobility is dispersing the young of the community in an ever-widening social and geographic radius.

The rituals which govern Orthodox life are intricate and they penetrate into all the routine activities of everyday life. Because the ideology of the community makes observance of these rituals the ultimate value, it requires considerable psychological and social talent to mesh sacred and secular norms without any symptoms of stress or upset. As we have seen in the previous chapter, all of the key institutions of the community are so organized as to enable individuals to navigate successfully between these two compartimentalized worlds. Yet, the occasions for stress are numerous, especially for those people who feel most exposed to the simultaneous tugs of both worlds. The young Hasid who works as a diamond polisher on Forty-seventh street in Manhattan must make his way to and from work among the movie theaters and pornographic bookshops of the Times Square area. The young *yeshiva* student who attends Brooklyn College at night, preparing to be an accountant, must choose between spending his free hours studying in a quiet corner of the library or mingling with mate-seeking coeds at an on-campus cafeteria serving only *kosher* food. One need not be either a Hasidic diamond polisher or a *yeshiva*-student–accounting-major to feel the multi-valent tugs of their world.

Not surprisingly, there are young men and women who find navigation between the two worlds either too difficult or simply unrewarding, and they withdraw from one or the other. Those who withdraw from the normative demands of the secular world are, undoubtedly, fewer in number than those who withdraw from the normative demands of the religious world. But both constitute deviant minorities in the community, whose presence is a relevant factor in the future of Boro Park Orthodoxy. Those who withdraw from the normative demands of the secular world seek fulfillment primarily in the world of the *yeshiva*, in personal piety, and perhaps in the supervision of the religious life of others (e.g. teaching children in *yeshivas*). A substantial minority of the young men, perhaps as many as ten percent, spend their late teens and twenties exclusively, in post-high school *yeshiva* seminaries, without a thought about further secular education or gainful career. Since such an option is not available to young women, one is less likely to find a pattern of religious overconformity among them. There are, however, many young women who are so enamored with the image of the overconformist *yeshiva bochur* that they spend their maidenhood in any menial employment, cultivating their religious zeal and ritual practice, in the hope of marrying and supporting such young men. Unfortunately, such marriages are often prone to early and severe economic hardships, and much personal disappointment.

Attempts to control religious overconformity are usually made by parents or other relatives. Their primary weapons are reason and ridicule. "How do you expect to support a family on a *blat Gemorah*?" they argue with their son. When the son replies, as he is likely to, that one must have *bitochon*, faith, that God will provide, parents are apt to grow more impatient. "Son," they argue, "you live in a world of fantasy. Besides, do you really mean to tell us that you spend your entire day learning? How much of your time do you *batl*, waste, with your *chavrusa*, learning partner? Couldn't you spend that time learning some useful profession? How long do you think your in-laws will support you?" Such exchanges undoubtedly curb the appetite of many a young man who would wish to cloister himself in the world of the *yeshiva*. But the religious ideology of the community, coupled with the authority of rabbis, provide the religiously overcommitted with potent sources of legitimacy for their deviant life style.

Since women are expected to marry and raise children, regardless of the intensity of their religious zeal, their religious overconformity is less likely to be perceived as a problem. Therefore it is less likely to be checked by any means.

Since religious overconformity is truly the problem of the minority, and, where it occurs, is only likely to be perceived as a serious problem by the immediate family, we must turn our attention to the reverse problem: deviance due to lack of conformity to religious norms, and overconformity to what are perceived to be the norms of the larger society. As we have pointed out time and again, the religious norms which govern life in the Orthodox community are numerous and pervasive. So, there are many opportunities to violate them, both in private and in public. The most serious form of deviance is public display of irreverence—violating dress codes, eating in public places which are acknowledged to be non-*kosher*, being seen transgressing the Sabbath restrictions. But those whose lives are devoted exclusively or overwhelmingly to success in academic pursuits, professions, or business are also likely to be suspect, particularly if those commitments interfere with their full participation in the religious life of the community.

Daily attendance in the synagogue as well as participation in the social programs of local religious organizations often run headlong into competition with the demands on one's time of extra-religious and extra-communal obligations or pursuits. Young adults, who are on the beginning rungs of some career, and who may have less leeway in controlling the competing demands on their time and energy than older persons might, are particularly prone to reject religious norms in favor of secular norms.

Among the dozens of boys and girls who were my own classmates in the *yeshivas* Toras Emes, and Kamenitz, and who were my peers and friends in such organizations as the Young Israel, the "Y," and the Agudah, several became reputable rabbis, Talmudic scholars, or traditional housewives. But I know a great many more who became doctors, lawyers, college professors, psychologists, editors, and executives. Many of the latter have remained Orthodox by their own definition of the term, but all have left the Boro Park community and settled in communities where religious demands do not have as direct and easy access to their private life as is the case in Boro Park. Although their successes are generally admired, they are usually held up to rebuke in rabbinic sermons, in *yeshiva musar* talks, and even in parental admonition. Unless they have moved to a community that is as religiously identified as Boro Park (e.g. Monsey, Lakewood, Washington Heights, and so forth), even their geographic mobility is likely to be interpreted as deviant.

Because secularization is the most serious of the chronic forms of deviance in Boro Park, most of the social controls are designed to stem it. As we have seen in earlier chapters, the community by and large has been successful in this regard. It has managed to control the problem, however, only by compartmentalizing it in the bifurcated value system. Therefore, the threat of secularization is a relentless and pervasive one, and the number of young people as well as of more established members of the community who are pulled away from the Boro Park milieu each year constitute a real and abiding threat to the future of the community.

Thus far we have dealt with those patterns of deviance that we have called chronic. These appear to be embedded in the very nature of the cultural system of the community and its relationship to the larger society. We have called these problems chronic precisely because of their embeddedness, and because efforts to control them do not appear to be effective. There are, however, more acute forms of deviance that, while less pervasive, will also play at least a potential part in shaping the future of Orthodoxy in Boro Park

Deviance: *The Acute Patterns*

Because they are chronic and fundamental, and wear away at the life of the community almost imperceptibly, the problems we have described thus far do not constitute dramatic elements in the life of Boro Park Orthodoxy. There are, however, dramatic occurrences of what may be called acute deviance as well. Outrageous sexual behavior, drug use, theft and violent crime, violence within the family—all occur very rarely in Boro Park. They do, however, occur.

A much-heralded divorce of some rabbinic figure, reports and rumors of criminal activity, rumors of drug use or sexual misbehavior among *yeshiva* students, all send ripples of gossip and shock through the community. Such events not only are viewed with alarm in the community—"How can such a thing happen in Boro Park?" people ask—but also evoke disbelief and rebuke. Women express their outrage at the grocery or vegetable stand, or on their way to work on the BMT subway line. Men linger a few minutes after the morning *davening* (prayer service) to probe the details of the particular outrage and to share frowns. Most importantly, relevant organizations (e.g., the Jewish Family Service, the "Y," the local Council of Jewish Organizations, and so forth) move into action.

Acute deviance triggers rapid responses from both formal and informal agents of social control. Police, parents, rabbis, and social workers—as well as lawyers, where necessary—are quickly activated to deal with any outbreaks of illegality or large-scale violation of community standards in matters of drugs, sexuality, or family life. If the problem does not involve any legal infractions, it is likely to be defined as one of psychological maladjustment or ill health. Beyong controlling the particular activities or persons themselves, the agents of control tend to collude in restoring the status quo and the veneer of normality by keeping the news of the deviance as quite as possible. Perhaps the greatest fear for everyone, professionals and lay people alike, is that the veneer of normalcy and religious probity will be shattered. Thus, the myth that such things, indeed, cannot happen in Boro Park is perpetuated.

The apparently marvelous efficiency with which the acute forms of deviance are controlled does contain the seeds of some ironic consequences. Because people recognize the swiftness and efficiency of the mechanisms of social control in the community, if they contemplate deviant behavior, they will very likely remove themselves from the community long before they violate communal norms. For example, in the course of my research I have become acquainted with several young men who, recognizing their own homosexual preferences, moved away from the community before their deviance could become noticed and subject to control. Undoubtedly the same anticipatory effect of social control must touch other deviants as well. Who can say how many individuals, or even families, leave the community each year because of this anticipatory effect of social control?

Two other ironic consequences of the effectiveness of the controls are heightened awareness of deviance, on the one hand, and increasing tolerance of it, on the other. Much of what is regarded in Boro Park as an *avla or shande,* that is, sinful, shameful, or deviant behavior, is thought by the residents to be rampant at the gates of the community, in New York City at large. Of course, they are not altogether wrong! Therefore, organizations such as the *yeshivas,* the synagogues, the Family Service agency, the Maimonides Mental Health Center, and community-conscious people in general, are constantly on the look-out for any signs of such problems cropping up in their midst. Some local *yeshivas* have gone so far as to obtain government funds for drug and alcohol abuse prevention. Undoubtedly at least some of these monies are used for less ominous activities, such as mending abused books and abused classroom furniture. But the conscious effort to be on the look-out for such problems necessarily raises awareness of such activities for everyone. And that awareness may be the very avenue of exposure for some.

Because acute forms of deviance, such as drug abuse, homosexuality, marital infidelity, or criminality are the most visible and dramatic disruptions of communal life, they pose the greatest threat to the Orthodox worldview and lifestyle. As the religious community has no recourse to punitive sanctions, at least not outside of the school system, it has increasingly turned to counselling therapies (e.g. family therapy, psychotherapy, group therapy, and the like) for dealing with non-criminal deviance. It is not at all uncommon to find synagogue rabbis, as well as rabbis in *yeshivas,* referring individuals to private therapists, or to the local Jewish Family Service, or to the Maimonides Mental Health Center. In these settings deviant behavior or heretical attitudes can be dealt with as adjustment problems, in the neutral language of psychology and social science. The irony is that, as deviance is dealt with increasingly from a therapeutic or mental health perspective, the language of this perspective seeps into the collective consciousness of the community. As *averas,* or transgressions, become maladies, and misbehavior becomes maladjustment, the rigidity of communal attitudes is bound to soften.

The ultimate effect of the variety of deviance on the future of Boro Park Orthodoxy is difficult to estimate. Just as an individual rarely dies of a chronic ailment, so too, we may prophesy that the community is not likely to be destroyed by its chronic problems of deviance. Chronic forms of deviance are likely to engender new values, new norms, and perhaps even new institutions in the long run. On the other hand, acute forms of deviance seem to occur so rarely that they cannot pose a threat to the survival of the community. In short, deviance of various kinds may alter the values and norms of the community in the long run, but Boro Park Jewry's social life is not likely to be eroded by any kind of deviance. There are, however, other threats of a less benign nature.

Structural Change and Ethnic Invasion

Sometimes it is the subtle shift in the climate of people's minds which changes the social world around them. At other times changes occur in the very make-up of the environment in spite of whatever notions and values people may harbor. As we have seen in the previous chapters, the evolution of Boro Park from a suburb into a *shtetl* has been shaped by changes in people's values and norms as well as changes in the environment. In the preceeding section of this chapter we also discussed the potential impact of changing values and norms on the future of the community. Presently we shall turn our attention to an aspect of the community which is quite independent of the wishes and thoughts of its members, that is, its social structure. We shall examine the shifting composition of this structure and probe its relevance for the future.

In the present context the concept of social structure refers to classes of people in the community and the neighborhood in general, as well as to the relationship between them. We shall be concerned with both the internal structure of the Jewish community and also with the larger structure, which includes the non-Jewish community. Changes in these two elements of social structure haunt the future of Boro Park Orthodoxy.

In our demographic overview of the Jews of Boro Park, in Chapter 2, we noted that from 1957 to 1970 the greatest growth in population in the community was among the over-forty age groups. Younger age groups underwent a steady decline—at least according to 1970 census figures. The increase in the older age groups, as we have pointed out, was due to the influx of upwardly mobile Jews from Williamsburg and Crown Heights. Their influx led to a boom in renovation and new housing starts, at least in the most densely Jewish quarters of the area. One knowledgable observer of Boro Park Jewish life has estimated that between 1965 and 1975 there occured a massive urban renewal in the Boro Park area, all of which was privately financed at a cost of perhaps as much as ten million dollars. What the 1970 census did not indicate is that many of the people who moved to Boro Park, partly because they were more religious than those who left Boro Park, continued to have children, despite the fact that they were in their forties or fifties.[3] Moreover, many of them brought teenage sons and daughters with them, all of whom came of age and married in the community subsequent to the 1970 census. Because of religious norms, these new families have proven to be extremely fecund, starting childbearing immediately after marriage and giving no thought to birth control at least until the third or fourth child.

The net result has been a veritable population explosion coupled with skyrocketing housing costs. This combination of structural developments has made the community a dynamic one, but it has also created one of the most serious problems facing the community. Because renovation and new housing construction have all been privately financed, the costs of houses as well as of rents have skyrocketed hand-in-hand. No one receives subsidies of any kind. Therefore, only those most secure financially can afford to purchase a home in Boro Park. Even the payment of rents requires a substantial income. People who earn only modest incomes, or who are at the beginning of a career (usually the two go hand-in-hand), must either try to find an apartment in one of the few apartment houses that are governed by the New York City Rent Stabilization Law or seek housing in other neighborhoods. In short, the older adults of the Boro Park Jewish community have priced their own children out of the local housing market.

The development of housing patterns in the Jewish quarters of the Boro Park community has probably done more to push young adults out of the community than any change in ideology, norms, values, or habits of life style. Places like Flatbush, Bensonhurst, and, more recently, Staten Island are simply more affordable. They are also less densely settled, offer more greenery and parks, and in general are more attractive to families just getting started.

The irony of this pattern of development is that the parents and grandparents whom these young adults leave behind are saddled with extraordinarily high rents and mortgages. Their properties retain the high values, however, only as long as the community remains a choice residential location. But with the outmigration of young adults and young families, the community is in danger of losing its desirable reputation. The impact of such a turnabout is bound to be calamitous. In short, structural developments in the Boro Park Jewish community during the past decade have manifested a combination of remarkable growth and enrichment along with a social time-bomb effect. While the cultural development of the community has served, in a very large measure, to cement the ideological and normative bonds between the generations, its structural development threatens, in the very near future, to dissolve the bonds of proximity.

Although the forces of change which haunt the future of the community originate, to a large extent, in its own socio-cultural dynamics, external forces also penetrate into its future. We have already seen in the preceding section of this chapter how the contact between normative demands of the community and the demands of the larger society (along with its attractions) creates problems of deviance. Structural changes in the immediate neighborhood have, at least potentially, an even greater impact on Orthodoxy's future in Boro Park.

The reader will no doubt recall that in our description of the social history of the community we saw that suburban Boro Park emerged in response to the residential needs of upwardly mobile Jews and Italians. Historically the neighborhood has harbored these two communities in just about equal proportions since the 1920s. Other immigrant groups, such as the Irish, Swedes, Poles, etc. constituted much smaller and less visible segments on the fringes of the neighborhood. While Jews and Italians remained socially aloof from one another, each group having a rich intra-communal life of its own, they did live amicably. They shared a great deal: their socio-economic conditions, their similar mobility strivings and achievements, their pride in being able to afford to live in such a choice neighborhood, and their common immigrant European ancestry. Italian mothers trying to raise their sons to be good Catholics, urging them to finish high school and to go to college, could find much in common with their Jewish counterparts as they picked out fruits and vegetables on the open stands along Thirteenth Avenue.

But the shifting demography of the neighborhood during the 1960s was to change this aspect of social structure as well. Just as the Jewish residents who had come to the area in the early decades of the twentieth century moved on to newer suburbs in the sixties, making room for the Jews streaming out of Williamsburg and Crown Heights, so too, their Italian counterparts were heading for greener pastures. But the houses and apartments which they left vacant were not taken over by other Italians. Some were taken over by the newly incoming Jews. But increasing numbers were taken over by Puerto Ricans and other non-white immigrants. The ownership of the housing stock, taken over by speculative businessmen, undoubtedly contributed to this development. Since the incoming non-Jewish residents were largely non-English speaking and poor, their residential areas were left to gradually deteriorate. Thus, in the mid-1970s the Jews of Boro Park find themselves ringed by an ethnically incompatible population who are also significantly poorer, less educated, and vastly different in culture and outlook. We shall have to wait for the census of 1980 to establish the precise figures of growth in this segment of the neighborhood. But the proliferation of *bodegas* (Spanish-American groceries) store-front churches, and graffiti along Thirteenth, Fourteenth, and Fifteenth Avenues on streets numbering in the Forties all impress the casual observer as unmistakable signs of expansion.

The commonalities which had made Jews and Italians familiar to one another simply do not apply to the current neighbors who surround the Jewish community. Hence, Jews feel more beleaguered, indeed, as if they were in a *shtetl* of old. Incidents of conflict, whether it be muggings, robberies, or fistfights between Puerto Rican youths and Jewish youths are on the increase and widely feared. The desecration of synagogues has also created tension in the neighborhood and fear in the Jewish community.

The ironies of structural change now reveal themselves in full detail. Even as the community grew in wealth and cultural vitality, Boro Park Orthodoxy has made it more and more difficult for its young people to continue to remain in the community. Simultaneously, real estate speculators and the shifting tide of demographic change have ringed the Jewish community with incompatible and even hostile neighbors. Even as the Jewish community financed its own urban renewal—thereby making it unaffordable for many of its own young—the housing stock of their new neighbors has deteriorated steadily. The juxtaposition of these twin developments has exacerbated the potential for conflict that already exists between the two communities.

With their young people priced out in increasing numbers, with deteriorating housing stock and hostile neighbors surrounding a community whose most stable and well-to-do residents have sunk literally millions of dollars into housing and institutional construction, it is not at all unimaginable that within a decade Jewish Boro Park will be a community of largely older residents. They will be burdened with high rents and heavy mortgages, living amidst neighbors whom they fear and dislike, longing for their children who have settled elsewhere. This is hardly a new scenario for Jewish communities in the United States.[4]

A Glimpse at a (Brighter) Future

Having lived with the evolution of Boro Park Orthodoxy for twenty years, and having studied it professionally for nearly a decade, it is difficult for me to accept my own prognosis for the future of the community as I have sketched it in the preceding paragraphs. The reader, too, must be puzzled by the incongruity between the robust development of this community's culture and institutions in the recent past and the ominous strains in its social structure which cast such a dark shadow over its future. Is it possible that such rich cultural developments and such active institutions will last no longer than a few decades? Is it possible that a community that has been built up by people whose efforts were strengthened by religious commitments, sustained by economic well-being, and enlightened by education and professional skills, will gradually disintegrate in a few decades?

The answer to these questions is an inescapable "yes and no." The "yes" thrusts itself at us from the previous analysis of the unforeseen and unintended consequences of structural developments in Boro Park and in the Jewish community in particular. It thrusts itself at us also from the history of Jewish communities in other metropolitan neighborhoods—in New York City and elsewhere—where decades of cultural and institutional vitality were eclipsed overnight, so to speak, as a result of structural changes.

The negative answer to those ominous questions requires a bit more faith, a bit more optimism, and a more imaginative reading of the available evidence. Since our pessimistic reading of the future of the community is based primarily on the gradual displacement of young Orthodox Jews from Boro Park, we should remark briefly on where they go, what they take with them, and what ties they retain with the community. In addressing this question we must discount deviants of various types who depart in unchartable directions. Except for religious overconformists who tend to gravitate to communities which are more religiously isolated than Boro Park, such as New Square, Monsey, Mt. Kisco, Lakewood, or *yeshiva* communities elsewhere, other deviants tend to disappear in the wider world of the metropolis. The future of the community, however, rests with the comings and goings of the non-deviants. Their movements are more readily observable and easier to interpret.

For the most part, young adults move out of Boro Park only after they marry. Unless in-laws who live elsewhere have a strong influence on the residential decision of the young couple, the communities which seem to have attracted the greatest number in recent years are Flatbush, Staten Island—the Willowbrook section—and, to a somewhat lesser extent, Bensonhurst. These communities either border Boro Park directly, or are within easy commute over the Verrazano Bridge. The contiguity of the communities which draw young people away from Boro Park proper suggests more than just a geographic relationship. It indicates something of the ties which bind them to the community in which many were born, most were raised, and in which their parents continue to reside. It also points to a continuity of commitment to the lifestyle which has developed in the Boro Park Orthodox milieu during the past couple of decades. One might almost say that the communities that are currently evolving in these neighborhoods, as a result of the outmigration of young Orthodox families from Boro Park, are satellites.

The young who move to these neighborhoods are not rebelling against the Boro Park milieu. They are merely trying to establish their lives at some slight distance from their parents in more affordable and more pleasant surroundings. But the culture they strive to establish in their new communities is an unalloyed Boro Park export. Small *shuls, yeshivas* for small children, and *kosher* food outlets have quickly made their appearance in all of the communities where the young emigres of Boro Park have settled in any appreciable numbers. Transportation services of various kinds tie all of these communities into a common social network with Boro Park. The school buses which ferry children from these communities to Boro Park *yeshivas*, in large numbers throughout the school year, further reinforce the cultural dependence and similarity between Boro Park and its satellites. The attractiveness of shopping in Boro Park, and the extensive visiting which flows between these communities—especially on a Sabbath or holidays—also insures that the bonds of community do not stop at the boundaries of Boro Park per se.

I believe that these observations should permit us to lighten the heavily gray shades with which we portrayed the future of the Orthodox community in Boro Park in the preceding section of this chapter. The development of satellite communities in the orbit of Boro Park Orthodoxy in no way diminishes our analysis of the structural strains in that community. Quite the contrary. It strengthens our gloomy forecast for the future. But the existence of the satellite communities—the continuity of culture and institutions, the close ties between the younger residents of the newer communities and their elders in Boro Park—assures that the communal life which has evolved in Boro Park since the end of World War II will not evaporate into passing history even if Jews should abandon the Boro Park locale. From roots planted in the *shtetl*, branches are already in bloom elsewhere, and new fruits and seeds are not far behind.

Methodology

Unlike surveys, which constitute the core of the sociological literature, studies of communities do not have a simple, well-organized methodology. The researcher invariably works in a complex field and encounters different layers of the social system, to which he must adjust as the work progresses. Particularly where the supposedly objective scientist is a participant in the social world he is studying—as I am—his questions, his perceptions, his adjustments, indeed, his very biography become part of his methodology. Therefore, this appendix will depart somewhat from the conventional methodological treatises which have become such predictable features of the social science literature. As someone who has lived in the Orthodox world all his life, and grew to adulthood in Boro Park, I would be less than candid if I did not include a capsule autobiography as part of a discussion of my methodology.

Autobiography of a Researcher

I immigrated into the Boro Park community at the age of twelve, a refugee from Hungary and its revolution of 1956. We came as a rather bourgeois family: father, a plastics factory manager; mother, a housewife. Both parents were urbanized and urbane, "cultured" by European standards. My younger brother and I were brought up as the scions of a prestigious family in the Budapest Jewish community. Whether our upbringing was based on fact or fiction is of little importance here. What is of importance is that it set the stage for my encounter with Boro Park.

Although we had no family living in the community in the spring of 1957, when we moved in, my parents chose to live in Boro Park because cousins, residing in Crown Heights and in Williamsburg, advised them that it was the community for "modern Orthodox Jews," Jews with a little refinement and money. In those early years we had considerably more of the former than of the latter.

My earliest recollections of this period are of frustration over my inability to speak the languages of the community. I say languages because it was as frustrating not to be able to speak or understand English as it was not to be able to speak or understand Yiddish. All the other boys in the *yeshiva* Toras Emes spoke both languages comfortably. To make matters worse, the *yeshiva's* double curriculum—secular and religious—was taught in both languages. Inability to speak them adequately not only was socially stigmatizing but also threatened academic failure. And academic failure in religious subjects carried the taint of moral failure.

I promised myself that I would master at least one better than my "American" peers or even my teachers. It is startling to think of the resentments that are bred by the inability to articulate. I am sure I was not aware then that my desire for mastery, and the obvious resentment which fueled it, made me very attentive to what people around me were saying, how they were speaking, and what shades of meaning they were conveying. I became particularly sensitive to contrasts or contradictions between what was said and what was meant.

Being "educationally handicapped," I was placed in the third grade with children who were eight years old, even though I was twelve, and soon to be Bar Mitzva. This experience, too, increased my resentment as well as my critical understanding of what my teachers and *rebbis* were teaching. Adults just speak differently to eight-year-olds than they do to twelve-year-olds. Being spoken down to infuriated me. But after my youthful anger (at what I then perceived as so much hypocrisy) wore off, I became curious about the construction of the culture and social world into which I had been dropped.

I was struck by the pride with which some children and adults flaunted their knowledge and performance of the most obscure religious commandments or restrictions. They always seemed to know which bubble gum or ice-cream cone had an impermissible, non-*kosher*, additive. I also noted how cowed others would become when, having purchased one of these delights, they would be informed by their more knowledgable *chaverim*, friends, that they were not only ignorant but were also about to transgress.

I was puzzled by the sense of accomplishment, almost joy, they exuded. Members of the community prided themselves, and continue to pride themselves, on their ability to find ever-new ways to be faithful to the technicalities of the *halacha*, the religious legal system, but contravene its spirit. For example, one may not carry any object from one's house into the public domain on the Sabbath. But if the object is worn as clothing it may, naturally, be carried on one's person. Thus, keys to one's home were fashioned into tie-clips for men or broaches for women. Handkerchiefs became scarves or wristbands. Similarly, one may not turn on electric lights or appliances on the Sabbath or holidays, but they may be activated by a preset electrical timer. Non-*kosher* foods, like bacon, may not be eaten. But imitations, made from soy bean extracts, may be used. One may not mix milk with meat dishes. But after a meat meal, one may serve coffee with a *pareve*, neutral, milk substitute. This—finding functional and aesthetic alternatives to religious restrictions—peculiar strategy of observance, drew my attention to the presence of a dual value system in the community. Insofar as contradictory elements contribute to a given culture, a faithful report on its structure and dynamics is impossible without knowledge of the techniques by which the "insiders" negotiate the multiple tugs of competing norms, values, and symbols in their daily lives. Thus, the purely biographical coincidence of where and how I learned these skills constitutes an inestimably important part of the method of research undergirding this study.

The dual nature of the Orthodox culture kept cropping up in school, in the synagogue, in the youth groups to which I belonged, and in the general atmosphere of the community as a whole. Although all the *yeshivas* I attended had a double curriculum, one for religious studies and one for secular (called, interestingly, "English") studies, the former were officially considered more important than the latter. More hours of the day were spent on *limudei kodesh*, religious studies, than on English, and teachers of the former were considered to have much more authority than teachers of the latter. Yet we were only loosely graded on our religious studies. Especially in high school, we all worried much more about receiving poor grades in English than in *limudei kodesh*. While we were morally bound to "study Torah," we received real homework only in secular subjects. And parents always seemed to be more upset if their children's report cards indicated poor performance in Math, Science, or English, than if the *rebbi* reported one's failure to master some passage in the Talmud. There did not seem to be any terrible sanctions for failure to master religious subjects—although mockery, shame, ridicule, or a cold shoulder may at times seem terrible. On the other hand, failure in English could mean not getting into a college, or not getting a job—ending up as a "bum." Nobody's parents ever feared that he would end up as a "bum" because he did not master *Rashi* or *Tosvos* (two ancient commentators on the Bible and the Talmud). Of course, anyone who mastered both curricula was considered a paragon.

In the synagogue, too, one was expected to master not only the techniques of prayer, its texts and its tunes, but also the social graces of conversation and banter at the appropriate intervals. During some prayers one was not to utter a word. But conversations could be continued through hand and facial gestures. Too careful attention to the actual meaning and spirit of prayers was simply not a normal form of synagogue behavior. Yet levity would also be regarded as an offense against group sentiments. One learned to attend half-seriously to the prayers which were led by a *bal t'fila* (literally, master of prayer, but actually a congregant knowledgable about text and tune), and at the same time continue social conversation with one's friends. It was a conspiracy of inattention—tacit, to be sure. But we all engaged in it, often two or three times a day.

The Sabbath and holidays were spent with friends at the Agudah or Young Israel (the former a more religious youth group for boys only, the latter a less religious co-ed group), or just "hanging out" on Fourteenth Avenue. No matter where we were, our most frequent activity was conversation, and the topic always seemed to be the tension between what was possible in the world at large and what was required by tradition. Would a Jewish astronaut have to say his morning prayers? When? If we keep crossing the International Date Line and never actually live to see a Saturday, would we still have to observe the Sabbath? If one could completely reconstitute milk from chemical ingredients in a laboratory, would the prohibition against mixing meat with dairy dishes still apply?

As we grew older, theoretical questions took on a more personal nature, having to do with relations between the sexes. Because I attended all-boys' *yeshivas*, discussions about girls, much less social contact with them, were officially forbidden. Yet from the age of about fourteen or fifteen, that topic seems to have been our central concern, albeit, in various guises. We suddenly took a serious scholarly interest in passages in the Bible and the Talmud dealing with sexual matters. How soon after his wife's menstrual cycle might a man have sexual contact with her? Could an unmarried woman become ritually pure if she went to a *mikva*? Would she then be allowed to have sexual relations with an unmarried man? What is the prohibition against having sexual relations with an unmarried Gentile girl? What does the *Rambam* (an eleventh century commentator on the Bible) say about oral-genital contact? Why does he even discuss it, if it is considered a perverse act?

Our questions, and the eagerness with which we sought answers, filled endless hours with "intellectual" delights. Later, as we became bold enough to actually meet girls on Fourteenth Avenue or at the Young

Israel, it was frustrating to discover how little those discussions improved our ability to relate to living, flesh-and-blood beings of the opposite sex. We had lots of ideas and designs on them—all quite divinely inspired. We only lacked opportunities. If I hardly had the courage to ask a girl for a date, how could I ask her to go to the *mikva* before it? Eventually, of course, we all mastered the art of dating. But I do not know of a single friend who ever asked his date to go to the *mikva* first, so that he could hold hands with her or kiss her good-night. Somehow, we learned to live with contradictions.

But this report is not simply the author's biography written as sociology. Universally recognized procedures of data collection were employed as well. These are discussed below.

Gathering the Data

The thesis of this study and its corollary propositions required a large variety of evidence. Hence, the methodology had to be rather multifaceted. Statements referring to such objective characteristics of the Boro Park Jewish community as socio-economic status, educational achievement, demographic characteristics, building and real-estate matters, and the like are based on available data.[1] Historical statements about the community and its residents are based on similar data. But the overall scheme of Orthodox Jewish life could be ascertained only through direct contact with individuals. Moreover, since an important aspect of this study is the question of how the community perpetuates itself, an effort was made to uncover the strains as well as the strengths of those relationships which seem central to the structure of the community. For this reason, surveys were conducted among four sub-groups within the community: (1) principals of *yeshivas*, representing the educational institutions of the community, (2) rabbis, representing the religious institutions of the community, (3) families, and (4) young adults, representing that generation which we might expect to be a source of change in the community. These groups were considered the most vital contributors to everyday social life in the community. The questions addressed to each dealt with their encounters with American society at large, and also their encounters with one another.

Sampling Boro Park's Jews

The method by which respondents were selected from among each of the four sub-groups undoubtedly has a strong bearing on the ultimate findings of this research. The following note on sampling is intended to allow the reader to judge its efficacy.

(1) The number of *yeshivas* in Boro Park is not so large as to warrant sampling. All were surveyed. An initial listing of *yeshivas* was obtained from Torah U'Mesorah, the National Society for Hebrew Day Schools.[2] From this listing twenty-seven *yeshivas* were identified as being located in Boro Park.[3] This listing was further checked against the 1972 edition of the Brooklyn Yellow Pages Telephone Directory, and also against the listing of the Maimonides Medical Center.[4] In the process four more *yeshivas* were added to the original list of twenty-seven. A total of thirty-one questionnaires were mailed to the *yeshivas* on October 12, 1972. Six weeks later all of the non-respondents were contacted by telephone. Ultimately, sixteen of the thirty-one questionnaires were returned in a usable form. Several telephone interviews were also obtained, yielding usable information about twenty-one out of the thirty-one *yeshivas*.

An examination of the list of *yeshivas* which failed to respond to the survey did not indicate any systematic bias in our usable sample. Thus, there is no obvious reason to suspect uniform bias in the results.

(2) The Yellow Pages of the telephone directory identify 'Clergymen' as a special category of subscriber. In the 1972 edition of the Brooklyn directory, 1,553 names bearing Jewish surnames were identified within the boundaries of the Boro Park Jewish community.[5] This list of names constituted our sampling frame for the survey of rabbis in the area. Due to limitations of time and budget, only five hundred of these names were selected as the sample that would receive a mailed questionnaire. Between the last week of December 1972 and the first two weeks of January 1973, a total of five hundred questionnaires were mailed out to rabbis. [6] The rate of return on these survey instruments was just over 10 percent. Ultimately, fifty-six of the questionnaires were returned, of which all but three were complete and usable.[7] Since the anonymity of the respondents was thoroughly protected in the design and administration of the survey, it was impossible to follow-up on those who failed to respond. And limited resources did not allow a second mailing to the entire sample.

Bias in results obtained from the survey of Boro Park rabbis due to the manner in which the instrument was administered, rather than the manner in which the sample was selected. Since a 10 percent rate of return for mailed questionnaires is not at all uncommon, there is little reason to suspect any special bias due to the nature of the cases (viz. rabbis) studied.[8]

(3) The families that were interviewed in connection with the present project were also selected from a phone-directory-based sampling frame. Using the *Brooklyn Address Telephone Directory*, all streets—block by block—were assigned a code number. A total of five hundred and four coded street segments were thus produced. From these segments a sample of thirty were selected using a table of random numbers. This phase of the sampling was intended to insure maximum coverage of the geographical area under study. From these randomly selected blocks, corresponding to the block arrangements in the address telephone directory, a list of Jewish surnames was randomly selected. In addition to a table of random numbers, the selection of names was guided by the proportion of Jewish surnames found on particular blocks. In this manner as few as one and as many as ten names were selected from any given block. A list of two hundred names was thus produced.

During the first week of February 1973, an introductory letter was sent to each of the two hundred names on our list, indicating that they should expect to be contacted by telephone in order to set up interview appointments. That letter also included an introduction to the re-searcher and the purposes of the work. Subsequently, undergraduate sociology majors who were enrolled in two sections of a methodology course at Brooklyn College made telephone contact with all the names on the list. There students were instructed to make every effort to obtain an interview appointment with the families or persons on the phone. If a respondent did not refuse outright but merely used polite techniques of delay, students often called back two or three times. In addition, students were instructed that, if the respondent refused to grant a personal interview, as a last resort they should attempt to conduct an *ad hoc* telephone interview.

Through the prodigious effort of my student assistants, fifty-five personal interviews were conducted. In addition, a dozen telephone interviews were obtained. In several cases the respondents requested a mailed questionnaire which they later returned anonymously. It should be pointed out that of the two hundred names selected from the phone directory, not one of those who were ultimately contacted failed to be Jewish. This finding certainly enhances the credibility of using surnames in estimating population size.

Despite an all-out effort to interview the entire sample of two hundred families on our list, we failed to obtain usable responses from nearly two-thirds of the original sample. In an effort to discover whether our results were tainted with any special bias, students were instructed to make *ad hoc* door-to-door visits to those respondents who refused to be interviewed when first contacted by telephone. The intent of these visits was to discover if those who refused to participate had any distingui-shable characteristics in common.

In about 5 percent of the cases, the persons we sought to contact had moved from the given address. The most frequently given reasons for refusal to participate were: (a) "we are not interested in this kind of thing"; and (b) "we do not let strangers into our home." The *ad hoc* visits did yield some useful results insofar as the student interviewers were able to get a look at the person(s) who had refused. With few exceptions, refusers occupied two broad categories, and many were in both. These categories were: (a) the old and infirm, particularly if they lived alone; and (b) the extremely Orthodox or Hasidic, particularly if they did not speak English. Perhaps as many as 15 percent of the refusals, however, did not fit in either category. These were due apparently, to a genuine lack of interest. The interviews were time-consuming, often lasting as long as two hours. Many people were simply not willing to give that much, or any, of their time.

(4) On December 1, 1972 a presumably current mailing list containing the names of two hundred college-age men and women, was obtained from the Intercollegiates of Young Israel, a modern Orthodox youth group of which I once had been a member. During the last two weeks of April 1973, a questionnaire was sent to all two hundred persons on the list. As of May 1973, forty-six complete and usable instruments were returned. The timing of this survey—coming at the time of the school year when college students begin to worry about finals—may have especially aggravated the problem of response rate. So a rate of return of nearly 25 percent—without any follow-up—is encouraging.

A possible source of bias in this survey was the sampling frame itself. Within the context of Boro Park Jewish life, the Young Israel Synagogue represents perhaps the most Americanized and modernized version of Jewish Orthodoxy.[9] And within the Young Israel organization, the Intercollegiates are the most modernized contingent. Hence, it is difficult to argue that the Intercollegiates are representative of the thousands of more conservative Orthodox or Hasidic youth, many of whom may belong to the more religious youth movements, such as the

Agudah.[10] Surprisingly, the attitudes expressed by the majority of the Intercollegiates were not too different from what one might have expected from a more fundamentalist or traditional group. Whatever biases this group might have introduced into the study would have run contrary to the basic thesis of this work.

Survey Research in the Orthodox Jewish Community

Reports on previous research in the Orthodox Jewish community have cautioned against the use of conventional survey techniques in this community. Poll has reported that "because of the members' distrust of any outsiders, I had to be extremely flexible in my approach and techniques. For this reason the more orthodox techniques which might normally be more effective in studies of this kind could not be used at the time."[11] Kranzler, at least by implication, worked under a similar constraint.[12]

My experience, however, seems to indicate that the pattern of response to survey research in this community is not all that much different from what survey researchers have come to expect from the population at large. In those instances where the legitimacy of the researcher was firmly established by means of a cover letter, as was the case in the survey of *yeshiva* principals, the survey of the Intercollegiates,[13] the rate of response was relatively high and the likelihood of sample bias minimal. Similarly, in the case of the survey of families, where an effort was made to contact every single member of the sample, a normally adequate rate of response was obtained.

The survey of rabbis is the only one of our four surveys whose results allow some suspicion of bias. Here, too, one must look to the way in which the survey was administered, rather than to the nature of the sub-population to which it was administered, as an explanation for possible bias in the results.[14] Thus, it may be concluded that systematic survey results constitute an indispensable and reliable source of data in the study of the Orthodox community.

Sociological Research in Boro Park: *Balancing Two Perspectives*

So-called "hard data" indicate the way the Boro Park Jewish community presents itself to an outsider. On the other hand, the argument of this study is that the way this community presents itself in terms of objective criteria does not fully disclose how its members perceive and come to terms with the "outside world." Only some of these perceptions can be tapped by means of the survey instrument, and only some of the coming to terms can be apprehended through systematic questioning and observation. The nuances of cognitive adjustment by which individuals seek, and are able, to integrate successfully a sacred system of values and symbols in the secular world can be apprehended only through what Max Weber called *Verstehen*: an empathetic understanding of the implicit language of the group, its dialect and subtle inflections, and its silences.[15]

Yinger once suggested that the sociologist can "see a stained glass window from the outside."[16] But there is no reason why one should opt for such a limited vision. Hence, this study tried to look through the stained glass window, so to speak, from both sides. The insider's view is much helped by the fact that I lived in the Boro Park community from 1957 through 1967. I had attended some of its *yeshivas*, and belonged to and participated in a number of its youth groups and synagogues. Many of my affiliations with the community have remained intact since, and I have continued to be a frequent participant in communal affairs and concerns. In addition, my professional affiliation with Brooklyn College during the past decade has enabled me to maintain something like an insider's contact with many of the young people who reside in Boro Park and pursue their advanced secular education at the college.

How well I have managed to balance the perspectives of the outsider with those of the insider will have to be decided by the reader.

Notes

Chapter 1

1. For a detailed listing of the myriad rules which govern Orthodox Jewish daily life, see the compilation of Solomon Ganzfried, *Code of Jewish Law*, trans. by Hyman E. Goldin (New York: Hebrew Publishing Co., 1961).

2. Judith R. Kramer and Seymour Leventman, *Children of the Gilded Ghetto: Conflict Resolutions of Three Generations of American Jews* (New Haven: Yale University Press, 1961), p. 11.

3. Ibid.

4. This estimate is based on calculations of the numbers of religiously tax-exempt properties in the area. See *Detailed List of Tax-Exempt Properties of the City of New York* (New York: New York City Tax Commission, 1961, 1972).

5. Temple Emanu-El of Boro Park (Conservative) was organized in 1904. The Boro Park Progressive Synagogue (Reform) was also organized sometime during the first or second decade of this century.

6. Isaac Metzger, ed., *A Bintel Brief: "A Bundle of Letters" to the Jewish Daily Forward* (New York: Doubleday, 1971).

7. Howard Polsky, "The Great Defense: A Study of Jewish Orthodoxy in Milwaukee" (University of Wisconsin, unpub. Ph.D. diss., 1956); George Kranzler, *Williamsburg: A Jewish Community in Transition* (New York: Philipp Feldheim, 1961); Solomon Poll, *The Hasidic Community of Williamsburg: A Study in the Sociology of Religion* (New York: Schocken, 1962); Charles S. Liebman, "Orthodoxy in American Jewish Life," in *The American Jewish Yearbook* (New York: American Jewish Committee, 1965); Samuel C. Heilman, *Synagogue Life* (Chicago: University of Chicago Press, 1976).

8. Marshall Sklare, *Conservative Judaism: An American Religious Movement* (New York: Schocken, 1955, 1972), p. 43.

9. Ibid., p. 75.

10. See his chapter "Recent Developments in Conservative Judaism" in the second and augmented edition of *Conservative Judaism* (1972).

11. Marshall Sklare, *America's Jews* (New York: Random House, 1971).

12. Herbert J. Gans, "The Future of American Jewry," *Commentary* 21 (June 1956): 555.

13. The work of Will Herberg, Nathan Glazer, Judith Kramer and Seymour Leventman, and Milton and Albert Gordon are among the more prominent in this area.

14. Sidney Goldstein and Calvin Goldscheider, *Jewish Americans: Three Generations in a Jewish Community* (Englewood Cliffs: Prentice Hall, 1968).

15. Louis Wirth, *The Ghetto* (Chicago: University of Chicago Press, 1928); Seymour

Leventman, "From Shtetl to Suburb," in *The Ghetto and Beyond*, ed. Peter I. Rose (New York: Random House, 1969).

16. Arthur J. Vidich and Joseph Bensman, *Small Town in Mass Society: Class, Power and Religion in a Rual Community* (New York: Doubleday, 1959), pp. ix–x.

17. Fred Massarik, "The Jewish Community," *in Community Structure and Analysis*, ed. Marvin B. Sussman. (New York: T. Y. Crowell, 1959).

18. This characterization and its consequences for the survival of Jewish communities in urban areas has most recently been the subject of the work of Yona Ginsberg, *Jews in a Changing Neighborhood: A Study of Mattapan* (New York: Free Press, 1975).

19. Massarik, "The Jewish Community," p. 250.

20. Marshall Sklare and Joseph Greenblum, *Jewish Identity on the Suburban Frontier* (New York: Basic Books, 1967), p. 44.

21. H. Laurence Ross, "The Local Community: A Survey Approach," in *Neighborhood, City, and Metropolis: An Integrated Reader in Urban Sociology*, ed. Robert Gutman and David Popenoe (New York: Random House, 1970); Peter H. Mann, "The Neighborhood," in *Neighborhood, City and Metropolis*, ed. Gutman and Popenoe; Eugene Litwak, "Voluntary Associations and Neighborhood Cohesion," in *Neighborhood, City, and Metropolis*, ed. Gutman and Popenoe.

22. Gans, "Future of American Jewry," p. 428.

23. Will Herberg, *Protestant-Catholic-Jew: An Essay in American Religious Sociology* (New York: Doubleday, 1955).

24. Nathan Glazer, *American Judaism* (Chicago: University of Chicago Press, 1957), p. 109.

25. Sklare, *Conservative Judaism*, p. 133.

26. Leventman, "From Shtetl to Suburb," p. 34.

27. Stuart E. Rosenberg, *The Search for Jewish Identity in America* (New York: Doubleday, 1965).

28. Sklare and Greenblum, *Jewish Identity on the Suburban Frontier*.

29. Major expositions on this theme are the works of Harvey Cox, *The Secular City* (New York: Macmillan, 1967), and Peter L. Berger, *The Sacred Canopy: Elements of a Sociological Theory of Religion* (New York: Doubleday, 1967).

30. Robert Alter, "A Fever of Ethnicity," *Commentary*, vol. 53 (June 1972); Andrew M. Greenley, *Unsecular Man: The Persistence of Religion* (New York: Delta, 1972).

31. Sklare, *Conservative Judaism*, p. 25.

32. Mervin F. Verbit, "Referents for Religion Among Jewish College Students" (Columbia University, unpub. Ph.D. diss., 1968).

33. Leon Festinger, *A Theory of Cognitive Dissonance* (Evanston, Ill.: Row & Peterson, 1957). To be sure, there are other theories of dissonance besides that of Festinger. But his work on the subject has achieved the greatest popularity in recent years.

34. Ibid., p. 260.

35. The phrase "cognitive minority" was coined by Peter L. Berger in his work *The Sacred Canopy*. It refers to the social psychological status of "those who continue to adhere to the world as defined by religious traditions [amidst a secular society]" (p. 152).

36. Goldstein and Goldscheider, *Jewish Americans*, p. 8.

37. Anton C. Zijderveld, *The Abstract Society: A Cultural Analysis of Our Time* (New York: Doubleday, 1960), pp. 70–72. For a more popular exposition, see Alvin Toffler, *Future Shock* (New York: Bantam, 1970).

38. In the present context the absence of cultural integration refers to a lack of any distinctly American norms which could challenge the legitimacy of the particular beliefs or rituals of any recognized religious system. The apparent resurgence and growing popularity of obscure and even bizzare ideas and practices (e.g., Black magic, Eastern Mysticism, charismatic Catholicism and neo-Pentecostalism) on what was earlier thought to be religiously arid terrain all attest to the capacity of modern American culture to accept diversity. It is quite likely that people who join one of the many cognitive minorities which dot the contemporary American landscape may no longer experience cognitive dissonance as a result.

39. Anton C. Zijderveld, *The Abstract Society: A Cultural Analysis of Our Time* (New York: Doubleday, 1970).

40. Ibid., p. 57.

41. Zijderveld, *Abstract Society* p. 81.

42. Ibid., p. 93.

43. Karl Mannheim, *Man and Society in an Age of Reconstruction* (New York: Harcourt, 1940), see especially his discussion of "functional" versus "substantive" rationality; Herbert Marcuse, *One Dimensional Man* (Boston: Beacon, 1964); Jurgen Habermas, *Toward a Rational Society: Student Protest, Science and Politics*, trans. Jeremy Shapiro (Boston: Beacon, 1971); Daniel Bell, *The End of Ideology: On the Exhaustion of Political Ideas in the Fifties* (New York: Free Press, 1961); Amitai Etzioni, *The Active Society* (New York: Free Press, 1968).

44. Etzioni, *Active Society*, p. vii.

45. It may be objected that these groups have always been in tension with a rationalizing technological society, but this objection can be easily met. The family and the community have been in tension with modern society to the extent that they called upon those resources of the individual which the rationalizing society sought to mobilize. A religious community calls upon resources of its individuals which are no longer required in an abstract society.

46. Berger and Luckmann, *Social Construction of Reality*, p. 108.

47. For a general overview of the resurgence of Orthodoxy in America see Egon Mayer and Chaim I. Waxman, "Modern Jewish Orthodoxy in America: Toward the Year 2000," *Tradition* 16 (Spring 1977): 98–117.

Chapter 2

1. Seymour Leventman, "From Shtetl to Suburb," in *The Ghetto and Beyond*, ed. Peter I. Rose (New York: Random House, 1969), p. 340.

2. Henry R. Stiles, *A History of the City of Brooklyn* (Brooklyn, N.Y.: H. R. Stiles, 1867), p. 43.

3. Lou Gody, ed., *New York City Guide* (New York: Random House, 1938), p. 470.

4. Rebecca B. Bang, *Reminiscences of Old New Utrecht and Gowanus* (Brooklyn, N.Y.: Mrs. R. B. Bang, 1912), p. 19.

5. *The Brooklyn Eagle*, October 13, 1964.

6. Stiles, *History of Brooklyn*, 3: 820–860.

7. Kehilla of New York City, *The Jewish Communal Register of New York City, 1917–1918* (New York, 1919), p. 122.

8. *The Brooklyn Eagle*, January 5, 1947; *Scrapbooks* 76: 16. There are two ways to spell

the name of the community. We have chosen to call it "Boro" Park because that is the way it is known by the people who live there.

9. Long Island Historical Society, *Scrapbooks* (Brooklyn, N.Y.) 53: 30; 126: 6, 72; 128: 82; 129: 171.

10. Long Island Historical Society, *Scrapbooks*.

11. *Scrapbooks* 94: 153–154.

12. Michael Gold, *Jews Without Money* (New York: Horace Liveright, 1930), pp. 155–156.

13. Ibid., p. 158.

14. Accounts such as this one are transcribed from taped interviews with our respondents. Names are disguised to protect confidentiality.

15. Moses Rischin, *The Promised City: New York's Jews, 1870–1914* (Cambridge: Harvard University Press, 1962), p. 93.

16. Kehilla of New York City, *Jewish Communal Register,* p.86; Morris Horowitz and Lawrence Kaplan, *Estimated Jewish Population of the New York Area, 1900–1975* (New York: Federation of Jewish Philanthropies, 1959), p. 233.

17. The subject of this interview gave special emphasis to the last sentence, indicating her appreciation of the community.

18. Sidney Goldstein and Calvin Goldscheider, *Jewish Americans: Three Generations in a Jewish Community* (Englewood Cliffs, N.J.; Prentice-Hall, 1968), p. 8.

19. Kehilla of New York City, *Jewish Communal Register,* "List of Congregations in Brooklyn, Queens, and Richmond."

20. Ibid., p. 366.

21. Samuel P. Abelow, *History of Brooklyn Jewry* (Brooklyn, N.Y.: Scheba Publishing Co., 1937), pp. 218–222, 326–327.

22. The boundaries used in the *Communal Register* to define the community are considerably more extensive than the boundaries which have been defined in this study.

23. Today the proportions may be quite the reverse. Makeshift quarters, however, may no longer be associated with lower social class.

24. This term originates from the German *shtube*, meaning "room." In Yiddish it refers to a room or several rooms in a house or store-front used for prayer, study, and general meetings of the membership. It was, and is, typically, an array of tables, desks, and chairs which are arranged *ad hoc* to suit the immediate purposes.

25. This observation about dress codes is based on a personal communication from Rabbi Israel Schorr, who has been serving Temple Beth El, one of the largest Orthodox synagogues in the area, for the past thirty-five years.

26. Rabbi Schorr also indicated that, during its early history, leadership was never interested in attracting the *arbeiter yidden* (working-class Jews). Membership requirements ensured a relatively affluent clientele: Jews in business and the professions.

27. Officers and clergy should be able to boast of business success or academic and professional degrees and achievements.

28. Two exceptions to this generalization are the Hebrew Institute of Boro Park, an elementary school for boys founded in 1917, and the Shulamith School for Girls, founded in 1928. Both were all-day *yeshiva* schools in which religious instruction was given in the morning and secular instruction in the afternoon.

29. Emma Lazarus, "The New Colossus," in *Poems* (Boston: Houghton Mifflin, 1889).

30. Covering one's head at all times is a principal way of identifying oneself as an Orthodox Jewish male.

31. The details of this argument are treated more fully in Chapter 1.

32. George Kranzler, *Williamsburg: A Jewish Community in Transition* (New York: Philipp Feldheim, 1961), pp. 34–37.

33. This assumption is based on the previous age profile in conjunction with the history of immigration into the U.S.

34. Community Council of Greater New York, "Population Characteristics" (mimeo.; New York, 1961), p. 88.

35. Ibid., pp. 91–92.

36. Kranzler, *Williamsburg*, p. 37.

37. *New York Times*, March 6, 1972, p. 22.

38. Kranzler, *Williamsburg*, p. 206–210.

39. Ibid., p. 210.

40. Kranzler, *Williamsburg*, p. 210. Hasidic leaders take on titles which derive from the name of the town from which they originate. Thus the Skvirer 'rebbe' takes his dynastic name from the town of Skvir. Interestingly, when he and his followers moved to a closed community in Rockland County, N.Y., they named it the Town of New Square.

41. Ibid.

42. Israel Rubin, *Satmar: An Island in the City* (Chicago: Quadrangle, 1972). This is a detailed, though not very original, account of the Szatmarer group.

43. An important exception to this statement is the Lubavitcher community whose headquarters are in the heart of the Crown Heights community. Cf. Michael Cohn, *Crown Heights and Williamsburg* (Brooklyn, N.Y.: The Brooklyn Children's Museum, Cultural Anthropology Workshop, 1964); Sydelle B. Levy, "Shifting Patterns of Ethnic Identification Among the Hasidim," in *The New Ethnicity: Perspectives From Ethnology*, ed. John Bennett (New York: West Publishing, 1975).

44. One sign of this growth is the establishment of the Association of Orthodox Jewish Teachers in October 1963. The headquarters of the group was, and is, in Boro Park. It focused its efforts on the protection of the interests of Orthodox Jews working for the New York City Public Schools.

45. Peter L. Berger and Richard J. Neuhaus, *Movement and Revolution* (New York: Doubleday, 1970), p. 130.

46. Nathan Glazer and Daniel P. Moynihan, *Beyond the Melting Pot: The Negroes, Puerto Ricans, Jews, Italians, and Irish of New York City* 2nd ed.; (Cambridge, Mass.: M.I.T. Press, 1970), p. xix and tables.

47. Ibid., pp. 67–76.

48. Specific elements of this effort were the Civil Rights Act of 1964, the Voting Rights Act of 1965, and the Civil Rights Bill of 1968.

49. The establishment of the Office of Economic Opportunity (OEO) and the Department of Housing and Urban Development (HUD) were the most significant elements of federal assistance. Of more temporary but provocative significance was the involvement, for example, of the Ford Foundation in the educational experiments of Ocean-Hill–Brownsville during the mid-to-late sixties.

50. Ben J. Wattenberg and Richard Scammon, "Black Progress and Liberal Rhetoric," *Commentary* 55 (June 1973): 4.

51. Open admissions programs at colleges and universities and affirmative action programs in hiring practices of both the public and private sector have had a most significant impact on the expectations of non-colored minorities.

52. For a brief survey of the scope of this "spirit of movement" during the 1960s, see "Violence in America," in *Encyclopedic Almanac, 1971* (New York: The New York Times, 1971).

53. The JDL was founded in 1968 in New York City. Its battle cry—NEVER AGAIN!—capitalized on the feelings of many Jews that they have experienced enough injustice.

54. COLPA was founded in 1965 and focused primarily on the protection of the civil rights of Orthodox Jews who have found themselves discriminated against due to their religious observances. For example, COLPA regularly defends persons whose jobs are threatened because they will not work on the Sabbath or Jewish holidays, or who are socially discriminated against because of their Orthodox practices.

55. Glazer & Moynihan, *Beyond the Melting Pot*, pp. xxviii–xxix.

57. *New York Times*, April 10, 1972, p. 22.

58. Just one year earlier, Israel had been engaged in the Six-Day War. That event, especially the great danger it posed for Israel and her near-miraculous victory, loomed large in the consciousness of the Jewish community—and, as of Spring 1973, continued to be a source of inspiration. The Yom Kipur War, in Fall 1973, had a far less buoyant effect on the consciousness of the community. But it, too, added to the community's assertiveness in defense of its security, as we shall see below.

59. Both P.S. 103 and P.S. 164 have been turned over almost entirely to *yeshivas* during the past five years. The sections of the buildings which have not been turned over are mostly filled by students who are bused into the neighborhood.

60. These statements are not direct quotes, but a composite of statements voiced by a large number of respondents.

61. These percentages are based on a total of forty-four respondents.

62. Spearheading the Nixon campaign in Boro Park was Rabbi Ronald Greenwald, formerly of Torah U'Mesorah, an umbrella organization for Jewish day schools. He subsequently moved to a position with the U.S. Department of Health, Education and Welfare, and has since continued his liaison work with various branches of the government on behalf of the Orthodox community.

63. Professor Marvin Schick's column, "In the City," appeared regularly in *The Jewish Press* from around 1967 to 1977.

64. *The Jewish Press*, May 25, 1973, p. 24. The general fear of crime, along with the increase in the Puerto Rican population at the periphery of the Boro Park community, have led to active involvement of Orthodox residents in the Auxiliary Police Force and voluntary patrols. For an earlier account of community reactions to crime and its control in the neighborhood, see *The Jewish Press*, April 27, 1973, p. 2. Community Planning Boards were established by the Lindsay administration in 1967. Their goal was to permit local groups a greater voice and participation in managing the affairs of their communities. The Jewish community of Boro Park is part of Planning Board No. 12 and has several representatives sitting on the board. Thus far the community has successfully resisted pressures that have plagued other communities in New York City, such as pressure to construct low-income housing in the area, or to establish public facilities which would serve noncommunity clientele.

65. The Maimonides Mental Health Center was established with federal money during the mid-sixties. Initial resistance of Orthodox Jews has been giving way to greater utilization of, and interest in, the services of the organization as well as its management.

Chapter 3

1. H. Laurence Ross, "The Local Community: A Survey Approach," in *Neighborhood, City, and Metropolis,* ed. Robert Gutman and David Popenoe (New York: Random House, 1970), pp. 557–568.

2. The presence of *shared meanings* as a criterion of community may be found in the works of Durkheim, Tonnies, Nisbet; also, from a different point of departure, in the works of Mead, Schutz, Berger and Luckmann.

3. Eugene J. Webb et al., *Unobtrusive Measures: Nonreactive Research in the Social Sciences* (Chicago: Rand McNally, 1966).

4. New York Telephone Co., *The Brooklyn Street Address Directory* (New York, March 1972).

5. A verified list of "Distinctive Jewish Surnames" was obtained from Mr. Alvin Chenkin, Research Consultant to the Council of Jewish Federations and Welfare Funds, Inc. The sample obtained on the basis of this list revealed no errors.

6. Ben Greenberg, "The Jewish Poverty Survey," *The Jewish Press*, August 24, 1973, p. 14.

7. Much of the data reported in the remainder of this chapter are taken from the 1970 U.S. Census. Where possible, I have tried to update them with less official but more current estimates.

8. Liebman, "Orthodoxy in American Jewish Life," *American Jewish Yearbook* (New York: American Jewish Committee, 1965), p. 22.

9. Ibid., pp. 23–25.

10. Robert Gutman, "Non-Conventional Methods of Obtaining Data on the Religious Composition of the U.S. Population: The Case of Jewish Population Statistics," (Belgrade, Yugoslavia: United Nations World Population Conference, 1965).

11. "Characteristics of Housing Units and Population by Blocks, 1970" in *1970 Census of Population and Housing* (Washington, D.C.: U.S. Department of Commerce, Bureau of Census, 1970), table 2.

12. Horowitz and Kaplan, *Estimated Jewish Population of the New York Area, 1900–1975* (New York: Federation of Jewish Philanthropies, 1959).

13. New York City Planning Commission, *The Plan for the City of New York*, 3 (New York: Department of City Planning, 1969): 131.

14. Community Council of Greater New York, "Population Characteristics" (mimeo; New York, 1961), p. 91.

15. One particular informant who has lived in Boro Park since 1913 furnished literally dozens of exemplary cases from her recollections to make this point. No contradictory reports were encountered.

16. The family survey we conducted bears this out.

17. "Percentage of Families at Seven Income Levels," *New York Times*, July 17, 1972, p. 1: also see *Statistical Abstracts* (93rd ed.; Washington, D.C.: U.S. Dept. of Commerce, 1972).

18. This figure actually exceeds the median income reported for all American Jewish households in 1970 by the National Jewish Population study. That figure was $12,630. See

Demographic Highlights of the National Jewish Population Study (New York Council of Jewish Federations and Welfare Funds, 1973).

19. Marshall Sklare, *America's Jews* (New York: Random House, 1971), p. 60ff.

20. All of these figures compare favorably with educational patterns of American Jewry as a whole; see *Demographic Highlights*, p. 18.

21. The theme of the Holocaust emerged in nearly every interview, particularly as an explanation for the need for a tight-knit and strong Jewish community like Boro Park.

22. Liebman, "Orthodoxy," p. 22.

23. Israel Grama, "From Yemen to Boro Park," *Jewish Life* 33: 4 (March/April 1966).

24. Ibid., pp. 37–38.

Chapter 4

1. Deut. 5: 12–14.

2. Lev. 11.

3. Phrased this way, the question cannot be answered without a lengthy historical dissertation that would exceed the scope of this study. Here we will be less concerned with the historical reason than with the social, and possibly psychological, consequences.

4. Joseph Kaminetsky, "Boro Park," *Jewish Life*, 21:1 (September-October 1953): 22–23.

5. A simple but useful text on these rules and their meanings is Isidore Grunfeld, *The Sabbath: A Guide to its Understanding and Observance* (New York: Philipp Feldheim, 1959).

6. The rules concerning carrying and lighting fire or electricity are somewhat modified during different holidays.

7. Max Weber, *The Sociology of Religion*, trans. Ephraim Fischoff (Boston: Beacon, 1963), p. 254.

8. The popularity of *kosher*-style foods with otherwise non-Orthodox Jews is an interesting, at times amusing, indication of the affective dimension of the *kashrus* laws.

9. Some businessmen who make extended trips abroad take along all necessary edibles as a matter of course.

10. The rules concerning hot and cold foods and utensils form a part of the complex rules of *kashrus*.

11. Sidney Goldstein and Calvin Goldscheider, *Jewish Americans: Three Generations in a Jewish Community* (Englewood Cliffs, N.J.: Prentice-Hall, 1968), pp. 201–204.

12. Ibid.; also Marshall Sklare, *Not Quite at Home* (New York: American Jewish Committee, 1969), pp. 11–22.

13. *The Authorized Daily Prayer Book*, trans. Dr. Rabbi Joseph H. Hertz (New York: Bloch, 1965), pp. 748–749.

14. Solomon Poll, *The Hasidic Community of Williamsburg: A Study in the Sociology of Religion* (New York: Schocken, 1969); also Israel Rubin, *Satmar: An Island in the City* (Chicago: Quadrangle, 1972).

15. Seymour Leventman, "From Shtetl to Suburb," in *The Ghetto and Beyond: Essays on Jewish Life in America*, ed. Peter I. Rose (New York: Random House, 1969), pp. 51–52.

16. This report is from a long-time resident in the community whose father had founded one of the earliest *shuls* in the area.

17. I. B. Singer, "The Extreme Jews," *Harper's* (April 1967), p. 56.

18. Singer, "Extreme Jews," p. 57; Poll, *Hasidic Community*.

19. Judith R. Kramer and Seymour Leventman, *Children of the Gilded Ghetto: Conflict Resolutions of Three Generations of American Jews* (New Haven: Yale University Press, 1961), p. 55.

20. George Kranzler, *Williamsburg: A Jewish Community in Transition* (New York: Philipp Feldheim, 1961), p. 207.

21. "Orthodox Fashions," *The Jewish Press*, June 22, 1973.

22. Louis Wirth, *The Ghetto* (Chicago: University of Chicago Press, 1928), p. 37.

23. Judith Kramer, *The American Minority Community* (New York: T. Y. Crowell Co., 1970), p. 68.

24. Kranzler, *Williamsburg*, pp. 110–111; Poll, *Hasidic Community*, ch. 7.

25. Milton M. Gordon, *Assimilation in American Life: The Role of Race, Religion and National Origins* (New York: Oxford University Press, 1964), p. 186.

26. Ibid., p. 190.

27. Kranzler, *Williamsburg*, p. 111.

28. Poll, *Hasidic Community*, p. 117.

29. Household conveniences, day-care centers for children, and a large number of *kosher* take-home food facilities in the Boro Park community have helped to modernize the role of the Orthodox woman to a surprisingly great extent.

30. George Vecsey, "Confronting Crisis in the Orthodox Jewish Family," *The New York Times*, Feb. 3, 1978, p. A14; see also "Family Collapse Spreads to Orthodox Ranks," in *The Jewish Week*, Feb. 5, 1978, p. 17.

31. Mark Zborowski and Elizabeth Herzog, *Life Is with People: The Culture of the Shtetl* (New York: Schocken, 1962), p. 78.

32. Kramer, *American Minority*, p. 68.

33. Jerome E. Carlin and Saul H. Mendlovitz, "The American Rabbi: A Religious Specialist Responds to a Loss of Authority," in Marshall Sklare, *The Jews: Social Patterns of an American Group* (New York: Free Press, 1958), p. 378.

34. Poll, *Hasidic Community*, p. 53.

35. Oscar Handlin, *The Uprooted* (1st ed.; Boston: Little, Brown, 1951), p. 254.

36. Hutchins Hapgood, *The Spirit of the Ghetto* (New York: Schocken, 1966), with notes by Harry Golden, pp. 30–33.

37. Carlin and Mendlovitz, "The American Rabbi," p. 377.

38. Leventman, "From Shtetl to Suburb," p. 52.

39. The importance of tradition in the curriculum of the Orthodox *yeshiva* must not be underestimated. See Joseph Kaminetsky, *Hebrew Day School Education: An Overview* (New York: Torah U'Mesorah, 1970), pp. 2–60. The point being argued here is that the very context within which tradition is imparted to the next generation has been rationalized, thus leading to a change in the nature of legitimacy.

40. Tamotsu Shibutani and Kian M. Kwan, *Ethnic Stratification* (New York: Macmillan, 1965), p. 288.

41. An examination of the choices of "majors" in Brooklyn College reveals that the most popular choices of Orthodox students are accounting, pre-law, engineering, and mathematics, and, for the women, education. These courses are expected to lead them into respectable and financially rewarding careers, and can thus be legitimated as

"accessory knowledge." Cf. Menachem Greenberg, "The Yeshiva World's Outlook on Torah and Secular Studies," *The Jewish Observer*, 6, no. 4 (December 1969): 11–14.

Chapter 5

1. Marshall Sklare, *America's Jews* (New York: Random House, 1971), p. 85. Surprisingly, Israel Rubin makes similar observations about the Hasidic family in his *Satmar: An Island in the City* (Chicago: Quadrangle, 1972), p. 107.

2. Solomon Poll, *The Hasidic Community of Williamsburg* (New York: Schocken 1969), p. 52.

3. Stanley Brav, ed., *Marriage and the Jewish Tradition* (New York: Philosophical Library, 1951), p. 88; also Ben Schlesinger, "The Jewish Family in Retrospect," in his *The Jewish Family: A Survey and Annotated Bibliography* (Toronto: University of Toronto Press, 1971), and Samuel Glasner, "Family Religion as a Matrix of Personal Growth," *Marriage and Family Living*, vol. 22 (August 1961).

4. Daniel Bell, "The Breakup of Family Capitalism," in *The Study of Society*, ed. Peter I. Rose (New York: Random House, 1967), pp. 565–570.

5. The New York Times, *Encyclopedic Almanac, 1971* (New York: New York Times, 1970), p. 399.

6. Rubin, *Satmar*, p. 125.

7. The pattern of the second generation in Boro Park, as far as occupations or careers are concerned, should be contrasted with the findings of Kramer and Leventman: "members of the second generation . . . continued to be located in the same area of the economy as their fathers . . . wholesale distribution, light manufacturing, and trucking. Real estate, construction, and investments . . ." *(Children of the Gilded Ghetto* [New Haven: Yale University Press, 1961], p. 52).

8. According to social workers at the local Jewish Family Service, "mistakes" do occur, and are often followed by divorce. Statistics are unavailable. See also "Divorce Overwhelming Even Orthodox, Rabbis Warned at Convention," *The Jewish Week*, Feb. 5, 1977, p. 4.

9. "Singles Who Shun the 'Rat Race' Prospering the Matchmakers," *The Jewish Week*, August 7–20, 1977, p. 10.

10. Sklare, *America's Jews*, pp. 76–77.

11. For an historical background to this controversy see Heinrich Graetz, *History of the Jews*, V (Philadelphia: The Jewish Publication Society, 1956): 274–294.

12. Morris Horowitz and L. Kaplan, *Estimated Jewish Population in the New York Area, 1900–1975* (New York: Federation of Jewish Philanthropies, 1959), and compare with our population estimates in Chapter 3 above.

13. Sklare, *America's Jews*, pp. 122–126.

14. Ibid., p. 127.

15. The much lamented disaffection of the young from the Conservative and Reform movements makes any statement about the survival of these movements overly optimistic.

16. Alfred Schutz, "Making Music Together," in his *Collected Papers*, II (The Hague: Martinus Nijhoff, 1964): pp. 170–173; see also Samuel C. Heilman, *Synagogue Life: A Study in Symbolic Interaction* (Chicago: University of Chicago Press, 1976).

17. Unlike in Eastern Europe, congregations do not have legally recognized juris-diction over their members; see Daniel J. Elazar, "The Legal Status of the American Jewish Community," *American Jewish Yearbook* (New York: American Jewish Com-mittee, 1972). On maintaining ethnic self-consciousness, see Marshall Sklare, "The Desire for Survival," in *The Study of Society*, ed. Peter I. Rose (New York: Random House, 1967).

18. *The Jewish Journal*, January 5, 1973, p. 21.

19. Alvin I. Schiff, *The Jewish Day School in America* (New York: Jewish Educational Committee, 1966), p. 48.

20. David Cole, "A Survey of Public and Parochial Schools Serving the Catchment Area of the Maimonides Community Mental Health Center," (mimeo.; Brooklyn, N.Y.: Research Unit of the Maimonides Community Mental Health Center, 1971).

21. All local observers concede that growth has occurred. In recent years, however, no systematic survey has been done to update specific figures. The Council of Jewish Organizations published a figure of 13,000 students in forty-one schools as of September 1978.

22. Solomon Poll, *The Hasidic Community of Williamsburg: A Study in the Sociology of Religion* (New York: Schocken, 1969), p. 73.

23. Joseph Elias, "The Hebrew and the General Studies Departments," in *Hebrew Day School Education: An Overview,* ed. Joseph Kaminetsky (New York: Torah U'Mesorah, 1970), p. 222.

24. Ibid., p. 224.

25. Ibid., pp. 225–226.

26. Rabbi Moses D. Tendler, "Science in the Day School Curriculum," in *Hebrew Day School,* ed. Kaminetsky, pp. 229–233.

27. A decision of the Supreme Court in the summer of 1973 has endangered some forms of governmental aid to *yeshivas*. Nevertheless, these schools still receive some financial assistance from governmental sources for their public functions.

28. Alvin Schiff, *Jewish Day School,* pp. 145–148 and tables 15 and 16.

29. "Yeshiva H.S. Seniors Are Regents Scholars," *Brooklyn Jewish Journal,* February 9, 1973, p. 18.

30. Immanuel Jakobovits, "The Strengths of the Yeshiva Movement," in *Hebrew Day School,* ed. Kaminetsky, pp. 86–87.

31. Samuel N. Eisenstadt, "Archetypal Patterns of Youth," in *The Challenge of Youth,* ed. Erik H. Erikson (New York: Doubleday, 1965), p. 38.

32. 3:7. Malachi was one of the twelve so-called minor prophets. He lived during the fifth century B.C.

33. Edward Bloustein, "Parents and Children of the Counter-Culture," *Hadassah Magazine,* vol. 52 no. 2 (October 1971).

34. Charles S. Liebman, "Orthodoxy in American Jewish Life," in *American Jewish Yearbook* (New York: American Jewish Committee, 1965), pp. 58–61.

35. Ibid., p. 59.

36. George Kranzler, *Williamsburg: A Jewish Community in Transition* (New York: Philipp Feldheim, 1961), p. 246.

37. Liebman, "Orthodoxy," p. 77.

38. Both the Young Israel and the Agudah occupy their own permanent buildings, which are well-equipped for the kinds of activities they normally sponsor.

39. Martha Wolfenstein, "The Emergence of Fun Morality," in *Mass Leisure*, ed. E. Larrabee and R. Meyerson (Glencoe, Ill.: Free Press, 1958).

40. According to Orthodox Jewish dogma, all time not devoted to procuring the necessities of livelihood must be devoted to learning Torah and meditating over sacred literature.

41. Marshall Sklare, *America's Jews* (New York: Random House, 1971), p. 106.

42. The long-standing debate between the leaders of Jewish Orthodoxy and secular Jewish leaders about government aid to *yeshivas* is a paradigmatic expression of the difference in attitudes towards extracommunal assistance. The early immigrants and their native-born off-spring took pride in being "self-made." The immigrants of the post-war era take pride in knowing how to "work the system."

43. "OEO gives $198,542 to N.Y. Jewish Poor," *The Jewish Press*, August 31, 1973, p. 3.

44. "465 Teenagers in Summer Projects," *The Jewish Press*, August 31, 1973, p. 35.

45. Delbert C. Miller, *Handbook of Research Design and Social Measurement*, 2nd ed., (New York: McKay, 1970), pp. 318–320.

46. "Boro Park Tenants Council Gets Underway" *Jewish Journal*, January 28, 1972, p. 8.

Chapter 6

1. Irving Howe, *World of Our Fathers* (New York: Simon and Schuster, 1976), p. 11–13.

2. Tom Wolfe, "Me," *New York*, Aug. 23, 1976, p. 26.

3. While most American-born Orthodox in Boro Park complete the childbearing stage of their life cycle by their mid- to late thirties, many post-war immigrants who had survived the Holocaust (and possibly lost their first families in the war) continued to have children until much later.

4. See Yona Ginsberg, *Jews in a Changing Neighborhood: A Study of Mattapan* (New York: Free Press, 1975).

Appendix

1. For a discussion of the uses of available data see Matilda W. Riley, *Sociological Research Vol. I* (New York: Harcourt, Brace & World, 1963), pp. 194–256.

2. Cf. *Directory of Day Schools in the United States and Canada, 1971–1972* (New York: Torah U'Mesorah, 1972).

3. The geographical definition of the community used for this and all further purposes will be the same as was indicated in Chapter 1.

4. David Cole, "A Survey of Public and Parochial Schools Serving the Catchment Area of the Maimonides Community Mental Center for 1970–1971" (mimeo.; Brooklyn, N.Y.: Research Unit of the Maimonides Community Mental Health Center, 1971).

5. The use of the Yellow Pages for the purposes of sampling this segment of the population was reported on by Hart M. Nelson et. al., "Ministerial Roles and Social

Activist Stances: Protestant Clergy Protest in the Sixties," *American Sociological Review* 38 (June 1973): 375–386.

6. Prior to mailing out the questionnaire, the instrument was pre-tested in personal interviews with a dozen rabbis who were selected as a qualitative non-probability sample.

7. Though this rate of return was meager, it was hardly surprising in light of what is generally known about mail-out questionnaires without follow-up. Cf. Riley, *Sociological Research Vol. I*, p. 190; see also Donald P. Warwick and Charles A. Lininger, *The Sample Survey* (New York: McGraw-Hill, 1975), p. 131.

8. Warwick and Lininger, *The Sample Survey*, pp. 130–131.

9. For a discussion of the Young Israel movement see Charles S. Liebman, "Orthodoxy in American Jewish Life," *American Jewish Yearbook* (New York: American Jewish Committee, 1965), pp. 58–61; also Bertram Leff, "The Modern Orthodox Jew: Acculturation and Religious-Identity," (Adelphi University, unpub. M.A. thesis, 1974).

10. Liebman, "Orthodoxy," contains an illuminating description of the Agudah movement.

11. Solomon Poll, *The Hasidic Community of Williamsburg: A Study in the Sociology of Religion* (New York: Schocken, 1969), p. 278.

12. George Kranzler, *Williamsburg: A Jewish Community in Transition* (New York: Philipp Feldheim, 1961).

13. In addition to the cover letter, the survey of *yeshiva* principles was also prefaced with an introductory letter from one of the directors of Torah U'Mesorah, a national umbrella organization for Jewish day schools. The cover letter to the Intercollegiates indicated that I had once been an active member of the organization.

14. It may be supposed that a survey instrument arriving at a rabbi's house from an unknown source, without any apparent community support, would not have a great deal of legitimacy.

15. For a systematic treatment of this complex method, see Max Weber, *The Theory of Social and Economic Organization*, trans. A. M. Henderson and Talcott Parsons (New York: Free Press, 1964), pp. 87–112.

16. J. Milton Yinger, *Sociology Looks at Religion* (New York: Macmillan, 1963), p. 17.

Glossary

All the words and phrases which follow appear in the text in italicized form and are followed by a brief definition. This glossary is offered, therefore, merely as a convenient reference. Both the spelling of terms and the definitions which follow are simplified and designed to reflect popular usage in the Orthodox community in general and the Boro Park community in particular.

Ahavas yisroel	love and concern for the Jewish people; or one who harbors such feelings
Avera (pl. *averas*)	a sin or transgression
Avla	a wrongdoing or action which is contrary to community religious standards
Balebos (pl. *balebatim*)	married adult men with children; also the lay adult male members of a synagogue
Bal t'fila	the lay leader (male) of prayer services
Batlan	one (male) who ostensibly spends his time in study, but in fact is an idler and dreamer
Beis hamedresh	a study hall, usually a separate room in a large synagogue, but may be used alternatively as a place for prayer
Beketch	long silken coat, usually black, worn as a light-weight outer garment by the very religious men
Bitochon	faith or trust in God's protection of the fate of the individual and the community
Blat Gemora	a page of the Talmud
Bochur	a male student in *yeshiva*
Bossor kosher	meat that is permissible to be eaten according to religious law
Chaver (pl. *chaverim*)	friend
Chnyak	a naive and overzealous follower of ritual practices
Cholov yisroel	milk that was processed only under religious Jewish auspices
Chumash	the Pentateuch or the first five books of the Bible known as the Old Testament
Chupa	a canopy supported by four posts under which the marriage ceremony is performed
Daven	to pray
Davening	the process or act of prayer; also the prayer service
Derech eretz	respect; civil behavior; common courtesy
Din	religious rule or law
Drasha	a sermon, or rabbinic exposition on some aspect of the Bible or Talmud

177

Erlach	used to describe a person who conducts his or her life faithfully according to all the religious laws and customs
Eruv	the religiously recognized boundaries of a Jewish community, usually designated by wire, within which one may carry objects in the public domain on the Sabbath
Frum	pious or observant Jew. See also *Erlach*
Galitzianer	any Jew who comes from Galicia (southeastern Poland, eastern Hungary); looked down upon by Lithuanian Jews who thought themselves to be generally more refined and better educated
Gartl	a cloth belt, usually made of black silken material, worn especially by the very religious during prayer
Gemora	the Talmud
Goy	any non-Jew
Goyish	used to describe behavior that is unbecoming a Jew
Greener	a new immigrant; a greenhorn
Halacha	the body of Jewish religious law (See, *Shulchan oruch*)
Hasid	a Jew who follows the teachings and customs of any one of the numerous rebbes, or charismatic religious leaders who trace their authority back to the eighteenth-century founder of the Hasidic movement, the Bal Shem Tov
Havdala	a prayer ceremony signifying the end of the Sabbath holiday on Saturday evening
Heimish	homey; emotionally warm and familiar
Kapote	black silken frock coat worn by very religious men in place of a modern jacket
Kashrus	the body of rules pertaining to the preparation of foods in order to make them kosher
Kidush	a ceremonial blessing over wine, conducted in each home on the Sabbath and holidays
Kohol hakodesh	a holy community; a community whose members conduct themselves according to religious precepts
Kolel	a seminary for post–high school students (men) for the advanced study of the Talmud
Kosher	describes all foods which meet the dietary rules found in the body of religious law
Koved	honor or respect
Lernen	to engage in learning of sacred subjects
Limudei kodesh	sacred subject matter, such as Bible or Talmud
Litvak	any Jew from the region of Lithuania; also one who is very cerebral in his approach to religious matters
Ma'ariv	daily prayer services conducted after sundown
Masmid	a scholarly student of the Talmud
Mikva	ritual bath used for self-purification by women after their menstrual period, and by men before the Sabbath and holidays (also used to purify new cooking utensils and dishes)
Mincha	daily prayer services conducted in the afternoon

Minhag	quasi-religious custom, often adhered to as religiously as if it were a law
Minyan	a prayer quorum of a minimum of ten men
Mitzva (pl. *mitzvas*)	a religious commandment, or a good deed
M'lamed	a teacher (male) of lower grades in a *yeshiva*
Mora	a teacher (female) of lower grades in a *yeshiva*
Musar	a homily, or discourse on morality aimed to revive the listeners' moral sensibilities
Nachas	joy, especially derived from family and a morally upright life through which one enjoys the respect of the community
Nagelwasser	water sprinkled on one's fingers upon awakening in the morning
Nido	a woman in the midst of her menstrual period
N'shomo yithera	an additional soul, symbolic of course, that the individual is thought to possess on the Sabbath
Nusach	the structure of the prayer service, inluding the texts, their sequence, tune, and style of enactment by both the worshippers and the leader of the service
Ol Torah	the obligation laid upon the Jew by the Torah to live according to the commandments
Pareve	the ritual status of foods which are permissible and which are neither meat nor dairy (e.g., vegetables)
Peyes	side locks of hair worn by very religious Orthodox and Hasidic Jewish men
Rebbe (rebbi)	head of an Hasidic sect; or teacher of advanced religious subject matter in a *yeshiva*
Rebbetzin	the wife of a rabbi, *rebbe,* or *rebbi*
Rosh yeshiva	the dean of a *yeshiva*
Rov	a rabbi who is also a recognized leader of a community or a major organization
Shabbos	the Sabbath
Shachris	daily prayer services which are conducted during the early morning hours
Shadchan	a matchmaker, usually a woman
Shamos	a beadle in a synagogue
Shande	shameful or improper behavior
Shatnes	any item of clothing which contains wool and linen sewn or woven together (such a combination is prohibited by religious law)
Sheitl	a wig (religious women do not appear in public with their own hair visible)
Shiduch	a marital match arranged by a *shadchan*
Shomer shabbos	one who observes the rules of the Sabbath
Shokl	to sway back and forth during prayer (an indication of zeal and religious intensity)
Shtetl (pl. *shtetlach*)	a small town or village largely inhabited by Jews

Shtiebl	a small synagogue, usually a single room in a basement or store front. See also *Beis hamedresh*
Shtreimel	a fur-rimmed cap worn by various Hasidic sects
Shul	a synagogue
Shulchan oruch	the code of practical Jewish law
S'lichos	penitential prayers said for a week prior to the High Holidays and during the intervening days between Rosh Hashono and Yom Kipur
S'micha	rabbinic ordination
Sukka (pl. *sukkas*)	hut covered with bamboo to commemorate the wandering of the Jewish people in the wilderness after their exodus from Egypt
Taharas mishpocho	family purity, specifically the purity achieved by proper use of the *mikva* by married women
Talis	a shawl with fringes on the four corners worn by Jewish men during prayers
Tashlich	prayer ceremony on the afternoon of Rosh Hashono conducted at the side of some body of living water, such as a well-fed lake or river
T'nach	the books of the Hebrew prophets (actually an abbreviation of the words "Torah," "N'viim" [the Prophets], and "K'thubim" [apochryphal literature])
Tomeh	ritually impure (e.g., a woman during her menstrual period)
Trefa	any food that is not *kosher*; usually used to refer to un-*kosher* meat stuffs
Tzedaka	charity
Tzuris	the pain of misfortune
Yarmulka	a skullcap
Yeshiva	a school (day school) in which children or young adults learn religious subject matter as well as secular subjects
Yeshiva bochur	a student (male) in a *yeshiva*
Yeshivaleit	all those who attend a *yeshiva*
Yichus	the prestige derived from one's ancestry
Yid (pl. *yidn*)	Jew
Yidishkeit	Jewishness in all its traditional religious and ethnic forms
Yordim	those who have emigrated from Israel
Yomtov (pl. *yomtovim*)	a Jewish religious holiday

Bibliography

Books

Abelow, Samuel P. *History of Brooklyn Jewry*. Brooklyn, N. Y.: Scheba Publishing Co., 1937.

Bang, Rebecca B. *Reminiscences of Old New Utrecht and Gowanus*. Brooklyn, N. Y.: Mrs. R. B. Bang, 1912.

Beard, Charles A., and Mary R. *The Beards' New Basic History of the United States*. New York: Doubleday, 1960.

Bell, Daniel. *The End of Ideology: On the Exhaustion of Political Ideas in the Fifties*. New York: Free Press, 1960.

Berger, Peter L. *The Sacred Canopy: Elements of a Sociological Theory of Religion*. New York: Doubleday, 1967.

_____, and Thomas Luckmann. *The Social Construction of Reality: A Treatise in the Sociology of Knowledge*. New York: Doubleday, 1966.

_____, and Richard J. Neuhaus. *Movement and Revolution*. New York: Doubleday, 1970.

_____, and Brigitte Berger. *Sociology: A Biographical Approach*. New York: Basic Books, 1972.

Boulding, Kenneth E. *The Meaning of the Twentieth Century: The Great Transition*. New York: Harper & Row, 1964.

Brav, Stanley R., ed. *Marriage and the Jewish Tradition*. New York: Philosophical Library, 1951.

Cohn, Michael. *Crown Heights and Williamsburg*. Brooklyn, N.Y.: The Brooklyn Children's Museum, Cultural Anthropology Workshop, 1964.

Coleman, James S., Amitai Etzioni, and John Porter. *Macrosociology: Research and Theory*. Boston: Allyn & Bacon, 1970.

Commager, Henry S. *The American Mind: An Interpretation of American Thought and Character since the 1880's*. New Haven: Yale University Press, 1950.

Cox, Harvey. *The Secular City*. New York: Macmillan, 1965.

De Tocqueville, Alexis. *Democracy in America*. Trans. Henry Reeve. 2 vols. New York: Schocken, 1961.

Durkheim, Emile. *Suicide*. Trans. John A. Spaulding and George Simpson. New York: Free Press, 1951.

_____. *The Elementary Forms of the Religious Life*. Trans. Joseph W. Swain. New York: The Free Press, 1965.

Etzioni, Amitai. *The Active Society*. New York: Free Press, 1968.

Festinger, Leon. *A Theory of Cognitive Dissonance*. Evanston, Ill.: Row & Peterson, 1957.

181

Ganzfried, Solomon. *Code of Jewish Law*. Trans. Hyman E. Goldin. New York: Hebrew Publishing Co., 1961.

Ginsberg, Yona. *Jews in a Changing Neighborhood: A Study of Mattapan*. New York: Free Press, 1975.

Glazer, Nathan. *American Judaism*. Chicago: University of Chicago Press, 1957.

—————, and Daniel P. Moynihan. *Beyond the Melting Pot: The Negroes, Puerto Ricans, Jews, Italians and Irish of New York City*. 2nd ed. Cambridge: M.I.T. Press, 1970.

Gody, Lou, ed. *New York City Guide*. New York: Random House, 1938.

Gold, Michael. *Jews Without Money*. New York: Horace Liveright, 1930.

Goldstein, Sidney, and Calvin Goldscheider. *Jewish Americans: Three Generations in a Jewish Community*. Englewood Cliffs, N.J.: Prentice-Hall, 1968.

Gordon, Milton M. *Assimilation in American Life: The Role of Race, Religion and National Origin*. New York: Oxford University Press, 1964.

Graetz, Heinrich. *History of the Jews*. Trans. Bella Lowy and others. 6 vols. Philadelphia: Jewish Publication Society, 1891.

Greeley, Andrew M. *Unsecular Man: The Persistence of Religion*. New York: Schocken, 1972.

Grunfeld, Isidore. *The Sabbath: A Guide to Its Understanding and Observance*. New York: Philipp Feldheim, 1959.

Gutman, Robert, and David Popenoe, eds. *Neighborhood, City and Metropolis: An Integrated Reader in Urban Sociology*. New York: Random House, 1970.

Habermas, Jurgen. *Toward a Rational Society: Student Protest, Science and Politics*. Trans. Jeremy Shapiro. Boston: Beacon Press, 1971.

Handlin, Oscar. *The Uprooted*. 1st ed. Boston: Little, Brown, 1951.

Hansen, Marcus L. *The Problem of the Third Generation Immigrant*. Rock Island, Ill.: Augustana Historical Society, 1938.

Hapgood, Hutchins. *The Spirit of the Ghetto: Studies of the Jewish Quarter of New York*. New York: Funk & Wagnalls, 1902; Schocken, 1966.

Heilman, Samuel C. *Synagogue Life*. Chicago: University of Chicago Press, 1976.

Herberg, Will. *Protestant-Catholic-Jew: An Essay in American Religious Sociology*. New York: Doubleday, 1955.

Hertz, Joseph H. *The Authorized Daily Prayer Book*. New York: Bloch, 1948.

Hillery, George A. *Communal Organizations: A Study of Local Societies*. Chicago: University of Chicago Press, 1968.

Hobbes, Thomas. *Leviathan*. Ed. Herbert W. Schneider. Indianapolis: Bobbs-Merrill, 1958.

Horowitz, Morris, and Lawrence Kaplan. *Estimated Jewish Population of the New York Area, 1900–1975*. New York: Federation of Jewish Philanthropies, 1959.

Howe, Irving. *World of Our Fathers*. New York: Simon and Schuster, 1976.

Kallen, Horace M. *Culture and Democracy in the United States: Studies in the Group Psychology of the American Peoples*. New York: Horace Liveright, 1924.

Kaminetsky, Joseph, ed. *Hebrew Day School Education: An Overview*. New York: Torah U'Mesorah, 1970.

Kehilla of New York City. *The Jewish Communal Register of New York City, 1917–1918*. New York, 1919.

Kramer, Judith R. *The American Minority Community*. New York: T. Y. Crowell, 1970.

—————, and Seymour Leventman. *Children of the Gilded Ghetto: Conflict Resolu-*

tions of Three Generations of American Jews. New Haven: Yale University Press, 1961.

Kranzler, George. Williamsburg: A Jewish Community in Transition. New York: Philipp Feldheim, 1961.

Landesman, Alter F. Brownsville: The Birth, Development and Passing of a Jewish Community in New York. New York: Bloch, 1969.

Lazarus, Emma. Poems. Boston: Houghton Mifflin, 1889.

Luckmann, Thomas. The Invisible Religion: The Problem of Religion in Modern Society. New York: Macmillan, 1967.

McNiff, William J. Haven on Earth: A Planned Mormon Society. Oxford, Ohio: Mississippi Valley Press, 1940.

Mannheim, Karl. Man and Society in an Age of Reconstruction. New York: Harcourt, Brace & World, 1940.

Marcuse, Herbert. One Dimensional Man. Boston: Beacon, 1964.

Medding, P. Y. From Assimilation to Group Survival: A Political and Sociological Study of an Australian Jewish Community. Melbourne: F. W. Cheshire, 1968.

Metzger, Isaac, ed. A Bintel Brief: "A Bundle of Letters" to the Jewish Daily Forward. New York: Doubleday, 1971.

Miller, Delbert C. Handbook of Research Design and Social Measurement. 2nd ed. New York: McKay, 1970.

Minar, David W., and Scott Greer, eds. The Concept of Community: Readings with Interpretations. Chicago: Aldine, 1969.

Myers, Jerome K., and Lee L. Bean. A Decade Later: A Follow-up of Social Class and Mental Illness. New York: Wiley, 1968.

Newman, William M. American Pluralism: A Study of Minority Groups and Social Theory. New York: Harper & Row, 1973.

Novak, Michael. The Rise of the Unmeltable Ethnics. New York: Macmillan, 1971.

Parsons, Talcott. The Structure of Social Action. New York: McGraw-Hill, 1937.

_____, and Neil J. Smelser. Economy and Society: A Study in the Integration of Economic and Social Theory. New York: Free Press, 1956.

Poll, Solomon. The Hasidic Community of Williamsburg: A Study in the Sociology of Religion. New York: Schocken, 1969.

Reisman, David, Nathan Glazer, and Reuel Denney. The Lonely Crowd. New Haven: Yale University Press, 1950.

Riley, Matilda W. Sociological Research Vol. I. New York: Harcourt, Brace & World, 1963.

Ringer, Benjamin B. The Edge of Friendliness: A Study of Jewish-Gentile Relations. New York: Basic Books, 1967.

Rischin, Moses. The Promised City: New York's Jews, 1870–1914. Cambridge: Harvard University Press, 1962.

Rose, Peter I., ed. The Ghetto and Beyond: Essays on Jewish Life in America. New York: Random House, 1969.

Rosenberg, Stuart E. The Search for Jewish Identity in America. New York: Doubleday, 1965.

Rubin, Israel. Satmar: An Island in the City. Chicago: Quadrangle, 1972.

Schiff, Alvin I. The Jewish Day School in America. New York: Jewish Education Committee Press, 1966.

Schutz, Alfred. Collected Papers. 3 vols. The Hague: Martinus Nijhoff, 1970.

Shibutani, Tomatsu, and Kwan, Kian M. *Ethnic Stratification*. New York: Macmillan, 1965.

Sklare, Marshall. *Conservative Judaism: An American Religious Movement*. 2nd ed. New York: Schocken, 1972.

_____. *America's Jews*. New York: Random House, 1971.

_____. *Not Quite at Home*. New York: American Jewish Committee, 1969.

_____, ed. *The Jews: Social Patterns of an American Group*. New York: Free Press, 1958.

_____, and Joseph Greenblum. *Jewish Identity on the Suburban Frontier*. New York: Basic Books, 1966.

Smith, C. Henry. *A Story of the Mennonites*. Newton, Kans.: Mennonite Publication Office, 1950.

Stember, Charles, and others. *Jews in the Mind of America*. New York: Basic Books, 1966.

Stiles, Henry R. *A History of the City of Brooklyn*. Brooklyn, N.Y.: H. R. Stiles, 1867.

Strauss, Anselm. *George Herbert Mead: On Social Psychology*. Chicago: University of Chicago Press, 1934.

Toffler, Alvin. *Future Shock*. New York: Bantam, 1970.

Vidich, Arthur J., and Joseph Bensman. *Small Town in Mass Society: Class, Power and Religion in a Rural Community*. New York: Doubleday, 1960.

Warren, Roland L. *The Community in America*. Chicago: Rand McNally, 1963.

Webb, Eugene J., Donald T. Campbell, Richard D. Schwartz, and Lee Sechrest. *Unobtrusive Measures: Non-reactive Research in the Social Sciences*. Chicago: Rand McNally, 1966.

Weber, Max. *Ancient Judaism*. Trans. Hans H. Gerth and Don Martindale. New York: Free Press, 1952.

_____. *The Sociology of Religion*. Trans. Ephraim Fischoff. Boston: Beacon Press, 1963.

Wirth, Louis. *The Ghetto*. Chicago: University of Chicago Press, 1928.

Yinger, J. Milton. *Sociology Looks at Religion*. New York: Macmillan, 1963.

_____. *The Scientific Study of Religion*. New York: Macmillan, 1970.

Zborowski, Mark, and Elizabeth Herzog. *Life Is with People: The Culture of the Shtetl*. New York: Schocken, 1962.

Zijderveld, Anton C. *The Abstract Society: A Cultural Analysis of Our Time*. New York: Doubleday, 1970.

Articles

Abelson, Robert P. "Modes of Resolution of Belief Dilemmas," in *Problems in Social Psychology*. Ed. C. W. Backman and P. F. Secord, pp. 136–140. New York: McGraw-Hill, 1966.

Alter, Robert. "A Fever of Ethnicity," *Commentary* 53 (June 1972): 68–73.

Berger, Peter L. "Some Sociological Comments on Theological Education," *Perspective* 9 (Summer 1968): 127–138.

_____, and Hansfried Kellner. "Arnold Gehlen and the Theory of Institutions," *Social Research* 2 (Spring 1965): 110–121.

Bloustein, Edward. "Parents and Children of the Counter-Culture," *Hadassah Magazine*, October 1971, pp 20–22.

Borgatta, Marie L. "The Concept of the Group," *Sociology and Social Research* 43 (Summer 1958). pp 83–89.

Carlin, Jerome E., and Saul H. Mendlovitz. "The American Rabbi: A Religious Specialist Responds to a Loss of Authority," in *The Jews*. Ed. Marshall Sklare, pp. 377–417. New York: Free Press, 1958.

Eisenstadt, Samuel N. "Archetypal Patterns of Youth," in *The Challenge of Youth*. Ed. Erik H. Erikson, pp. 29–50. New York: Doubleday, 1965.

Elazar, Daniel J. "The Legal Status of the American Jewish Community," *American Jewish Yearbook*, pp. 3–94. New York: American Jewish Committee, 1972.

Elias, Joseph. "The Hebrew and General Studies Departments," in *Hebrew Day School Education: An Overview*. Ed. Joseph Kaminetsky, pp. 219–228. New York: Torah U'mesorah, 1970.

Etzioni, Amitai. "The Ghetto: A Re-evaluation," *Social Forces* 37 (March 1959): 255–262.

Friedman, Norman. "Jewish or Professorial Identity," *Sociological Analysis* 32 (Fall 1971): 149–157.

Galtung, Johan. "Rank and Social Integration: A Multi-Dimensional Approach," in *Sociological Theories in Progress*. Vol. 1. Ed. Joseph Berger, Morris Zelditch, Jr., and Bo Anderson, pp. 145–198. Boston: Houghton Mifflin, 1966.

Gans, Herbert, "The Future of American Jewry," *Commentary* 21 (June 1956): 555–563.

Geschwender, James. "Continuities in Theories of Status Consistency and Cognitive Dissonance," *Social Forces* 46 (December 1967): 160–171.

Glasner, Samuel. "Family Religion as a Matrix of Personal Growth," *Marriage and Family Living* 22 (August 1961): 291–296.

Grama, Israel. "From Yemen to Boro Park," *Jewish Life* 33 (March/April 1966): 30–38.

Greenberg, Ben. "The Jewish Poverty Survey," *The Jewish Press* August 24, 1973, p. 3.

Greenberg, Menachem. "The Yeshiva World's Outlook on Torah and Secular Studies," *The Jewish Observer* 6 (December 1969): 11–14.

Gutman, Robert. "Non-Conventional Methods for Obtaining Data on the Religious Composition of the United States Population: The Case of Jewish Population Statistics." Belgrade, Yugoslavia: United Nations World Population Conference, August 1965.

Jackson, Elton F. "Status Consistency and Symptoms of Stress," *American Sociological Review* 27 (August 1962): 469–478.

Jakobovits, Immanuel. "The Strengths of the Yeshiva Movement," in *Hebrew Day School Education: An Overview*. Ed. Joseph Kaminetsky, pp. 86–91. New York: Torah U'mesorah, 1970.

Kelman, Herbert C. "The Induction of Action and Attitude Change," in *Problems in Social Psychology*. Ed. C. W. Backman and P. F. Secord, pp. 141–152. New York: McGraw-Hill, 1966.

Lazerwitz, Bernard, and Louis Rowitz. "The Three Generation Hypothesis," *American Journal of Sociology* 69 (March 1964): 529–538.

Leventman, Seymour. "From Shtetl to Suburb," in *The Ghetto and Beyond*. Ed. Peter I. Rose, pp. 33–56. New York: Random House, 1969.

Levy, Sydelle B. "Shifting Patterns of Ethnic Identification Among the Hassidim," in *The New Ethnicity: Perspectives from Ethnology*. Ed. John Bennett, pp. 25–49. New York: West Publishing, 1975.

Liebman, Charles. "Orthodoxy in American Jewish Life," *American Jewish Yearbook*, pp. 21–98. New York: American Jewish Committee, 1965.

Lipset, Seymour M. "Jewish Sociologists and Sociologists of the Jews," *Jewish Social Studies* 17 (July 1955): 117–178.

_____. "The American Jewish Community in a Comparative Perspective," in *The Ghetto and Beyond*. Ed. Peter I. Rose, pp. 21–32. New York: Random House, 1969.

Litwak, Eugene. "Voluntary Association and Neighborhood Cohesion," in *Neighborhood, City and Metropolis*. Ed. Robert Gutman and David Popenoe, pp. 583–599. New York: Random House, 1970.

Mann, Peter H. "The Neighborhood," in *Neighborhood, City and Metropolis*. Ed. Robert Gutman and David Popenoe, pp. 568–582. New York: Random House, 1970.

Mannheim, Karl. "The Problem of Generations," in *Essays on the Sociology of Knowledge*. Ed. Karl Mannheim, pp. 276–320. New York: Oxford University Press, 1952.

Marsh, Judith. "Patterns of Conflict in American Society, 1952–1968," *Sociology and Social Research* 57 (April 1973): 315–334.

Massarik, Fred. "The Jewish Community," in *Community Structure and Analysis*. Ed. Marvin B. Sussman. New York: T. Y. Crowell, 1959: 237–252.

Mayer, Egon, and Chaim I. Waxman. "Modern Jewish Orthodox in America: Toward the Year 2000," *Tradition* 16 (Spring 1977): pp. 98–112.

Mazur, Allan. "The Socialization of Jews into the Academic Subculture," in *The Professors*. Ed. Charles H. Anderson and John D. Murray, pp. 265–287. Boston: Schenkman, 1971.

Nelsen, Hart M., et. al., "Ministerial Roles and Social Activist Stances: Protestant Clergy Protest in the Sixties," *American Sociological Review* 38 (June 1973): 375–386.

Robison, Sophia M. "A Study of Delinquency Among Jewish Children in New York City," in *The Jews*. Ed. Marshall Sklare, pp. 535–541. New York: Free Press, 1958.

Rosenthal, Eric. "Acculturation Without Assimilation: The Jewish Community of Chicago, Illinois." *American Journal of Sociology* 66 (November 1960): 275–288.

Ross, H. Lawrence. "The Local Community: A Survey Approach," in *Neighborhood, City and Metropolis*. Ed. Robert Gutman and David Popenoe, pp. 557–567. New York: Random House, 1970.

Schlesinger, Benjamin. "The Jewish Family in Retrospect," in *The Jewish Family: A Survey and Annotated Bibliography*. Ed. Benjamin Schlesinger, pp. 3–14. Toronto: University of Toronto Press, 1971.

Singer, Isaac B. "The Extreme Jews," *Harper's*, April 1967, pp. 55–62.

Sklare, Marshall. "The Desire for Survival," in *The Study of Society*. Ed. Peter I. Rose, pp. 738–744. New York: Random House, 1967.

Snyder, Charles R. "Culture and Jewish Sobriety: The Ingroup-Outgroup Factor," in *The Jews*. Ed. Marshall Sklare, pp. 560–594. New York: Free Press, 1958.

Tumin, Melvin. "The Cult of Gratitude," in *The Ghetto and Beyond*. Ed. Peter I. Rose, pp. 69–82. New York: Random House, 1969.

Wattenberg, Ben J., and Richard Scammon. "Black Progress and Liberal Rhetoric," *Commentary* 5 (April 1973): 35–44.

Weinryb, Bernard D. "Jewish Immigration and Acculturation to America," in *The Jews*. Ed. Marshall Sklare, pp. 4–22. New York: Free Press, 1958.

Wolfenstein, Martha. "The Emergence of the Fun Morality," in *Mass Leisure*. Ed. Eric Larrabee and Rolf Meyersohn, pp. 86–95. Glencoe, Ill.: Free Press, 1958.

Other Sources

Cole, David. "A Survey of Public and Parochial Schools Serving the Catchment Area of the Maimonides Community Mental Health Center, 1970–1971." Mimeographed document, Brooklyn, N.Y., 1972.

Community Council of Greater New York. "Population Characteristics." Mimeographed document, 1961.

Deets, E. L. "The Hutterites: A Study in Social Cohesion." Columbia University, Ph.D. diss., 1939.

Leff, Bertram. "The Modern Orthodox Jew: Acculturation and Religious Identity." Adelphi University, M.A. thesis, 1974.

Long Island Historical Society. *Scrapbooks*. Brooklyn, N.Y.

New York City Planning Commission. *The Plan for the City of New York*. 5 vols. New York: Department of City Planning, 1969.

New York City Tax Commission. *Detailed List of Tax-Exempt Properties of the City of New York*. New York: Department of Taxation and Finance, 1961, 1972.

Polsky, Howard. "The Great Defense: A Study of Jewish Orthodoxy in Milwaukee." University of Wisconsin, Ph.D. diss., 1956.

United States Bureau of Census. *1970 Census of Population and Housing*. Washington: Department of Commerce, 1970.

Verbit, Mervin F. "Referents for Religion Among Jewish College Students." Columbia University, Ph.D. diss. 1968.

Index of Names

189

Subject Index